PENGUIN BOOKS

I DREAMED OF AFRICA

Kuki Gallmann was born in Italy and in 1972 moved to
Africa with Paolo Gallmann and her son. As a tribute
to their memory, she created the Gallmann Memorial
Foundation, which is devoted to exploring new ways
of combining development with conservation. She cur-
rently lives on her ranch in Kenya with her daughter
and eight dogs.

THE GALLMANN MEMORIAL FOUNDATION
P.O. BOX 45593 • NAIROBI

KUKI GALLMANN

I Dreamed of Africa
_____

PENGUIN BOOKS

PENGUIN BOOKS
Published by the Penguin Group
Viking Penguin, a division of Penguin Books USA Inc.,
375 Hudson Street, New York, New York 10014, U.S.A.
Penguin Books Ltd, 27 Wrights Lane, London W8 5TZ, England
Penguin Books Australia Ltd, Ringwood, Victoria, Australia
Penguin Books Canada Ltd, 10 Alcorn Avenue, Suite 300,
Toronto, Ontario, Canada M4V 3B2
Penguin Books (N.Z.) Ltd, 182 –190 Wairau Road,
Auckland 10, New Zealand

Penguin Books Ltd, Registered Offices:
Harmondsworth, Middlesex, England

First published in Great Britain by Penguin Books Ltd., 1991
First published in the United States of America
by Viking Penguin, a division of Penguin Books USA Inc., 1991
Published in Penguin Books 1992

1 3 5 7 9 10 8 6 4 2

THE LIBRARY OF CONGRESS HAS CATALOGUED THE HARDCOVER AS FOLLOWS:
Gallmann, Kuki.
I dreamed of Africa / Kuki Gallmann.
p. cm.
ISBN 0-670-83612-5 (hc.)
ISBN 0 14 01.7102 9 (pbk.)
1. Kenya—Description and travel—1981– 2. Gallmann, Kuki—Homes
and haunts —Kenya. I. Title.
DT433.527.G35 1991
967.6204 —dc20 90–50742

Printed in the United States of America
Set in Palatino

In memory of Paolo and Emanuele

A hope beyond the shadow of a dream . . .

John Keats, *Endymion*

Contents

PART III   *Emanuele*

PART IV *After*

List of Illustrations

All photographs taken by the author except where indicated

Acknowledgements

I had a story to tell. If you have the patience to read it to the end, you will understand why I wrote it, although it meant exposing an intimate and deep part of my life to a large number of people, mostly unknown to me.

Without the support of my friends, too many to be mentioned, I might never have finished it. My gratitude to them will be understood from the pages of my book. Particularly, I would like to thank:

Adrian House, the first to encourage me to go on writing in English, for his generosity, ruthless criticism, and for offering me his time and accepting my ouzo.

Aino Block, Carol Byrne, Amedeo and Josephine Buonajuti, Rocky Francombe, Hilary Ruben, John and Buffy Sacher, for reading my script; and Oria and Iain Douglas-Hamilton, for the special part they played in my story.

Toby Eady, for agreeing to be my 'brother'.

Mehmood Quraishy for his impeccable work on my old photo-graphs and slides.

Cecilia Wanjiru, Simon Itot and all my Laikipia and Nairobi friends, for looking after me and my daughter with love and loyalty in sad and happy times.

And, last but not least, my daughter Sveva, for her graceful way of bearing with me, and for agreeing to share her childhood and her mother for months with a computer and all those papers.

18 August 1990

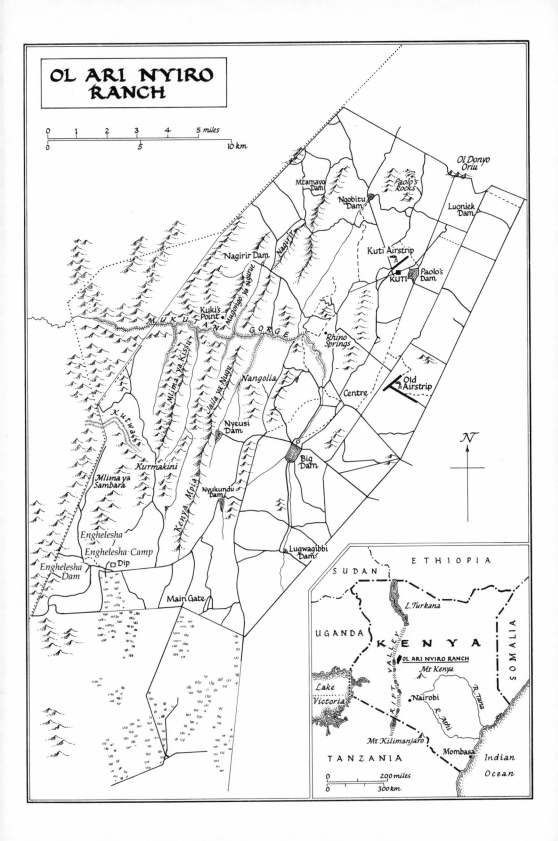

Prologue

A song of friends long dead, and times now past,
of children, grown and gone . . .

Lyall Watson, *Gift of Unknown Things*

Often, at the hour of day when the savannah grass is streaked with silver, and pale gold rims the silhouettes of the hills, I drive with my dogs up to the Mukutan, to watch the sun setting behind the lake, and the evening shadows settle over the valleys and plains of the Laikipia plateau.

There, on the extreme edge of the Great Rift Valley, guarding the gorge, grows an acacia tree bent by timeless winds. That tree is my friend, and we are sisters. I rest against its trunk, scaly and grey like a wise old elephant. I look up through the branches, twisted arms spread in a silent dance, to the sky of Africa. Darkness gathers fast, red deepens into purple, a sliver of white moon sails over the horizon. A last eagle flies majestically back to her nest on steep cliffs. The same primordial breeze rises from the gorge with a rustle of leaves and scuttling snakes, trills of hidden tree-frogs, the call of the first nocturnal birds, and sometimes the snort of a buffalo, the cry of baboons, or the rasping cough of leopard.

The world of crowds and Europe is far and alien. Does Venice really exist, and the evening fog from sleepy canals drift over the ancient palaces? Do the swallows still dart to their nests under the eaves of my grandfather's abandoned home in Veneto?

And did the car really skid that summer night, on the edge of the lagoon?

The screeching of brakes brought me to my senses with a jolt. The stars looked small and far away. The grass was wet with night dew. The crickets had stopped singing. In the eerie silence the only sounds were laboured breathing, and a feeble lament which soon ceased. The right side of my body felt wet and sticky. I touched my dress with my hand, and even in the darkness I knew that it was soaked with blood, oozing from the mouth of the man whose head rested heavily on my shouder. I called him gently, but he was too deep in the coma from which he would only emerge six months later. At the time, I thought he was dying.

I could feel no real pain, only a throbbing numbness in the region of my left leg: when I reached out to check I could only find swollen pulp where my thigh had been. My right femur had exploded in tiny fragments of bone. As a surgeon's daughter, I knew that it would be a long time before I could walk again, if ever. It was ironical that when the car overturned and crashed we were all going out to dance.

My main worry was that no one would find us. I could see neither the car nor the road. I had no idea where we were. I only knew the friend was dying, and Mariangela . . . I could see just her white dress, almost translucent in the pale starlight speckled with fireflies. The lament was coming from her, but she did not answer me. I had been talking to her when the beams of a lorry blinded us all, and the car lost control, hit some trees and threw us out into a field of lucerne.

Now there was the sound of a car, then others screeching to a halt . . . voices, screams of horror . . . 'Here!' I shouted at the top of my voice. 'Three of us are here . . .'

The first to find me was Chiara. Their car had been following ours after dinner; we had all been going to the same place, an open-air night club. We were young, and it was summer.

I saw her slender feet walking awkwardly through the grass.

She was barefoot, and I remembered her saying that when something really worried her, the first thing she did was to kick her shoes off. Quiet, aristocratic Chiara, whom we all respected and loved.

'My femur's gone. Don't worry about me. Check on Mariangela over there, and him, here: they're not answering.' The mute friend's head was heavy on my shoulder. 'I'll wait for the ambulance. Don't let anyone move us.'

Afterwards I wondered how I could have been so cool. I felt an almost totally detached calm. I had just to take one thing at a time . . . be in control. I could not know that this need for calm had only just begun: my newly-found capacity to keep my head in moments of drama would be tested again. Again and again.

Chiara gave me her light sweater as I had started shivering with shock, but I shook my head. She spent only a few moments with the shape a few metres away from me. When she returned, I could read on her face what had happened. Gently, she covered me instead.

'She will not need this any more.'

In this way I learned that Paolo's wife was dead.

Paolo himself was badly hurt. His jawbone was fractured and several vertebrae, and a cracked rib had penetrated his lung. They had found him on the road, unconscious in a pool of his blood. It would be weeks before they could tell him what had happened. From now on our stories and those of his two little girls who had lost so much in that warm June night would be forever intertwined by this absurd tragedy.

Still lying on the ground, waiting for the only ambulance in the small seaside resort to arrive, I felt a deep pity for us all, but mostly for Paolo: not only would he suffer physically, but his wife was dead and his small daughters orphans. And he was the one who had been driving. When, days after, they discovered that the tendon of his left index finger had been cut, it was too late to do anything about it, and to the end of his life it remained crooked, like a hook.

*

The bed was hard and narrow. An almost unbearable pain radiated from my leg, spreading through my body, and I sank in its vortex.

Someone was murmuring in a foreign, yet familiar, language. It was a prayer: '*Ego te absolvo ab peccatis tuis.*'

I tried to open my eyes. The sharp light above my head blinded me. The priest was bending over me, administering the Sacraments for the dying. He smelt of incense. I blinked. This was not really happening to me. There was a mistake. I was alive and I was going to live. 'Save your prayers, Father,' I told him fiercely with all my remaining strength. I tried to sit up, and failed. 'I am not dead yet. My time has yet to come.'

Perhaps I screamed. A dry hand soothingly touched my forehead. A needle penetrated my arm, and almost immediately I was pervaded by a pleasant dreamy numbness, through which a hoarse, gentle voice I would have recognized anywhere reached me: 'You will be all right, Kuki.' I looked up in relief. Green, serious eyes were watching me behind thick glasses. I was safe. It was my father.

PART I

Before

1

A Child of Italy

I learned what every dreaming child needs to know — that no horizon is so far
you cannot get above it or beyond it . . .

Beryl Markham, *West with the Night*

The first memory I have of my father is of a slim young man with
a straight nose and a beautiful mouth, black hair and grey-green
eyes behind glasses, dressed in strange greenish trousers and a
shirt which had some golden stars and birds on it. I remember
being embarrassed that he did not wear a jacket, like all the other
men in our household. That they were old men and he young —
he was in fact in his late twenties — did not make any difference to
my childish sense of propriety: all men in those days wore jackets
and ties, even in the morning, in the country.

I lived in my grandfather's country house attached to his silk
factory, in a village in the hills of Veneto, with my mother and her
family of women and old men: all the young men were at the war.
We had moved here to escape the bombing in town. I was a
pampered little girl, inquisitive, and always seeking adventure and
magic. As a baby and then a toddler, and the only child in the
household, I had everyone's attention and time. In those days of
fear, I must have represented for them the hope for the future. In a
world of doting adults, surrounded by their love and kindness, I
grew up with great self-confidence.

My earliest memories of the war are of being carried through

3

the night by a running adult towards the air raid shelter at the end of our garden, and of people running with us, looking anxiously up at the sky, where some small red and green lights moved in the dark with a threatening noise of thunder.

They talked in front of me of my father, and of their apprehensions about his fate, a parachutist and a medical officer, fighting somewhere on the front line a war in which he did not believe. When Italy was divided by civil war, he had been posted to the free south. Approached by an officer of the British Intelligence Service, he had agreed to go back to fight in the north, in the mountains around Udine which he knew extremely well. A passionate mountaineer, like all his ancestors from the Val D'Aosta, he had climbed alone and for pleasure since he was barely eleven, twelve years old.

From the warm, balmy coast of Puglia they parachuted him, in the dark of an autumn night, on to the hill of Col Di Luna in northern Italy, in hell again, to fight.

For nearly two years my father was in the mountains of Friuli, leading the free but lonely life of the partisans, starving and freezing in barns, stalking and being stalked, seeing destruction and friends die. Then one day he was captured by fellow Italians belonging to the extreme right wing of the Fascist party, the notorious Decima Mas. He was thrown into prison in the sinister Castle of Conegliano, a theatre of grotesque torture. No one had ever walked out of it alive. My father did. When he heard that the end of the war was approaching, and that the prisoners' days were numbered, he managed to escape in the night with a friend. My mother, alerted by a spy, carried me that same night through a wood to a monastery, where we were given asylum. She was just in time. They came to take my mother and me in retaliation, but found us gone. They arrested my grandfather instead, as a hostage. Later, they had to let him go.

There was always tension in the air in those days, of which with my alert little senses I was perfectly aware. The repeatedly murmured name of my father, whom I had never seen, made me perceive him as an elusive superman, and I wondered if I would ever meet him.

Then, one day he was there.

The war had just finished, and he came back still in the khaki uniform of the Allies, with an Englishman by the foreign name of Nicholson — a war name, his real name was Roworth — to whom I owe my nickname of 'Cookie'. My father had brought tins of condensed milk, which I liked, and corned beef, which I did not: the taste of metal and grease was alien to my tentative tongue. The Englishman gave me my first chocolate bar.

With the return of my father and of the others who had survived, the streets of the village and our house were suddenly crowded with young men. There was an atmosphere of excitement and euphoria. People sang and danced outside in the spring evenings, and my father's voice sounded clear and high in the nostalgic songs of the partisans. My mother laughed often; she was expecting another child, and my life changed with the spirit which had entered it.

My father had the gift of making me believe, and of believing himself, that there is always a new adventure, something waiting to be discovered, if we can only find the time to look for it, and the courage to jump. His drive and his energetic attitude to life galvanized me, making me perceive that there were no limits to what one could achieve. I was keen to explore, eager to follow in his footsteps. Like him, I have never known a moment of boredom.

He loved nature, creatures wild and tame, and he could not bear cruelty to animals. He instilled in me these same feelings. Once he found an innocuous grass snake which had been almost cut in half by the blade of the lawnmower. He stitched the wound and, to help me overcome my natural revulsion, he insisted that I should assist him, passing him the instruments one by one. Later he rescued a baby fox and a vervet monkey from a pet shop, where they had been imprisoned and exposed to the hurried indifference of passers-by. I remember the small, inquisitive, whiskered red face peering from the folds of his winter coat. The monkey became a real menace, possessive towards him and jealous of all females. In the spring I would take her to my school, where she sat on a tree outside during lessons, jeering at the students, under the protection and to the joy of the school's caretaker. He loved anything connected with Africa, having been in his youth a soldier in Somalia, where he had found a beautiful girlfriend, but lost his dreams.

For as long as I can remember there were pets in our house. Both my parents were particularly fond of dogs, especially fox terriers. Small and compact, brave and intelligent, fox terriers have little sense of their diminutive size, for which they compensate with aggressiveness and a highly-strung character. They need a great deal of exercise. My father walked the dogs every evening and I usually accompanied him.

At the time of day when bats fly low, and the barking of our dogs pursuing a cat or a water rat grew fainter in the distance, I walked at my father's side. Talking came easily in the twilight, and my youth did not matter. Some of those sunset conversations are embedded in my memory for ever. So are special moments which I shall always treasure, like the times he came home with books for me to read.

'Kuki!' he would call from the hall. 'Come and choose a book.' With a great sense of anticipation I would run to meet him. From an open suitcase, assorted volumes supplied by a dealer in second-hand books, whom he had once cured of kidney stones, spilled out on to the grey marble floor.

My father always gave me first choice, and once I had picked up from the scattered pile the books which most interested me, he told me something about the content, the story, the style and the author. He allowed me absolute freedom to select whatever I wanted, regardless of my age. Thus I accumulated, without any effort, a vast, if unmethodical, knowledge of literature and poetry, at an age when most children are concentrating on comics or novels. From Edgar Allan Poe – in translation, as were all the non-Italian writers – to Boccaccio, from Mark Twain to Victor Hugo or Ibsen, from Hemingway to Machiavelli, from Sappho to Saint-

Exupéry, Byron, Tolstoy, Leopardi or Lamartine, my late childhood and early adolescence were spent devouring any book I could lay my hands on. My father's only condition was quality, and I shall always be in his debt for moulding my taste to his high standards. Many of his friends were writers or artists, and our house was always open to them. I loved listening to their conversations.

I loved poetry and was fascinated by its harmonious rhythms. Often my father and I recited classic Italian poems in duet, reading from the same page. We both enjoyed those unique and inspiring times, and verses still live dormant in my subconscious, often to emerge as quotations to underline a moment, a feeling, a particular event. Those are among the happiest memories of my childhood, and in every man in my life perhaps I looked for a reflection of my father.

He had a passion for archaeology. Together we would explore caves in the hills of Montello, probing the walls with torches, discovering bones and teeth of neolithic cave bears. He taught me to look for pointed arrowheads, chipped out of pink and grey stone by some skin- and fur-clad ancestor. We found Roman coins in recently ploughed fields, and amphorae in drained river beds. We would visit abandoned country cemeteries, or I would follow him up steep mountains, aiming for some cloud-covered peak.

Many times in later years I asked myself how it all began. I had sometimes this urge to find the link, the reason why, and when people ask me why I decided to come to Africa, the answer lies in the days of my childhood.

A bird's nest hung grey in a corner of the verandah in my grandfather's home in the country. That nest had been there for as long as anyone could remember. During autumn and winter it was empty, crumbling fragments of dry mud. Then the skies of May once again filled with darting birds, screeches and chatters animated the twilight, and in a flurry of activity the nest was renewed and inhabited. The swallows were back. Where they came from, how they knew how to find again exactly this spot on the Earth, puzzled me for years. I realized later that they could not for ever be the same swallows, and that it was an ancestral memory which guided young birds to the place chosen by past generations.

The desire to go to Africa seemed to have been an obscure yearning to return, a nostalgic inherited need to migrate back to where our ancestors came from. It was a memory carried in my genes. The urge to fly home, like the swallows.

One day, the subject of the essay was: *'Io, tra ventanni'* ('Myself twenty years on'). My paper was returned without being marked.

I was twelve, and my marks in composition were usually good. I did not understand what had gone wrong this time. I had put my heart into the effort of explaining what I wanted to do, where I wanted to be in twenty years' time.

The teacher, a middle-aged lady with dark mahogany hair, looked at me over her spectacles: 'It is well written, as usual,' she said, 'but it is totally absurd. You should have described something possible, as your friends have. You certainly must have some feasible desire for your future? Like being a . . . teacher, or a doctor, a mother, perhaps a writer . . . or a dancer, with your long legs . . . something you can do right here where you were born, where your family and friends are, something normal. Why did you have to write about Africa?'

I can still remember the day: a cold, foggy November. Months of school and winter lay ahead. Until the summer I had my books and my dreams and I clung to them as to the only light; my fantasies of a hot land of unending horizons, herds of animals in the savannah, and a farm in the Highlands where I lived with my family, riding in the early morning through hills and plains, camping out at night on a river bank . . . where dark-skinned people lived who spoke strange languages I could understand, and were still close to nature and knew its secrets . . . dusty red tracks in the thick bush, ancient lakes with flamingoes, lions roaring in the vast darkness and snorting buffalo . . . sunsets of gold and fire with silhouetted giraffe, drums in the night . . .

'But I do want to live in Africa. I do not want to stay here all my life. One day I shall go to Africa. I shall send you a postcard from there, signora, in twenty years' time.'

Twenty years later, I did.

When I was about thirteen years old, my father's voice suddenly changed, and became a hoarse, raucous whisper. A surgeon, he recognized the symptoms as being serious, and the tests confirmed his own diagnosis: he had cancer of the throat.

Although we were never told anything, both my younger sister and I felt there was something different in the house. Conversations were hushed, and a cloud of gloom hung over it on the day of our father's operation. They explained to us that he simply had a benign growth in his throat. But I knew that this was a lie, and that he might be dying, and for nights I stared at the ceiling of my room, crying hot tears of desolation. My father survived his malignant cancer, which, diagnosed at an early stage, was successfully removed, together with a vocal chord. His beautiful voice never came back. I missed his stories and the flair of his enunciation. I felt his infirmity as crippling for me as he must have felt it: but soon his spirit took over and his voice gradually became stronger, although it never found its music, and it was to remain hoarse for the rest of his life.

He began, in those days, to talk to me about Africa and the nomad tribes of the desert, which fascinated him. Soon he started travelling there regularly, beginning a love affair with the Sahara which will live as long as he. I joined him a few times. The Tuaregs of the desert rode tall fast camels, their lean bodies were wrapped in flowing blue robes, fastened at the waist by belts inlaid with silver. They moved like shadows, leaving hardly a track. In the chilly nights of stars, around the fires, we shared stringy goat stews laced with pepper which made my mouth smart, and sweet mint tea in glasses small as thimbles. Black *ganduras* sheltered them from the wind and turbans protected their slit eyes from the fine penetrating sand. Lost jackals whined their sadness to the waves of barren dunes unending like the sea, and the night listened.

But it was not my Africa.

Mario and Emanuele

Emanuele's eyes: 'an old and secret sadness . . .'

I met Mario when I was barely out of school, during my first year of Political Sciences at university, and I fell immediately and totally in love with him. Within a few months we were married, and I never finished my university course.

Mario came from a wealthy half-Sicilian and half-Piedmontese milieu, and the mixture of Arab and northern blood had resulted in uncommonly good looks: his straight hair was brown and his almond-shaped eyes glinted gold; the olive skin set off gleaming even teeth and a perfect sensuous mouth below a slightly aquiline profile. Although only a few years older than I, he had the self-assured and chivalrous manners of good breeding, and of an unusual culture. He knew deeply – and loved with equal passion – art and music, antiques and racehorses, fast cars and beautiful women. His *savoir-faire* and aesthetic sense were far more developed than in any of his contemporaries, and he had the irresistible gift of making the teenager I still was feel like a woman. He was my first man, and he swept me off my feet.

My father, who loved me and knew me well, was strongly opposed to our marriage, as he felt it could not last, and only agreed to put his signature to the document permitting his under-age daughter to marry because he respected me, and felt the decision was, after all, mine. I was nineteen. Although there was no bigotry in my family, in the early sixties in Italy there was no way a girl could live with a man without being married.

It was with Mario, a couple of months before the date set for the wedding, that I had my first serious accident.

It was 7 January. Our son Emanuele would be born two years later on the same date. Mario did not stop at a crossroads, and the side of his black Jaguar was hit by a passing car. The door on my side opened, and I was flung out. My feet were trapped, and I was dragged face down on the tarmac, until the swerving car came to a stop.

It was a horrible, if brief, feeling of total impotence, being pulled suddenly, at such speed, by my legs, like a lifeless rag doll. My face hit the tarmac once, but, as I was conscious, I used all my willpower to contract my neck and lift my head from the road, to avoid being grazed all over. I was wearing a fur coat, and this, which was shaved bare by the friction, protected the rest of my body.

My left leg and shoulder, and my face, were partly tattooed with minute black tar particles, and the burning pain was excruciating. But there were no major cuts or lesions, and, all in all, I regarded myself as lucky. It took some months of treatment and dressings for the scars to heal completely, and to this day some tiny fragments of tarmac from an otherwise forgotten road in Conegliano Veneto, are still embedded, barely visible, in my shoulder and below my jaw. Mario, who was driving and naturally clung to the steering wheel, was shocked but unharmed.

Whatever the omens were, we were married one day in April. My father gave me away in a church packed with friends and peach blossoms. I wore white and a long veil, but somehow something was lacking from the very beginning. Perhaps it was the magic which purifies and blesses all things.

Two years later I gave birth to a son. We called him Emanuele. He was born in a cold night of rare snow in Venice, in the old Hospital of S. Giovanni e Paolo. In winter Venice, always an enchanted town, is at her most subtly charming when, the tourists gone, it remains to the Venetians, the pigeons and the cats.

There was nothing in the long, high-vaulted ancient corridors, in the greys of the first silent dawn after he was born, which could anticipate the golden freedom, the sunny landscapes which, in a few years, would be the background to Emanuele's extraordinary childhood and youth.

From the beginning, he was a quiet, serious and solitary little boy, with intelligent brown eyes and a small aristocratic nose like his father's. He inherited my smile and, I think, my physique. From a very early age he could speak a varied and correct Italian, uncannily able to converse with adults on their own level. At four he could read fluently and had already developed an unusual knowledge of what was going to be his abiding passion: animals. By the time he was six he had accumulated a remarkable collection of dozens of books and wildlife encyclopedias. He read them all in a methodical and scientific way, remembering the characteristics, the habitat and Latin name of every animal. Like Mario, Emanuele was a born collector, and like my father he was gifted with a remarkable memory. But what was most noticeable in Emanuele were his eyes. In them there was a wisdom and a strange sadness, as if he knew more than his years could allow.

Our marriage lasted just over two years. My lack of experience and my love for Mario could not disguise my intuition that our relationship could not stand the test of time, and I felt that the pain of an early separation was better than the unavoidable bitterness which wasted years of youth would one day bring. So, soon after Emanuele was born, with a heavy heart one evening of Mozart I spoke to Mario in the quiet of our library. Still in the dawn of our twenties, we agreed to separate amicably, and for the child's sake, we remained for years very good friends. Another stage of my life ended that night.

My parents chose this occasion to separate also. My mother for years now had concentrated on her interest in the history of art and had gone back to learn, and then to teach, at the University of

Padova. My father was absent more and more often in Algeria, Niger and Sudan, and spent most of his time writing about his adventures.

I went to live with my mother in a large old villa on the river Brenta, to whose cool banks, shadowed by ancient trees and beautiful formal gardens, Venetians — who only moved by boat — would traditionally escape the steamy summers of the lagoon. The Riviera del Brenta was the fashionable retreat of Venetian society some two or three hundred years ago, and its Palladian villas, now mostly museums, still stand to witness these departed grandeurs.

In this somewhat rarefied atmosphere, in a world mostly made of women and dogs, in an unusually large but gloomy garden, Emanuele spent the first years of his life.

Friends in Veneto

They are not long, the days of wine and roses . . .

Ernest Dowson, *Vitae Summa Brevis*

Near my mother's house lived Carletto Ancilotto and his wife Chiara, whom I had known since my childhood. He was a count, and their country place on the Laguna was always open to friends. There I met Paolo, who was married to an artistic and intelligent woman, Mariangela, and they had two small daughters, Valeria and Livia. It was impossible to ignore Paolo. He radiated energy; his aura of intense liveliness and awareness was extremely attractive. He had a special way of walking tall and straight, and of giving his interlocutor the undivided attention of his direct, intelligent and arresting blue eyes. Paolo had a doctorate in agriculture, and was interested in and successful at farming. Like most country gentlemen in those days, he enjoyed fishing, hunting and shooting, passions which he shared with Carletto.

Paolo's father had left Switzerland, where he was born, while still in his teens, to live in the southern United States, where he had learnt all there was to know about cotton; he had later settled in India and had dedicated himself to this prosperous trade. Paolo's maternal grandfather had been a pioneer in the world of aviation, and, at the beginning of the century, had founded in Italy the famous Macchi aircraft factory. His mother had studied at the Conservatoire, and had become an accomplished violinist. From his mother, Paolo inherited a passion for music, and from his father, a love of travel and a fascination with the tropics.

As soon as he finished university, Paolo took a year off and travelled by ship to Africa. He arrived in Mombasa one day in 1959: it was the beginning of his love-affair with this continent.

There he made friends: particularly with the Block brothers, Jack and Tubby, from the pioneering family who controlled the hotel business in Kenya, and with the Roccos, an extraordinary clan, half Italian half French, who lived on a farm on the shore of Lake Naivasha. During his peregrinations Paolo discovered a farm on the Kinangop, at the foot of the Aberdare Mountains, with a river full of trout running through it. It was for sale, and he set his heart on it. He went back to Italy, married Mariangela, the girlfriend of his schooldays, and returned to Kenya with her, having persuaded his father to acquire the farm.

Kenya in 1960, just before Independence, was still under the spell of the Mau Mau. People in isolated farms still went to bed with their guns. It was a very different life from that of Milan, and Mariangela found it difficult to adapt to it. When she realized she was going to have a child, she persuaded Paolo to return to Italy.

They returned to Europe and settled in Veneto, in a property on the lagoon, Cavallino ('Little Horse'), teeming with wildfowl and fish. Often the Blocks, or some of the Roccos, came to visit them, and rekindled Paolo's nostalgia for Africa.

They were adopted immediately by the community of landed gentry in Veneto. I saw them often, and got on extremely well with both. Paolo's intelligence and culture, his agile mind, and his way of telling stories of Africa, were fascinating to me. Often in the summer, our group of friends went out to dine in various open-air trattorias, famous for their food and excellent wine.

One night like many others, with Carletto, Chiara and several other friends, we decided to try a new fish restaurant on the shores of the river Sile. Fatally, that day Paolo had lent his car to Dorian Rocco, who had come from Kenya on holiday, and the one belonging to his wife was being serviced. Carletto and Chiara collected them in their car at the jetty on the mainland, and I went with them.

The food was excellent and our spirits were high. Afterwards we split up and changed vehicles, since Carletto and Chiara had decided to go home and all the rest of us wanted to go dancing. The night was balmy and luminous with fireflies. We laughed and talked in the car, unworried by that a lorry approaching us at full speed, headlights ablaze.

A bang, some screams, the noise of broken glass and screeching metal. The feeling of being torn apart, pulled backwards violently in a powerful vortex towards a dark tunnel from which there was no return. A lock of my blonde hair, plastered with blood, hanging on the smashed back window.

The fireflies kept dancing, unconcerned.

Through the tragedy I had shed what remained of my youthful naivety. Wrapped in heavy plaster like in a giant chrysalis, for over eight months I lay horizontal in different hospital beds. My multiple fracture was complicated by the discovery that I was already suffering from acute anaemia: before the accident I had simply been extremely thin.

One afternoon they lifted me laboriously on to a stretcher and wheeled me to another room where I watched bewildered on a black-and-white television screen the first tentative steps of a man who seemed himself weighed down by clumsy plaster, on the luminous surface of the moon. Later that evening I lay in the darkness, catching in my hand-mirror the silver moonlight which man had conquered, but which was so far from my bed that summer.

I learned to drink and to eat with my head barely lifted, and not to feel humiliated by being totally dependent on nurses for my physical needs.

During the unending hot summer nights, when the peculiar silence of hospitals breathing with suffering strangers closed upon me, I stared at the white aseptic ceilings, patiently waiting for my body to heal, aware that what happened afterwards was largely up to me.

The key to my future was Paolo. Through operations and blood transfusions, through physical pain and the agony of soul-searching, I started to look forward to his visits. He began to represent the link with a different world, the hope of change and of a new life.

His legs were not affected, and his fractured jaw, ribs and spine could not confine him to his bed indefinitely. Paolo could never stay still. He brought with him a sunny aura of adventure. He sat close by my bed, and through clenched teeth he started talking of the place where he had once lived, and to which he felt he belonged beyond explanation or reason. Lean and straight, and with a perennial suntan, his sparkling blue eyes full of suffering but also of invincible energy, Paolo evoked for me images of unbounded freedom, of wild open horizons and red sunsets, of green highlands teeming with wild animals. His presence lit the hospital room with golden light; I could smell the dry grasses of unknown savannahs, the first rains on the dust of a long drought, and feel the wind in my hair, the sun burning into my skin. The dream of my childhood revived through his vivid stories.

He told me once about the eels which leave the canals and rivers where they are born and swim back through the perilous seas to breed and to die in the Sargasso Sea, thousands of miles away. And of the baby eels which swim their way back to the same rivers and canals their parents came from. I remembered the swallows.

We never spoke, in those days, of what had just happened and changed our destiny for ever. We both needed, in order to heal our deeper wounds, and to forge ahead, to look forward to a completely different existence, where shadows of the past would not hover, where memories would not haunt us, and where we could discover again the sense of life. We both instinctively knew that this could only happen in a place where we could start again from the beginning. Somewhere far away, somewhere where everything was still practically unknown. His enthusiasm totally besotted me. My enthusiasm warmed him, and gave him new hope. We were bound together by the same vision of this far-away continent beyond the sea, and by the will to survive.

By the time the weather grew cold and foggy, and the trees again lost their leaves, we were in love.

'You must get better. You must walk again. Then I will show you Kenya.'

I could not wait. I exercised my muscles constantly under the heavy plaster, to be as fit as possible when they finally could free me of that shell.

When they did, Paolo was there. He helped me to sit up in the bed, and I could look out of the window at a grey winter sea. But when I tried to stand, I could not. My leg was not just weak, it was shorter, twisted. I was a cripple.

4

Africa

I speak of Africa and golden joys.

Shakespeare, *2 Henry IV*

It was as a cripple that I set foot for the first time in the country where I had dreamed I would one day walk tall, looking out at the breathtaking spaces of the Great Rift Valley.

I was pushed to the plane for Nairobi in a wheelchair, but on board I was helped by Paolo. From the moment I saw his lean suntanned face shed all the night tiredness as the African dawn lighted up the sky, I knew we had arrived. He was peering out of the aeroplane window with intense concentration, smiling. It was as if a light had sprung up in him, and for the first time since Mariangela had died, I saw his genuine self return and take over.

There was a new spring in his long easy step, a glorious progression, as if he walked again on safe territory where he felt he belonged and ought to be living, a land he was familiar with and which he understood; where he could be at his very best. He showed me Kenya as I had always known he would, with the enthusiasm of one who only there had been truly happy, and who had never wanted to leave. Even if it had to be with crutches, this was Africa at last. Kenya in February 1970 was at its hottest and driest. The yellow grass and the first acacias on the way from the airport; a gazelle – perhaps an impala – grazing in the long strange grass; the African faces of smiling porters; women in

19

bright cloths balancing baskets on their heads: these were my most vivid impressions, after the fog and dampness of Venice.

The strange tropical plants enchanted me. I was astonished by my first jacaranda in full bloom, in a glory of blue. Here was a totally different continent, where every physical stimulus was accentuated, strong and almost aggressively beautiful, as if painted by a sure and powerful hand. The subtle watercolour gentleness of sophisticated and waning Europe now seemed more alien to my nature than the burning, merciless, splendid sun which welcomed us.

We drove straight to Nairobi. Our room at the Norfolk Hotel, the gem of the Block Hotels group, looked into an internal court-yard with cages of exotic birds. I could not sleep. A large bush of red hibiscus, Paolo's favourite flower, grew just outside our room. It was ten times the size of the one I had tried to grow in Italy. I limped out into the sun, and observed the large scarlet flowers, their sharp yellow stamens crowned with red dots. Dew drops, like jewels, were trapped in their silky throats dusted with luminous pollen. I inhaled the subtle perfume. From the first breath I felt a new energy and an extraordinary sense of well-being, but it was from Dorian's aeroplane, I think, that I discovered that I, too, was in love with Africa.

The first morning, as we arrived at the Norfolk Hotel, Paolo decided to phone Dorian Rocco immediately. He was told Dorian had gone to Wilson, the private-aircraft airport of Nairobi. Paolo decided to go straight there to find him, driven, I knew, by the desire to renew contact with Kenya and his past life there. Dorian had been staying with Paolo in the Venetian lagoon at the time of the accident. Dorian's parents had come to Kenya in the thirties, walking their way through Africa. His mother, Giselle, belonged to a French family and was an artist. His father, Mario Rocco, called Pappi, was Neapolitan. They settled on a farm on the shores of Lake Naivasha, where they built an unusual Italianate villa of great charm, with an avenue of tall cypresses, like those in Tuscany, striding down to the lake. They were an unconventional and adventurous family, constantly involved in exploits out of the ordinary. Dorian had two younger sisters, Mirella and Oria.

Dorian was flying to the coast for the weekend, and invited us to join him. Without a moment's hesitation we accepted. Paolo's eyes sparkled as he tried to fit my crutches in the back of the little plane. I had nothing with me but the clothes I wore, a pair of jeans and a khaki shirt, and the bursting desire to fly high above Africa in a small aircraft. Nothing else mattered. Before we took off, Dorian said: 'Lower your heads while we taxi in front of the tower. I haven't got a licence to fly passengers yet.'

I lowered my head, to see the tarmac sliding fast through a hole torn in the tattered floor. Then, blurred burnt grass and blue sky. There was no going back. We were airborne.

Nairobi National Park is just outside Wilson. Soon the first herd of giraffe ambled, long-necked and graceful, just below us. Dorian steered the plane deep into a nose dive. They ran as if in slow motion, kicking away the dust. Feathery thorn trees on a river bank barely hid some sleepy buffaloes. I shouted with delight. I was intoxicated with the heat, the noise of the plane, the incredible feeling of my first flight in a small aircraft over the African plains. Dorian seconded my mood as only a Rocco could. We circled over herds of elephant when we reached Tsavo, and followed lazy rivers looking for hippos and crocodiles. I took in the vegetation of low bushland and savannah, the small groups of Grant's gazelles with twitching tails, troops of baboons running away down yellow fever trees, Doum palms with fan-shaped balanced branches, and the first amazing, silvery, gigantic baobabs.

Then a tented camp appeared, bright green canvas in neat rows on a river bend where a black rhino drank placidly, a grass airstrip close by. 'Oh, let's land, please!' I pleaded over the engine noise.

'Tomorrow,' Dorian said, 'tomorrow we will land for tea. We are really late.'

We were.

The sun seemed still high and bright to me, but I was not yet familiar with the sudden sunsets on the equator. Soon the sky was tinged with red and purples, as if a vast fire had been lit just below the horizon. The rare clouds became rimmed with gold, while the sun, orange and round like an incandescent coin, moved lower and lower and was gone. I had time to see the uncanny indigo expanse of the Indian Ocean, flat as a mirror, rippled only around the coral barrier. Palm trees darkened fast, car lights appeared on the thin tarmac road, and it was night.

I was not prepared for the tiny airstrip among thick palm groves and huge baobabs where we landed in almost total darkness, having first circled low over a group of thatched cottages to signal our arrival. We taxied on the bumpy, sandy strip, escorted by a dozen bare-chested children who screamed with excitement as they ran in front of us, and finally we stopped in what looked like a car park, in front of a dimly lit, pleasantly old-fashioned door, on which was written: 'Mnarani Club'.

'Here we are,' Dorian said. 'We'll spend the night at Mirella's.' An open Land-Rover approached and my door was opened. A heavy scent of frangipane and warm spiced sea air enveloped me, and I found myself looking into teasing, bulging blue eyes. It was a man with his long fair hair in a ponytail, his skin deeply tanned, and skinny bare feet emerging from a flowing turquoise caftan.

'I am Lorenzo Ricciardi,' he said in Italian. 'Welcome to Kilifi. I'll drive you to my house.'

Overwhelmed and dizzy with all the new sensations and discoveries, already totally won by the incredible beauty of this country, and intrigued by the exotic, unusual looks of our host: 'You look like a pirate!' I could not help exclaiming.

Lorenzo grinned. 'I am,' he said.

Lorenzo was married to Dorian's sister Mirella, a famous photographer. Her book, *Vanishing Africa*, had recently been published and I had a copy. It was an extraordinary book, the work of an artist who knew and loved Africa and had managed to capture the elusive yet haunting quality of the landscape, and of a people still living in the past, and their traditional culture. I was curious to meet her.

Mirella was more than just beautiful. Green eyes and full lips, curly hair in a halo, dark skin, a slim figure swathed in colourful cotton kangas and arms dangling with silver bracelets were the first things one saw. But her husky voice told more. Her Italian was heavily but pleasantly accented, her manner direct, almost masculine, and she gave the immediate impression of being an original and gifted woman with the courage and drive to live her life as she chose. Paolo knew her from the old days. Her approach was natural and uninhibited, and she shared the plans, memories and adventures of her unconventional life with me as if she had known me always. I felt welcome and completely at home.

Her house right on top of the cliff was open to the evening winds and the sea was as close as if we were on the deck of an Arab dhow. Bright cushions lined the walls, and straw mats covered the floors where one could only walk barefoot. There was a magic about that house, and the fact that I was not destined to sleep in an anonymous hotel room on my first night in Kenya seemed like an omen. I already belonged.

That night, in the large carved Lamu bed, with the windows open to the breeze from the ocean, the mosquito net gently moving, I lay listening to the noise of the surf mixed with the new mysterious voices of the African night — bushbabies and nocturnal birds. Paolo held my hand, and for a long time neither of us spoke. Only one day separated us from the cold European winter, but it was more than time and distance. I knew I had already crossed a barrier into a new world and that this was going to be more than just a holiday.

If my first day in Africa was virtually spent in the air, on my second I discovered the true heat of a merciless equatorial sun burning deep into my skin, the warmth of the salty water alive with a thousand creatures, the whiteness of the sand, the glory of colours and smells, the surprise of a school of dolphins playing out on the shimmering reef.

In the early afternoon we took off again, and I could see this time how close to the Kilifi creek we had landed the night before.

Dorian kept his word. 'Let's go for tea at Cottar's Camp.'

The green tents squatting on the river bank appeared again out of the parched bush, Dorian circled low, reached up, steadied the plane pointing to the grassy strip, and we were landing.

The grass was taller than we had realized, and concealed a large pig-hole. Before we knew it, one of the wheels had sunk into it, the propeller hit something, and a baobab at the end of the airstrip came closer and closer. Paolo's eyes were on mine, his fingers dug deep into my arm.

'Hold on, we're crashing,' said Dorian unemotionally, and with a terrific noise of broken branches the plane came to a halt, tilted to one side. 'Jump out! It might catch fire.'

It was not easy, with my crippled leg. Paolo propelled me out and I limped away as fast as I could, hanging on to his arm, my crutches abandoned.

The plane did not catch fire. We stopped, breathless, to look back at the contorted wreck. There was a smell of freshly mown hot hay, of dust and resin. Insects buzzed around us and the inevitable African children had already gathered in a silent, bare-footed little group, staring. Paolo took both my shoulders in his strong gentle hands to steady me, the dizziness cleared away, and I smiled back. 'We made it.'

There had been no time to think. My African adventure had begun, and I could only accept whatever came with it.

Across the airstrip, a strange couple was approaching from the camp. A thin elderly man with a beard, short khaki trousers, a pipe hanging from his mouth. A rotund woman in a flowered frock and rubber sandals. The managers. We must have looked weird — dishevelled, covered in dust and twigs, with the mangled wreck of the plane behind us. The man came forward unperturbed, as if nothing unusual had happened.

'Do you have any luggage?' he asked in clipped English. He did not wait for the answer. 'Come and have a cup of tea.'

'That's what we came for,' I said, and we were all laughing.

Rather than radio-calling Nairobi for another aircraft, we decided to spend the night there. This was going to be my first night ever in a tent. We sat outside in the mess tent, sipping sundowners and watching a rhino drinking on the other side of the river. In a few years this would become an extremely rare sight, but then I did not know it.

After putting out the paraffin lamp, I lay before sleep listening to a far-away hyena, giant croaking toads, strange rustles. A lion's sudden deep-throated roar, swallowing all other noises, was so startlingly close that the canvas seemed to vibrate at the sound. It was only my second night in Africa, yet something had begun to grow inside me which I could not stop, as if my childhood dreams had finally found the place where they could materialize. I had arrived where I was always meant to be. I did not know how it could be practically achieved, but I was certain beyond any shadow of doubt that it was here that I wanted to live.

Much had to be done before it was possible, and the crutches at the foot of the bed were the first reality. I did not want to, nor could I, be here as a cripple. I would need strong legs, to run if need be, and to walk straight at Paolo's side on the land I hoped we would one day find for ourselves in Africa. This meant, I knew, more operations, more hospitals, more pain and patience. It would take time. But I would make it. Yet again I could see with great clarity that a will is a way, and that having a worthy goal is what truly matters. Another bond tied me to Paolo now. I, like him, was in love with Africa.

'I must walk,' I murmured to Paolo before sliding into the best sleep I had had in months. 'I must learn to walk and run again, however long it takes.'

It took three more years.

5

To Walk Again

We have to change our patterns of reacting to experience. For our problems do not lie in what we experience, but in the attitude we have towards it.

Akong Rimpoche

Venice was covered in yellow fog when we landed, and our dark glowing skin and sun-bleached hair seemed incongruous among the pale crowd at Tessera airport. A little boy with a blond fringe, dressed in a dark blue coat, ran ahead of the small group who had come to meet us, and I kneeled to hug him. Every day, for the time I had been gone, I had sent him at least two postcards with photographs of animals, as I knew he would look forward to the arrival of the postman ringing his bicycle bell, and to little messages from across the sea assuring him that his mother cared, and thought of him constantly. The only thing I had been really looking forward to during the splendid two months abroad was to be reunited with Emanuele. He was four. He had been left in the care of his nanny, and of course of my mother, who adored him more than anyone else in the world.

Sitting at his bedside in his blue room, the first night I was back, I told him of Kenya and of the places I had visited, of the animals I had seen and the people I had met. He listened in silence, absorbed in all the stories. In his face there was that concentrated, focused look beyond his years and experience, which always made me think. Without having planned it, I heard myself saying, 'One day, we shall live there.' There was no surprise in his eyes, and he said quietly, 'Yes.'

When I told my mother, she thought I was mad. Yet she knew me well enough not to contradict me. 'You know nobody there. You speak no English. You hate driving. You ... cannot yet walk,' she protested.

'I will learn. It is the place where I want to live. If Paolo asked me, I would go tomorrow.' In the end, I was to ask him.

As we were landing from our second Kenya holiday, I said to Paolo, 'Supposing that instead of living in Italy and spending our holidays in Kenya, we did the opposite?'

I had timed my question to match the gloom lining Paolo's face at the prospect of going back to a life for which he had lost his enthusiasm, tuning it to the changed sound of the engines. I knew that, once said, there was no taking my words back, and that with them I had decided to help my destiny on the path which I was always meant to tread.

Paolo fixed his luminous blue eyes on mine, and seized my wrists. 'Thank you,' he said simply. 'Now we must get married.'

The law permitting divorce had recently been passed in Italy. I had been legally separated for years, and it took only a few weeks to obtain the divorce.

The institution of marriage had no particular appeal for me; no contract drawn up to legalize it would add to my love for Paolo. Yet it would be simpler, living in Africa, if we were married. Moreover it would give a sense of security and identity to our children to know that we had committed ourselves to each other, and thus, indirectly, to them.

The months and years which followed were of preparation.

I will not talk about the operations, the hospitals, the new doctors, the tedious hours spent in unending exercise. I feel I must, however, give a word of praise to the surgeon in Berne, the greatest in his field, who, with rare patience and skill, fractured my leg again, twisted it back to the right angle, lengthened it and set it once more: Professor Müller. He was the best, and I was lucky. From the first visit, when he took away my crutches and asked me to walk up and down the room in front of him, and I caught an unprofessional glint of pity in his eyes at my awkward limping, a relation of total trust was established between us.

'I can make you walk as before, but you must help me. You will have to work hard. You must be patient. It will be worth it. You are too young to be a cripple.'

Several operations were needed, and time to heal in between, but I had absolute confidence in him, and he kept his promise.

He used to come to my room in the early afternoons of yet another short European summer spent in a hospital bed. He sat at my bedside, and we talked. He spoke French, the language of my grandmother, and, as all the nurses spoke only German, he was the only person I could talk to. As Paolo, in Italy with his daughters, could only come for short visits, and Emanuele was away with my mother, Professor Müller was my one friend at the Lindenhof.

He, and the birds. I had once fed the birds crumbs from my breakfast, in the hope that they would come again. Soon they started to arrive first thing in the morning, before the fräulein came to pull the curtains, pecking with their beaks sharply at the glass windows to wake me up. I looked forward to their good-morning, and when I left I worried for weeks about them flying to my window as usual and finding me gone, and I hoped the next patient would befriend them too. At each return for the next two years, I found new birds to feed and to keep me company – or were they the same ones? – and this taught me that small things can often make big things bearable.

6

The First Fire

. . . burnt-out ends of smoky days . . .

T. S. Eliot, *Preludes*

We were married by the mayor of the small village where my mother lived. I wore a white dress printed with red strawberries, the children were dressed in a matching red pattern and Paolo sported a red silk tie. In all the photographs I have, we are smiling at one another, and we look happy.

Only a week before, I had come back from Switzerland, where the last piece of metal had been extracted from my leg. It was perfectly cured and of exactly the same length as the other. Professor Müller had kept his word. Only that very morning I had discarded for ever the stick I had used in recent months. The luggage was ready, and so were our tickets for Nairobi.

For our wedding lunch we went by boat to the small island of Burano, where the famous fish restaurant 'da Romano' had prepared a glorious feast of delicacies from the lagoon.

Wind in our hair, smell of seaweed, screams of seagulls, and the island fading like a mirage in the wake of the boats.

There was one more thing to do before leaving. From the age of twelve, I had kept a diary. Almost every day I filled page after page with my impressions and emotions, facts and events. The pleasures and doubts, questions and answers of my adolescent awakening were diligently recorded. During my convalescence, during the long nights in hospital, I had found refuge and solace in writing about my feelings, my hopes and my fears. My diary was to me what a psychoanalyst might be to others: a healthy way of getting things out of my system, pouring them out on the blank, unjudging, tempting pages. I kept the two dozen volumes in a green travelling trunk. When the decision was taken to leave Europe and live in Africa, I thought for weeks about what to do with those journals — all my life so far. Now that way of life had come to an end, a new page, literally, had been turned. I could not take that bulky trunk to Kenya, where we had as yet nowhere to live, and where it might well take years to find a home. I could not, however, leave my diaries behind. They contained nothing particularly secret which would have embarrassed me, but they were my private account of my past, and of all the people and events which were part of my story so far. Even if I locked the trunk and left it in the care of my mother, I would not feel at ease knowing that I had left a part of my life unguarded and vulnerable to the possible curiosity of people unknown. I regarded going to Africa as a rebirth, and I had learnt from my accident that for a new plant to sprout, the seed pod must crack and die. Holding on to the old was no way of progressing. I decided to burn my diaries.

At the back of my mother's large garden, on my last afternoon in Europe, with Emanuele's help I gathered a pile of firewood and placed my diaries on it as if on a ceremonial pyre. I poured some paraffin on them, and lit a match. The paper began burning at once, sending up waves of heat in the clear July afternoon. I sat on the grass, yellow and blue with buttercups and forget-me-nots, watching my past burn away for ever and go up in smoke before my eyes. Seeing the smoke, my mother came out in alarm. She stood petrified, realizing what was happening, for she, like the rest of my family, had known about my journals. All that was left was a small mound of papery ashes and glowing wood. I reached out to poke at the embers with my walking-stick. Some pages rose, half charred, flying up with the heat like leaves in a bush fire. A blackened shape appeared, smouldering still. My mother gasped.

A human shape, a torso, a stretched leg ... I grinned at her reassuringly: it was only my discarded plaster, and beneath that the melted plastic and blackened aluminium of my crutches. I stood up and threw my walking-stick in the fire. I was ready to go.

The following day, with Paolo's daughters and my son, and a great deal of luggage, we took off from Venice airport, bound for Africa and our new life.

PART II

Paolo

7

A New Life

A journey of a thousand miles must begin with a single step.

Chinese proverb

We had planned to look around for a place to buy, where we could settle. Paolo had thought of a ranch, where he wanted to raise cattle, but more importantly where wildlife had to abound. We knew it was not going to be easy, but we were determined to try. One thing was clear in both of our minds: we were not coming here to seek our fortune. We were choosing a way of life.

The children were excited at the idea of moving to a mysterious and different country, where summer lasted all year round. Emanuele fell in love with Kenya immediately, and with a passion which never left him. It was the place which embodied his dreams, where the animals lived which he had learnt about only from books, and his life in Kenya was, from the very first moment, a glorious and joyous adventure.

In the beginning, our main contact was Paolo's sister-in-law. Paolo's older brother had come to Kenya a few years earlier, drawn by Paolo's enthusiasm, and had bought a prosperous coffee farm close to Thika. It was still the time of big-game hunting, before the pressure of poaching and the destruction of the environment had made this sport anachronistic and, eventually, forbidden; still the time of the famous white hunters, of the grand camping safaris not very different from the ones celebrated by Hemingway.

One evening at Voi, in a hunting block near the coast, Paolo's brother shot an elephant in a herd and killed it. Instead of running away, the other elephants went for him. He was found next morning in a pool of blood, the dead elephant beside him. A tusk had penetrated his groin and he had bled to death. Three months later, his infant son, who had been staying with the grandparents in Italy, died in his sleep; the cause was never discovered. His widow chose to stay in Kenya. She eventually remarried a much older man, and it was they who took care of us in Nairobi in those early days.

We had arrived in July, one of the coolest months of the year in the Kenya Highlands. We stayed first at a quiet hotel in Nairobi which had rooms opening on to a large wild garden overlooking a river. The first morning Emanuele, who had been up exploring since first light, burst into my room flushed with excitement, an unusual occurrence, for he was usually very calm.

'Pep,' he said breathlessly, using his favourite nickname for me, 'Pep, I have seen a snake. I am sure it was a *Naja nigricollis*. I must check in my book.'

His book confirmed he had been right: the snake was a cobra.

Many years, many events later, during the longest night of my life, when the most unexpected and forgotten details came back to my tortured mind like clues for solving the absurd puzzle, I remembered this incident: the first animal Emanuele had seen in Africa had been a snake.

As it would take time to find what we wanted and we could not live in a hotel for ever, we decided to buy a house in Nairobi. We found a pleasant two-storey house in grey stone, set in about three acres of garden with many indigenous trees, in an area called Gigiri, close both to Muthaiga, where many of our friends lived, and to the school where the children would go to learn English.

For my own English, I decided to read books written in the

language. I prefer biographies, history, the classics, poetry, philosophy or religion, but I certainly could not plunge head first into these subjects in a foreign language, so I chose something I seldom read: novels. With a dictionary on my lap, I went through endless novels written in impeccable English. I learnt about scores of governesses, younger daughters of vicars or of teachers, usually orphans and penniless, who went to teach scores of spoilt and/or unhappy noble brats in grand gothic manors in Cornwall, and who inevitably fell in love with the widowed, darkly handsome and sinister master of the house. The plots were similar, and after the final pages of suspense, they ended − predictably − happily. Paolo, who spoke faultless English, was amused, and used to tease me about my choice of textbooks, but, always inquisitive, he became interested in these sagas and I ended up having to tell him most of the stories. I acquired many old-fashioned words like 'petticoats', 'becoming', 'duenna', 'philanderer' and 'bombazine', but I finally managed to master a decent vocabulary. I was now able to read what really interested me, and, mostly, to understand what people said. Once I could enjoy word-play and make jokes as I did in Italian, I felt I had won my battle with English.

Swahili was less difficult. Like Italian, Swahili is written phonetically. With no problem in pronunciation and a decent memory, I found it easy to master. We had chosen Kenya as the place to stay. It was inconceivable for me not to learn at least the principal language of my new home. I embraced it as I had the new country: with curiosity, interest and love.

8

Friends in Kenya

Friends are all that matters.

Guy Burgess

In our love of Africa we were not alone.

The people of European origin who lived in Kenya by choice, not as part of their career like diplomats or managers of international companies, formed a tightly-knit community. They had either been born there, of early settlers or pioneer ancestors, and had decided to stay on, or had chosen Kenya because, like us, they had fallen in love with it. This was the shared base from which the bond grew: we could fit in happily nowhere else; we were haunted by this country, and in different ways we felt we had to make the most of it.

Paolo wanted me to get to know his friends of earlier days, and we spent the first weeks visiting these people, some of whom I had already met, and most of whom lived up-country. One of the first places Paolo took me to was Lake Naivasha, about one hour's drive from Nairobi along a panoramic road overlooking the Escarpment. The Blocks had a place, Longonot Farm, on the south shore, and the Roccos had a villa on the opposite side. Their farm D.D.D., 'Dominio Di Doriano', had been named after our friend, their son.

One reached D.D.D. by way of sweeping steps which climbed in a gentle curve through palms and fig trees. Pappi Rocco and

Giselle spent most of their days in the spacious, high-ceilinged rooms on the ground floor. It was permeated by the Art Deco atmosphere of its design, its murals, Giselle's paintings and sculptures. In the panelled library, black-and-white photographs lining the walls and every possible shelf unfolded the unusual story of their daughters Mirella and Oria. I met Oria, and her Scottish husband Iain Douglas-Hamilton, first in those photographs. There was Oria on her wedding day, a gypsy air to her long dress and fringed shawl, against the background of a windswept island off Scotland. Iain stood beside her, long fair hair on a velvet coat with a lacy jabot, horn-rimmed glasses and the inevitable kilt. There was a wide photograph of an entire herd of elephant in Lake Manyara, closer to the photographer than one would think possible for safety. Oria's naked child reached up from an ant-hill, touched the outstretched trunk of a peaceful matriarch. A group of slight, naked Rocco children, hair glowing light around the darkly tanned faces, played with lean, naked African children: their bodies plastered with mud, they drew strange arabesques on each other, and were transformed into living clay sculptures.

The old Roccos had a way of telling stories with great flair, making them sound like legends.

The intriguing combination of aromatic Neapolitan food and French cuisine, concocted by old Kimuyu, was served by red-fezzed servants on the panoramic terrace guarded by tall cypresses. During one of these lunches, the noise of an engine approached from the sky and a small aeroplane appeared, aiming — or so I thought — straight for us at full speed, like a mad kamikaze on his target. The china seemed to clatter on the table, the wheels seemed to miss the roof by inches. I almost spilled my wine, the children cheered, the old Roccos looked not at all perturbed. 'Iain and Oria,' they commented casually. 'Good. They have made it for lunch.' That is how I met them, and their angelic little daughters, Saba and Dudu.

Like Mirella, Oria was dark-skinned and feminine, colourful and exotic, with a deep, low voice, lively eyes, and a ceaseless drive to achieve the unusual. Iain, of aristocratic Scottish descent, had written his D.Phil. for Oxford on the elephant of Lake Manyara in Tanzania, where they had lived for years. This choice, like all choices, was to influence the rest of his life for ever, and made of him, in time, a famous and respected elephant expert. They were a handsome, happy and original family of intelligent people, a mixture of Italian creativity and spontaneity, French flair, and Scottish determination and love of adventure and challenges. I knew at once that they would always be deeply involved in something stimulating and interesting. I was instantly drawn to them, and over the years our friendship naturally grew and our lives became inextricably involved. The warmth and culture of the Roccos made me feel welcome and at home, and I always looked forward to visiting them, for nothing obvious or boring could ever be found within their aura.

On the southern shore of Lake Naivasha was Longonot Farm, called after the crater which dominates the lake above the haunting gorge of Hell's Gate, today still teeming with antelope and giraffe, and it was the Blocks' domain. Their father had arrived from South Africa at the beginning of the century, his only wealth a sack of seed potatoes; and from this he created an empire. The Blocks' hospitality was renowned. Friendship was important to them and in their house you always met a mixture of talented and outstanding people from all over the world. For all their polish and social commitments, in different ways both Tubby and his Swedish wife Aino loved nature, and the peace of country life. Tubby adored taking you round his impeccable vegetable garden and the luxuriant orchard, going from plant to plant to taste a fruit, with a naive delight and a rural pride unexpected and refreshing in a man of the world. He had the gift of being happy with simple things. He adopted us, and became the staunchest and most dependable of loyal friends. Aino was an elegant and sophisticated hostess. But there was a side to Aino that few people knew, and as she once shared it with me it created a strong bond between us, which made her very close to me. She had lost her much-loved first-born boy of a few years to an incurable disease, and the way she explained her experience at that time was unforgettably touching.

Their house looked over the lake, where Paolo liked to go fishing for black bass with Emanuele in Tubby's boat. It skidded on the calm water through waterlilies and carpets of the infesting salvinia, barely missing some sleeping hippo. Pelicans, fish eagles and a breathtaking variety of water birds circled in the air and called from half-immersed tree stumps. These idyllic weekends at the Blocks' became a feature in our early days of search for our own Eden, and when we returned to Nairobi, the car bursting with fresh fruits and vegetables, the memory of Aino's desserts of meringues and strawberries lingered for days.

Other guests came to stay at Longonot Farm, and there we met the Rubens. Of the same Russian-Jewish background as the Blocks, old man Ruben had also come to Kenya at the turn of the century as a small boy, and at the end of the First World War, starting with two donkeys, he founded Express Transport, later a giant in the transport business, with fleets of lorries and hundreds of employees. Monty Ruben was a zoologist, with a passion for photography, medicine and gadgets. There was a strong base of loyalty and generosity in Monty, a sensitivity and a deep love for the country, and like Paolo, he felt himself very much an African. In the African tradition, he eventually adopted me as extended family, and I learnt that I could always count on him for advice and constructive help. Temperamentally, his wife Hilary was his absolute opposite. Spiritual and living in a world of her own, she loved beauty and culture, poetry and mysticism, music and nature. She combined this with compassion and caring for others. I found her company enriching and inspiring. Hilary and I had a spiritual affinity which created a common intuition of the meaning of what really mattered, and in this was the root of our friendship.

Among these new-found friends, there was Carol Byrne. She was so evanescent that somehow I cannot even remember how we first met. She entered our life on gentle feet, and she was there as if she had always been. She was a woman like the shadow of a cloud, untouched by age and not worn by life. Fate had been hard to Carol. Her man had died in an aeroplane crash, leaving her with a small child, Sam, an adorable and sensitive little boy a few years younger than Emanuele. Yet the preoccupations and the problems we knew she had been through had left no mark in her beautiful, youthful, spiritual face, nor had they affected her quiet manners. She took everything gracefully in her stride; her company was a privilege, and her presence always a gift which left us refreshed. She loved reading, music and Eastern philosophy. She was one of those rare people who fully practised her beliefs, and her life shone with harmony. She lived in a house built out of stone, thatch and great planks of wood, on the side of the cliff on the Mbagathi River at Kitengela. It was filled with books, carpets and cushions, music, and objects with a story, and like its owner, her house had a transparent soul. From the large windows, one could watch the animals of the Nairobi National Park coming to drink at the river. One often found lions sitting in her drive way, and rhino scratched their backs against her creepers.

Sooner than I could have imagined, I had been adopted by my new African family.

Exploring Lake Turkana

. . . giunta era l'ora che volge al desio
*e ai naviganti intenerisce il cuore . . .**

Dante Alighieri, *La Divina Commedia*

Exploring was our priority, and absolutely necessary in order to find the place we were looking for, so among the first things we purchased was a four-wheel-drive car and camping equipment. On the map of Kenya, Paolo pointed out the places we would visit next. From Naro Moru at the foot of Mount Kenya to Lake Naivasha and Lake Baringo; from Lake Nakuru to the parks and reserves of Amboseli, Tsavo, the Shimba Hills, Samburu, Marsabit, the Mara; from the wilderness of the Nguruman and of the Aberdare Mountains to the Arab towns on the coast, Lamu, Kiunga, the Bajuni Islands and Shimoni in the south, where fishing was supreme, we enthusiastically explored the country.

One of our favourite places was Lake Turkana, then still called Lake Rudolf, in the north after the Austrian Crown Prince.

The last stretch of road to Lake Turkana is a slow progression through black volcanic rocks. A last hill smouldering with heat and lava, barren landscapes, and then the purple, grey, black and

* '. . . the hour had come for remembrance
which saddens the heart of wandering sailors . . .'

jade expanse of the prehistoric lake appears, silent and majestic, with its islands immersed like immense sleeping dinosaurs.

In our early days we spent weeks and months there during the children's holidays. Sometimes we camped at Sandy Bay, a bare yellow cove fringed by a beach of brown pebbles and black sand, where Paolo always managed to catch, even from the shore, the most unexpectedly gigantic Nile perch. These are enormous but lethargic fish, easy to catch once they have taken your bait. Some are bright golden yellow, some grey-pink with the large round surprised eyes of all fish, in which we humans cannot read any expression of pain or suffering, so that – as with insects and molluscs – we feel absolved of their deaths. Sometimes we camped on long stretches of dunes, protected by very large *Acacia ethiopica*, under the shade of which the children, in their swimming costumes, would do their homework in the afternoons. The wind seldom stopped blowing and rain was rare at Turkana, except during the long rainy season of April, when sudden storms darkened the sky. Then huge waves altered the perfection of the lake, which became inkblack and violet, threatening and untameable, and torrents of water swirled, filling the sandy luggas.

One of those times the storm broke out at night, while we were camping north of Loyangelani, below Mount Por. We had two tents and the children shared one of them. At midnight the wind started howling with fury, and the violence and noise of the rain beating on the canvas was deafening. It was as if the sky was exploding, and the earth seemed to crack and tremble as before a volcanic eruption. I was worried about the children, but there was no way we could get out of our tent. The wind was so strong that we could not even manage to unzip the flap door. Then one of the posts collapsed and we were in total darkness.

The wind dropped as suddenly as it had started. For a time the only sound came from the newly-born river which flowed for a few hours into the lake. Then a chorus of birds and frogs came to life in the dripping silence of the night. We struggled out of our tent, to find the children's miraculously intact with them peacefully

1. Kuki at Mugongo ya Ngurue

2. Ol Ari Nyiro: Enghelesha from Sambara Hill

3. Ol Ari Nyiro: cattle drinking at a dam at midday

4. Paolo: the elephant hunt

5. Emanuele had a feeling for all reptiles. With a giant tortoise on Bird Island, Seychelles

5

6. Paolo

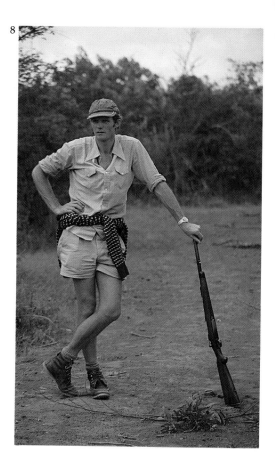

7. Mirimuk

8. Colin

9. Aerial view of the house at Kuti

10. Paolo's funeral

11. Mirimuk, Luka and the security at Paolo's funeral

9

12. The baby: Kuki, Sveva and Emanuele

13. Sveva and Wanjiru

asleep inside it. Next morning they woke as early as ever, and were amazed to discover that practically nothing remained of all our light camping gear which had been left outside. It was as if a tornado had come through the camp, carrying away all our pots and pans. Chairs and tables were upturned and blown for quite a few metres, and trees were festooned with kangas and toilet paper.

Life in Turkana followed ancient patterns. Paolo went fishing daily with Emanuele. I cooked. Plates were cleaned in the rough soda-saturated sand. We swam in the warm soda water, spying birds and crocodiles. Emanuele looked for chameleons and often found small black scorpions below the rocks, or, at night, that fat and evil-looking poisonous pale spider called the 'sole fugens'. He had several pet chameleons at that time, with names of early British kings — Alfred the Great, or Robert the Bruce. Funny creatures, with their careful, tentative walk, crafty eyes rotating in all directions, and interesting behaviour patterns, Ema just loved them. He used to have a favourite recurrent dream of a wood of blue bamboo alive with orange chameleons. We went for long walks, and in the evening we flew kites along the shore.

Occasionally, for more serious fishing, Paolo hired a boat at Loyangelani and we all went out. I remember coming back at sunset, the boat full of enormous fish, sitting at the prow with Emanuele, a little boy of seven or eight. The warm wind, which smelt of soda and of waterfowls' guano, blew through his straight fair hair streaked pale by the sun. His skin was dark, his eyes deep, brown and gentle. His head rested against my shoulder while I recited old Italian poems, which he would never study in his English school, Leopardi's *Silvia* and Dante's Quinto Canto in the 'Inferno' of the *Divina Commedia*, Pascoli and Foscolo, Jacopone da Todi, and Carducci's *Jaufré Rudel*. I hoped to try and communicate to Emanuele the same emotion, the same love for the harmonious beat of verses, which I remembered and treasured from those times with my father. It was strange and beautiful to be there in the heart of equatorial Africa, slowly crossing this vast, ancient

lake where our ancestors lived millions of years ago, reciting
classical Italian verses to my son.

> *Passa la nave mia con vele nere*
> *con vele nere pel selvaggio mare.*
> *Ho in petto una ferita di dolore*
> *tu ti diverti a farla sanguinare . . .**

or

> *. . . il volo d'un grigio alcione*
> *prosegue la dolce querela*
> *e sopra la candida vela*
> *s'affigge di nuvoli il sol . . .*†

Emanuele listened, gazing out at the distance. His skin had the
warm smell of healthy sunbaked boy, and I loved him with a
subtle pain, the premonition that it would not last.

---

* 'There goes my ship with black sails
with black sails over the wild seas.
My heart is wounded with a wound of pain
and you love to make it bleed.' (G. Carducci, *Passa la nave mia*)

† . . . The flight of a grey kingfisher
continues the sweet song
and over the white sails
the sun gathers clouds . . .' (G. Carducci, *Jaufré Rudel*)

10

The Coast

In the afternoon they came unto a land
In which it seemed always afternoon.
All round the coast the languid air did swoon,
Breathing like one that hath a weary dream.

Alfred, Lord Tennyson, *The Lotos-Eaters*

Paolo and I decided to spend the next summer on our own, and to
explore the north coast. We sent the children to their grandparents
in Europe, and we set off in our Land-Rover with a tent, an
inflatable Zodiac rubber dinghy, fishing gear and, of course, a gun.
We wanted to visit Lamu, Kiunga and Kiwayu.

I have always perceived Lamu as a sort of smaller and poorer
Venice, with similar characteristics. The narrow paved alleys, the
Arab architecture, the tall, crowded, arched buildings, and the
promenades facing the lagoon ... even the smells and dirt, and,
somehow, the cats.

Like Venice, it attracted a cosmopolitan crowd of eccentric and
educated wanderers, artists and hippies. For a short visit it was
pleasant, especially if one had the chance of a boat or could hire a
dhow to go out exploring. The endless sleepy shallow channels,
thick with mangroves, never failed to remind me of the Venetian
lagoon's smaller islands, still deserted and unpolluted in the days
of my childhood. There were ruins to visit, and over everything hung an ancient and decaying scent of old civilization and

mouldering stones, which I found fascinating and familiar; but I much preferred the solitary, more open and sunny, places inland. We passed through stretches of deserted forest, where often, at a turn of a sandy track, we surprised huge elephants drinking deeply in stagnant waters, blue with waterlilies, while white egrets rested on their grey backs.

One night we camped at Kiunga, then a forsaken group of fishermen's houses, facing the Bajuni Islands. Paolo hired a fishing-boat with a small crew, and decided to take off next morning for the Melango, where huge rock cod — *tewa* in Swahili — were known to hide in deep caves. Next morning we woke to a strange sight: during the night a ship had gone aground on the reef. Prow pointing up at an awkward angle, sides lapped by the high waves of the mid-monsoon, its silhouette on the horizon looked like a fallen seagull with a broken wing. It was surrounded by the fishermen's small canoes, balancing on their outriggers, like leaves or nutshells, and they brought back the news: it was a Greek cargo ship, bound for Kilindini Harbour in Mombasa, carrying animal fodder. The hold had been damaged, and water was filling it fast; they would have to abandon it before high tide, when it would certainly sink. The captain was trying to get in touch with his company to get instructions, which were delayed because of radio failure, and the crew were holding on. They did not want any help.

It was weird, going out fishing in sight of that sad reminder of man's inefficiency and fragility compared with the sea and the elements. The tide started coming in in the early afternoon, and I could distinguish figures moving on deck and checking over the sides. White-crested waves foamed closer and higher by the second.

I was keeping an eye on it, thinking that our help might be required, when a grey figure, looking ragged and windblown, climbed to the upper deck and raised his arm to the sky, where clouds heavy with monsoon rain were gathering; a faint bang, and a red rocket lined the dull sky for a few instants, like an inverted meteorite ... a short pause, and another rocket went up. Many craft started converging towards the ship, and we joined them, just in time.

The haggard, distressed crew descended silently into the canoes. We took four on board, our boat being the largest and sturdiest. One was the captain, a middle-aged Greek who spoke no English, and who, like the rest of them, was dirty and unshaven. He was hugging the ship's log wrapped in yellow oilskin, and brooding on his fate and the impending confrontation with his masters, to whom he would have to answer for his misfortune or negligence; his eyes were bloodshot and somehow sad, but vacant. They looked a ragged bunch, exhausted, shocked and drunk. The only undamaged cargo was a considerable number of cases of very good whisky. They distributed the bottles, and I was amused to see with what speed the Muslim fishermen took them, no doubt to sell them. It was good Black Label whisky, which Paolo much appreciated. The crew took slugs in turns and were fairly inebriated when, unexpectedly, the ship suddenly rose up, keel pointing to the slate sky, from which rain was starting to fall; in seconds it sank, disappearing into the ink-black turmoil of the ocean. It was an odd, unforgettable scene, which made me feel part, as in a Melville story, of the numberless past dramas of the sea.

From Kiunga we drove down through Mambore to the village of Mkokoni, a few palms scattered on a tongue of sand facing across the idyllic bay to the island of Kiwayu. Only the villagers lived there in those days. A few years later, a small exclusive tourist camp would be built further along that beach, but in the summer of 1973 Kiwayu and Mkokoni were for us alone. We pitched our tent just outside the village, on the beach where sea vines grew in intricate patterns making a carpet of green leaves and pale mauve flowers, just out of the reach of the high tide.

The dinghy allowed us the freedom of moving with speed to Kiwayu island and its channels lined with mangroves, to the fishing grounds. Because of the monsoon and the currents, August is not a good month for fishing. The water was murky, so Paolo resorted to bottom fishing. The fisherman we employed as a guide daily brought us fresh lobster, in huge quantities. I became rather adept at cooking them in various ways – boiled, poached, sautéed in butter and cognac, curried, fried, as a ragoût for spaghetti, in a wine sauce on rice, with herbs, with spices, in tomato and oregano, with ginger and shallots ... after ten days Paolo swore he could not face another lobster and would do anything for a good piece of roasted meat.

We motored across to Kiwayu, and walked to the village to buy a goat. As in all villages in Africa, the person to ask was the local chief. The chief was a fat man with yellow-brown skin, who sat under an ancient nim tree in front of his hut, a loose chequered *kikoi* around his ample belly, naked children and chickens scratching around him in the dusty sand. He wore an embroidered Muslim cap, and chewed betel nuts, occasionally spitting straight sprays of stained, rusty saliva at dangerous angles. He was blind from sarcoma. Women with large velvety eyes came and went, some giggling shyly at our strangeness, others made bolder by age and experience. They wore amber or red glass beads around their necks, their heads were covered with thin coloured cloth, in Arab style, with minute silver earrings on their earlobes and rings through their thin Nilotic nostrils.

Flies buzzed and landed everywhere; no one took any notice. We sat with the chief while Paolo bargained for a young goat which was still out, browsing with the rest of his small herd, soon to return. The man sat cross-legged, ignoring the filth, with a dignity and a curious worldliness about him. He suddenly addressed us in fairly good Italian, with a surprising Trieste accent: he told us he had been at sea for many years, working in freighters, and had visited many harbours in Europe, and the Middle and Far East. He spoke a little of many languages. He had seen more than any of his fellow villagers could hope to in a lifetime, until he became blind.

I asked him if he ever missed the wider horizons and freedom of the cosmopolitan contacts to which he had been accustomed.

He grinned a wise smile with almost toothless gums. He beckoned to a woman who brought him a piece of cloth containing a few thin, knobbly rolled reefers. He chose one, and a young boy was quick to light it. The sweet, drifting, aromatic smoke of cannabis pleasantly masked the smells of dried fish, overripe mango, coconut, jasmine and humanity which is the smell of most coastal villages, and his grin widened beatifically: he stood straight and proud, and with a round gesture of his hand he seemed to involve and gather everything which surrounded him there, and which he could no longer see.

'I have all this,' he said solemnly. 'This is my home and these are my children. What else should I want? I have seen the world, travelled to strange countries. Now that my eyes are blind and I can see no longer, I can still remember; and where could I remember better than here, sitting under this tree, in the village where I was born?'

His majestic movement encompassed the shabby huts, naked children, goat pellets, chickens, nets hung to dry: the same scene as hundreds of fishing villages on the Indian Ocean; this was a happy man. Paolo's eyes met mine through the smoke of his stubby joint, and we told each other mutely that he was right, and we could understand his wisdom.

The little goat was white and skinny, with a bloated stomach. It bleated pitifully when one of the younger sons of the chief took it aside and stuck a long sharp knife in its throat. The bleating stopped abruptly.

'How could you!' I turned outraged to Paolo. 'Such a sweet baby goat. I refuse to cook it for you. I shall not eat it!'

Paolo grinned his hungry dancing smile. 'That's fine. You don't have to. I will.'

Back at the camp, even though the smell of barbecued roast meat was tempting and succulent after days of lobster, I resisted and did not touch the goat, and Paolo, true to himself, remorselessly ate it all, with huge enjoyment.

I remember those days as a time of pure bliss and enchantment.

In the night, pink sand crabs came curious to our campfire to steal bits of food, running away obliquely and disappearing with it into their round new holes. They often managed to enter our tent through the zip closure, and we had to find them with the torch or the hurricane lamp to put them out, as their scraping legs scratching on the canvas prevented our sleep.

Late one night, excited voices and lanterns approached the tent. Paolo quickly wrapped a *kikoi* around his waist and went out, to discover a group of men from the village who, as he had a gun and ammunition, wanted him to help in shooting a rogue lion that had killed a bull. Paolo went, but to my relief the lion did not return to the kill.

One day a delegation came from the village to ask Paolo for his dinghy to bring back from the island the body of a man who had been killed by a swarm of bees. He agreed, and the thin corpse, wrapped in white linen like a mummy, was carried ashore amidst much wailing, to be buried in a shallow sand grave at the Muslim cemetery in the forest.

It is normal, in remote villages in Africa, for the local people to ask for medicine from the passing European's safari, especially if there is a woman in the party. I would wake up each morning to find the tent surrounded, at a respectful distance, by a circle of women with young children. They sat cross-legged in the sand, wrapped in their bright *kangas*, silent, just waiting for a sign of my being awake. They wanted medicine for a variety of ailments: malaria, aches of all sorts, coughs and diarrhoea were the most common, or, sometimes, a festering tropical sore. I learned quickly that it was easier to help daily at a regular time, and then have the day to ourselves.

The fisherman Paolo had hired as a guide was a thin, wiry man the size of a child, called Mote. His brother had been eaten by a shark while diving for lobster out of the Melango at Mkokoni. He knew all the coves and special spots along the mangrove channels where fish abounded. He was happy-natured, and gregarious. Soon all the villagers greeted us as longstanding friends, and invited us

to drink spiced Bajuni tea in their dark Arab-style houses, built
with coral rock and mud, which smelt of smoke, perfumed sandal-
wood oil and musk. The women offered me small gifts of shell
necklaces, a posy of wild jasmine. I reciprocated with soap, salt,
sugar, and once a small mirror, which they all shared and
treasured.

On the way back, Paolo planned to spend the night at Kipini, at
the mouth of the Tana River, north of Ras en Ngomeni. We
reached the village in the afternoon. The golden light was fading.
Behind the tall dunes, we could hear the ocean waves beating on
the invisible reef. We drove up to a spot Paolo knew along the
main track, and thought perfect for camping. It was a clearing
where the remains of a house still stood. The whitewash was
peeling from the coral walls, and purple bougainvillea grew wild
through the cracks, where colonies of gekko nested, up to the
rotting *makuti* roof. A dry stone well gaped empty in the middle
of the sandy courtyard. Whoever had lived there had long gone,
and the place looked abandoned and forsaken.

Below the dunes the evening tide was coming in fast, bringing
to the thin stretch of beach seaweeds, driftwood and the debris of
every evening tide on every beach in the Indian Ocean. I felt an
inexplicable gloom, and was seized by one of those rare, sudden
but strong, oppressive feelings of foreboding which occasionally
get hold of me. I felt I could not − simply could not − spend the
night there.

I did not want to be unreasonable. It would have been so much
easier to camp where we were; after all, we wanted to leave for Kilifi at
first light. But there was something tangibly hostile and evil hovering
about that spot for me, a wreath of unsolved mystery, unhealthy and
eerie beyond explanation. The pearly twilight which precedes night
on the equator was translucent, and as unreal as if we were inside an
oyster shell. I turned to Paolo. The last light reflected turquoise gleams
in his eyes, setting them in clear and stunning contrast with his
sunburned face. The halo of windblown hair, curly, dark blond, gave
him a glorious yet fey aura, like a vanishing prophet painted in the sky.

He looked at me. The same light, the same wind in my long blonde hair, my still unexpressed presentiment and fear, must have reflected the same fey look. Nothing had really happened, I had said nothing, but the air was charged with electricity and emotion. I had seldom felt more attracted to Paolo and I had seldom felt more afraid than in that forlorn place, over the dunes at Kipini. Our eyes locked.

'Not here,' I just managed to say in a hoarse whisper, 'anywhere else, but I cannot sleep here. On the beach, in the car, anywhere. Please. This place is haunted. We cannot spend the night here.'

The tension was unbearable, and the attraction between us dried my mouth. His hot dry hands were suddenly on my shoulders, his hot dry lips on mine. My cheek grazed against his jaw, unshaven since the early morning. His slim muscular chest pressed against mine through the thin cotton shirt and I could feel the beating of his heart against my own like a trapped swallow.

'Of course,' he whispered quietly in my ear,' 'I know you. I'll pitch our tent down in the bay.'

It had happened to me a few times before, it has happened a few times since: a grey cloud of doom over a place, a grey, shrinking aura around a person who is soon going to die. I have never been wrong. Apparently it runs in my family, on the female side, this uncanny gift of 'seeing'. Paolo respected it.

I learnt years later that there had been a mission there. Two people had killed themselves, one after the other, overwhelmed by inexplicable depression. The place had then been abandoned. Now it had a reputation for being haunted and for bringing ill-fortune and untimely death to whoever stayed there. To my dismay, Paolo confessed that he had once spent a night in that place, and this was why he knew it.

The night on the beach, in the tent hurriedly pitched by the light of the hurricane lamp, the warmth and perfect blending of our bodies compensated amply for the lack of comfort, for the lack of food.

Laikipia

Delamere, in the meantime, climbed the precipitous gorges on which Lake Baringo lies – a rocky escarpment rising about 4,000 feet – and emerged on the northern level of the Laikipia Plateau.

Elspeth Huxley, *White Man's Country*

One weekend, Paolo decided to go to Laikipia, a region which stretches from Mount Kenya to the edge of the Great Rift Valley. It was here that, at the end of the last century, Lord Delamere, a young English aristocrat and a gallant explorer, had emerged after trekking for months through the dusty and thorny savannah of Ethiopia and Somalia. The place, teeming with wildlife, green with pastures, rolling hills, rivers and springs, appeared as a mirage to the weary traveller. Its potential as agricultural land was not lost on Delamere. Back in England, he obtained a concession to farm it, and this was the beginning of the celebrated White Highlands of British colonial East Africa.

We stayed at a farm called Colobus on the southern slope of the Enghelesha hill, overlooking Lake Baringo, which belonged to an Italian family, the Buonajuti. Antonietta Buonajuti was newly widowed; her only son Amedeo was finishing university in the United States. She was considering whether to sell the farm, surrendering to the growing demand in the area for fertile arable land.

Across the Enghelesha hill, then still covered with thick forest teeming with the colobus monkey from which the farm had taken its name, Antonietta's land bordered on Ol Ari Nyiro, an enormous ranch spreading through hills, gorges and plains, which was famous for the abundance and variety of wildlife, mainly black rhino, elephant and buffalo.

The various owners were mostly absentees. The new young General Manager, Colin Francombe, a pleasant man with frank manners and an open smile, met Paolo and invited him over for a buffalo hunt.

There was possibly nothing in the world which Paolo liked more than hunting buffalo on foot in thick bush. It was a passion he had developed to a fine art. The instinct of the hunter, which involves perseverance, endurance, the skill of tracking a particular animal for hours and often days, checking the changing wind which could betray the human scent, was intricately mixed with Paolo's fatal love of risk. Although, as I have never killed anything, I could not share his passion for hunting, I always respected — and sometimes admired — Paolo's way of doing it. His was the ancient and refined wisdom of the warrior. Paolo was not a killer. He was a hunter in the best sense of the word, and I have no doubt that his passion for hunting would have logically evolved one day into pure conservationism.

Paolo came back from his first visit to Ol Ari Nyiro enthusiastic and dazzled. He went back a few times, and one unforgettable day he told me seriously, 'I think I have found it — the place for us. But you must come and see how you feel.'

Ol Ari Nyiro is 400 square kilometres of diverse landscapes, from dry open plains to thick impenetrable bush, from the luxuriant untouched cedar forest of Enghelesha to the steep dramatic cliffs of the breathtaking Mukutan Gorge. Blue hills and groves of acacia; open savannah dotted with trees; unending views of craters and volcanoes made purple and pink by the heat and the distance, as in a trembling mirage, and Lake Baringo shimmering with all its islands 3,000 feet below. A cool light air, dry and golden, and the feeling of being at the top of the world. The ranch, which ran thousands of head of cattle and sheep, was also teeming with game. One of the first animals we saw was a rhino, trotting away, silhouetted on the ridge of a hill. The area then was still 'literally swarming with them', as Delamere had written over eighty years before.

I was overcome by the beauty and amplitude of the land, but even more by the uncanny feeling of *déjà vu*. The profile of the hills seemed inexplicably familiar, as if I had already been there. I felt as if I had walked before down those gorges and known the hidden paths. It was more than I could have dreamed, yet it was, at the same time, exactly what I had dreamed.

Standing on a hilltop looking down at eagles gliding silent and free in the depth of the gorge, under the shadow of the one solitary gnarled acacia growing like a twisted bonsai at the edge of the long ridge of Mugongo ya Ngurue ('The Hog's Back'), I was silent for a long time. I touched the rough grey skin, worn at the joints, of that extraordinary tree, as if to draw strength and counsel from its ancient wisdom. Africa was there below us in all its unsolved mystery.

'Yes,' – I turned to Paolo – 'I think we have arrived.'

Here in Laikipia our African story could begin.

Years later, that favourite spot of mine, where I have stood so often, my back to the tree, thinking my solitary thoughts and trying to find reasons for all the events and make sense of them, became known locally as 'Kuki's Point'.

Here in Laikipia there would be other stories whose end I could not yet know.

12

Buffalo Hunt

Oh give me a home where the buffalo roam . . .

Home on the Range, song (19th century)

We spent the night at the Francombes'. Colin had recently married, and his wife Rocky was expecting their first child. They were a happy couple. Rocky was red-headed, with hazel eyes and freckles, slim, tall and extremely efficient. She came from a family of pioneers and farmers. During the war her father had commanded a column of Chindits in Burma under General Wingate, and as a result of his bravery had become one of the youngest brigadiers in the British Army; he was known as 'the Happy Brigadier'. Colin was tall, good-looking and good-natured, with an open smile of white, even teeth, capable and very much in charge, self-assured and dedicated to the ranch and its wildlife. His father had been a Wing Commander in the Royal Air Force, who had retired to Kenya after the war. When King George VI died, Princess Elizabeth was visiting Kenya with her husband, the Duke of Edinburgh. Colin's father was given the task of flying the new Queen from Nairobi to Entebbe, from where she proceeded to England; he was the first person in history to pilot an aircraft carrying an English Queen.

It was clear that both Colin and Rocky loved the place. They welcomed us with the warmth and hospitality which I came to know well in the years to come. It was a cold night, with gusts of wind that brought on its restless wings cries of hyenas and of nocturnal birds. It was hard to sleep under the many blankets. Before retiring, Colin had set a huge alarm clock for an extraordinary time, and given it back to his house servant, a Luo by the name of Atipa, a gesture which later became familiar to me, and which at the time of writing still occurs daily.

Paolo was woken by Atipa in the darkest hour before sunrise, with the inevitable early-morning tea — a Kenyan habit to which I always found it difficult to reconcile myself — and off he went in the chilly night with Colin after a rogue buffalo. They returned at breakfast: the buffalo had been wounded, and they were going to follow it with the dogs.

'Come!' said Colin.

I went.

I remember every detail of that first buffalo hunt. It was my first encounter with that unknown side of Africa: tracking for hours in the sun, kicking the dust to check the wind, going at a steady pace through the thorny bush and the dry leleshwa in total silence, careful not to step on twigs, ears alert to any noise, the hot smell of aromatic sage, dung and resin in my nostrils, mouth dry, heart pounding, eyes darting around to check any shadow, following the agile little African tracker, trying to repeat every movement he made . . . looking for a drop of blood on a thread of grass, the dogs running ahead, nose on the spoor, panting. Then their barking, high-pitched and urgent, told even my untrained ears they had found the buffalo.

The men froze. Sweat ran down their necks and stained the back of their khaki shirts. Slowly, precisely, without a word, they lowered their guns, ready.

A crashing of broken branches, closer and louder than I expected, startled me. Colin and Paolo turned to me together: 'He's coming. Quick, climb a tree!'

The barking drew close. With a terrific crash the leleshwa parted, and an enormous snorting black animal came straight for us. There were no real trees to climb, and if there had been, there would have been no time. Quick as lightning I climbed to the top of a thorny young acacia no taller than a man, which was just behind me, sending a mental blessing to Professor Müller who had put me back on my feet. Paolo and Colin fell to their knees just in front of it. They both aimed, and fired.

The noise shattered the lazy midday insects and silenced the cicadas and the birds. The following silence was only broken by the panting and low growling of the dogs. My ears throbbed with the drumbeat of my heart.

The buffalo had dropped dead a few feet from us. It lay black and massive, a darkening pool of oozing blood soaking the stubby grass. The dogs cautiously sniffed it. Bluebottle flies were already buzzing around the foaming mouth, the round bullet holes, the open opaque eyes, searching for moisture. Before approaching, Colin threw a pebble. I learnt that day that many buffalo, believed dead, have recovered, to gore their hunters. You cannot be certain that a buffalo is dead until he fails to react to a stone in the eye. This one did not move, and we approached.

The stomach seemed bloated, the horns enormous, and ticks of all types were already crawling away from the carcass. The leader of the pack of dogs put a proprietorial paw on the dead animal. He would be the first to be fed a slice of liver. The little Tharaka tracker who had led us with such amazing skill took his knife and slit the belly open. Air gushed out in putrid gusts, and the knotted intestines erupted. Elbow deep in the guts, the man found the liver, and gave the dog some. Then, nimbly, he cubed a piece with his sharp knife, as one would a mango. He squeezed the dark green liquid of the bile on to it, as if it were lemon juice. Politely, he offered me some.

Although I was generally adventurous in trying new food, I just did not dare to taste this, and I shook my head. Both Paolo and Colin declined. With a grin the little man shovelled the warm poultice into his mouth, bile dribbling down his chin. Smacking his lips in appreciation, he cleaned his hands on the half-digested stomach content – dry cud – and dried them on the back of his short, patched trousers. The pungent smell of dung and blood was thick in my nostrils. He smiled. For the first time I noticed the sharp eyes, the thin moustache and wide-spaced pointed white teeth. A bright red bead necklace encircled his short, strong neck. The beret at a rakish angle on his head sported a silvery rhino brooch. The small agile body was lean and muscled: perfect for coping in the bush.

Before beginning the laborious task of skinning, he pointed a bony finger to the sky. I looked up. In the merciless cloudless blue of the sky at noon, huge birds were circling high. More and more were gathering. My first vultures.

My first contact with Laikipia had been my blood baptism.

'Ndege,' the little man grinned.

This is how I met Luka Kiriongi.

13

Death of an Elephant

Nature's great master-piece, an Elephant, the only harmelesse great thing; the giant of beasts . . .

John Donne (1612)

While the negotiations for Ol Ari Nyiro were under way, Paolo decided he wanted to shoot an elephant. We had a serious argument about what appeared to me to be a futile and cruel desire I could not justify.

Had he known what we now know about elephants, their sensitivity and gentleness, their family patterns and loyalty, and most of all their uncanny intelligence, I have no doubt that Paolo would have never gone for that elephant. But he was a hunter and those were different days. Shops supplying all sorts of hunting equipment flourished in Nairobi; so did taxidermists, and curio shops offering ivory trophies and skins. Now it seems a distant and different era, but it is not twenty years ago. Decent people, respected game wardens, the rich and the famous now turned impeccable conservationsists, hunted then as a matter of course, and no one raised an eyebrow. How much rarer has wildlife become and how much has man's regard for it changed.

Paolo decided to go north, and booked a hunting block around Garbatula, and Isiolo. Grinding my teeth, but drawn by curiosity to see a part of the country I did not yet know, I accepted the offer to join the safari. Paolo invited Colin and Luka as well. Colin wanted a 'hundred-pounder' or nothing. Even then, hundred-pounders were practically impossible to find. Now they have all been killed. Colin, in fact, never found his hundred-pounder.

Doum palms, hot dry country, dust, sand and camels were the background to our adventure among the Somali and Boran tribes. Handsome and wild, they were still clad mostly in their traditional robes: long chequered *kikoi* and turbans for the men, long dresses and veils and shawls, or skin skirts and amber and silver jewels, for the tall proud women with eyes of dark velvet.

Our days were spent stalking through the bush on foot, with a Somali guide, looking for a large male with big ivory; going through villages and nomad camps, in the heat and flies; meeting people carrying gourds filled with sour, dense camel milk; inspecting for tracks near murky waters, where, through the footprints of camels, donkeys, goats and cattle, one could sometimes detect the majestic, soft-wrinkled, rounded elephant spoor.

Our evenings were spent around the campfire, the men with a beer and their stories of hunting adventures, I with a glass of ouzo, feeling a bit alien, and short were the nights of deep tired sleep: I do not have especially good memories of those two long weeks after the elusive elephant, which was always ahead, invisible, and — I secretly gloated — unreachable. We met many small and large herds, and once again I could appreciate Luka's skills, the dexterity and suppleness with which he led us straight into the middle of a group, literally between the legs of those huge creatures, and surrounded by their pungent smell, so that we could almost touch them.

One afternoon, finally, unexpectedly, we came across three elephants feeding up-wind. One was a large male with thick if not too long tusks, the largest sighted so far; the others, his two younger askaris.

The hunter nodded to Paolo. Paolo looked at Colin in offer, but he shook his head: the bull was obviously not a hundred-pounder . . . perhaps a seventy, eighty?

I think Paolo was growing tired of what must have seemed

even to him a pointless search. He could see I was not happy. I was consciously being a pest, subverting the safari in subtle ways. Perhaps I should not have joined the party in the first place, but I wanted to be with Paolo, and, of course, I was curious about any adventure which promised to be out of the ordinary.

Paolo looked briefly at me: I shook my head vigorously. We both turned to the elephant, no more than fifty metres away, who, intermittently flapping his ears, ignored us and kept quietly feeding from the nearby bushes.

Now and again he shook his large grey head. Then he turned towards us, undisturbed and unseeing, aware of our presence but, not being able to smell us, unbothered by it. I saw Paolo's jaw harden in determination, and my heart skipped a beat. On soft quick feet he approached the elephant, and I could only follow him closely out into the open, looking up at the grey powerful mass and feeling vulnerable. Paolo put the gun to his shoulders and aimed.

The elephant looked at him with alert ears. I protected my own ears with my hands: I knew the shattering blast of the .458.

The air exploded, dazzling the flies and lizards, and the old bull lifted his head backwards abruptly, tusks pointed to the sky, without a sound.

For a few instants there was just this stillness. Then he collapsed, a majestic tree stricken by lightning.

Nobody breathed: my heart beat wildly. Everything was suspended, as in a soundless slow-motion film. His companions, stunned and uncomprehending, searched the air for explanation with extended trunks, trumpeted furiously, opened their ears wide in a mock charge, then unexpectedly turned away in unison and disappeared, crashing through the bush.

Paolo started running towards the elephant for the *coup de grâce*, with me at his heels. When we reached him, we could see that a round dark hole had sprouted, like a small evil flower, in the middle of his forehead.

It had been an accurate brain shot: but the elephant is the largest animal to tread the earth. His big brain takes some time to die. I could see one of his eyes, so close that I could easily have touched it, brown-yellow, large and transparent, fringed with straight, dusty, very long eyelashes. The pupil was black and mobile. He was looking at me. I looked into that eye, and as in a mirror, I saw a smaller image of myself reflected, straight, in khaki shorts. I felt even smaller, realizing with shame and shock that I was the last thing he saw. It seemed to me there was an expression of hurt surprise in his dying yellow eye, and with all my heart, I tried to communicate to him my sorrow and my solidarity, and to ask his forgiveness.

A large white tear swelled up from the lower lid and rolled down his cheek, leaving a dark wet trail. The lid fluttered gently. He was dead.

I swung around to face Paolo, my own eyes full of tears, a knot of rage and shame blocking my throat. 'What right . . .' He was watching me.

The hunter came up and patted his back as was the custom. 'Well done. A clean brain shot. Congratulations.' Paolo kept watching me. As so often happened with us, that special link was established, and the rest of the world had receded, as if only he and I were left in it. And the elephant.

My eyes were glaring. Suddenly, his became sad and weary. He shook his head as if to cancel the scene of which we were part. 'No more,' he said. 'No more, I promise. This is my last elephant.' It was also his first.

Luka was sharpening his knife. The car was miles away and together we went to fetch it. When we came back, we found that the two younger askaris had returned and in blind fury had destroyed bushes and small trees around their friend, and covered his body gently with green branches.

I spoke no more that day. Paolo was strangely quiet. In the dark of the night, just before sleep, I remembered that an elephant had killed his brother.

14

Good Companions

... for golden friends I had ...

A. E. Housman, *The Welsh Marches*

We moved to Laikipia.

Ol Ari Nyiro supported, and was supported by, 5,000 Dorper sheep, a white, black-headed animal renowned for its superb meat, and 6,000 head of Boran cattle, a hardy variety of brown, white, black, or maculated bovids descended from the zebu, from which they had inherited the fatty hump on their back, their kind, patient eyes, and a resistance to harsh conditions, rocky terrain and poor grazing. In Ol Ari Nyiro, they were divided into many herds of a few hundreds each, depending on their sex, age and colour: this last criterion a clever way of discovering immediately to which herd a group of lost cattle found wandering through the bush belonged. It often happened that predators or sudden storms of rain scattered the animals grazing through the thick vegetation, and their disappearance was only noticed at night.

After sunset every day, cattle and sheep were gathered and counted by their herders – called the *wachungai* – into their respective *bomas*, rudimentary traditional round enclosures made of thorny branches. If some were lost a search was launched immediately, as a night out could certainly end in the animals being killed by lion, leopard or hyena. This happened often anyway: undeterred by the flimsy enclosures, lions jumped over them and took off with some young steer or weaner, creating havoc in the herd huddled together. Leopard and hyena preferred sheep and young calves. In the pitch dark of the night there was not much the *wachungai* could do but scream, beat metal drums, fire their shotguns into the air and hope for the best. When a lion persisted in eating domestic stock he developed a taste for the fat meat, and, lazy as cats are, resorted to killing only those docile animals which could not escape or put up a fight. In such cases, a bait was prepared and a hide of branches was built up-wind during the day, and Colin or Paolo, or both, went out with Luka in the night to wait for the lion.

Cattle and sheep were dipped regularly to free them from parasites, mostly ticks carried by buffalo, which they picked up while grazing and which gave them a variety of diseases, fatal if not discovered and cured in time. In this, Colin excelled, and so did the people he had trained, a Meru tribesman called Garicha, a natural veterinarian, gifted with a gentle hand with every animal, and the headmen Ngobitu and Tunkuri. The dipping exercise was called *menanda*, and from this Swahili word were named the areas where it was performed.

Once a week, in a cloud of dust, amidst whistles, bleating, mooing and the high-pitched calls of the *wachungai*, the mobs advanced in the early morning, were grouped within wooden fences, and meekly went through the spray race, one by one. When dry, they scampered back to their respective grazing, kicking in relief through the low shrubs, under the watchful eye of their ragged herders. Flies and a pleasant aromatic smell lingered for hours, dancing in the warmth of noon.

I was amazed by the skill of these people in recognizing the animals entrusted to their care, by how they noticed small details or any alteration in their behaviour. They gave them names as we do pets, and remembered every characteristic of each of a few hundreds of creatures.

Cattle and sheep grazed freely, sharing with the wildlife the same ranges that they had since their introduction in Africa. In the heat of the day I often met cattle drinking from one side of a water reservoir or a dam and elephant from the other, tolerant of each other's presence. I loved that.

No day passed, in those first happy times in Laikipia, without my learning or experiencing something new. If there was no end to my curiosity, there seemed to be no end to what Africa had to share.

We settled, in the beginning, in a small shack of a house which had been built by our predecessors with a spartan disregard for comfort, in an area named Kuti from the tallest hill around. Kuti was situated at the north-west side of the ranch, about eight kilometres from the Centre where the workshop, the principal village, the office and the Francombes' house were. The house was so basic there was not much for me to do there, and I had much time left to explore. In Ol Ari Nyiro, there was everything one imagines of Africa: the vastness and wilderness of the landscapes, the skilled people, the animals and the plants.

For Paolo, it was the embodiment of all his dreams. His love of nature, animals and freedom was linked, as is often the case, with his love of hunting. One does not hunt alone in Africa. But, of course, there was Luka.

Even before we built our permanent house, Luka was there every afternoon, a grin painted all over his acute face, ready for adventure. Luka's diminutive figure became the familiar shadow accompanying Paolo in his daily expeditions. A very special and close relationship was built up between them, as can only happen in Africa through sharing danger, and the elation of long hours and days and nights of following the same prey, the same tracks, the same dream. When Paolo and Luka left together for yet another buffalo hunt, often I went too. Those times became for me the penetrating and gradual discovery of this continent and its secret creatures, its mysteries and dramas, its strong emotions and the unavoidable facing of my inner and most unprotected truths.

If Luka was Paolo's companion in those early days, Gordon was mine. He helped me to come to terms with the facts behind the romantic dream of living in Africa, with the inescapable solitude and sometimes loneliness of those days, when I had to learn to cope with a reality which was totally opposite to the genteel life I had led in Italy, adapt to different values and different routines. Gordon was my own silent shadow. His patient, solid presence comforted and protected me, and to the end of my days I will remember him with gratitude and with love as one of the important presences in my life.

The fact that he was a dog does not make any difference.

'Choose one,' my friend had said. All the puppies were playful, fluffy and sweet, but there was one who already had a wise, serious and eager air. He looked straight at me as a person would, and I knew he was the one. I called him Gordon after the friend who gave him to me.

From my childhood I had felt that you could only call a place 'home' if you could share it with your dog. Gordon was an Alsatian puppy, round and furry, his eyes alert and intelligent. A black Belgian shepherd grandmother had added that exotic touch to his genes which I regarded as essential for originality. From the first moment I saw him he was special to me, an intense little puppy with a long way to go.

I acquired the habit of going for walks out into the bush with Gordon, a notebook and a pen in the pocket of my short khaki trousers. I walked through the dry bushland, and Gordon followed close behind. Occasionally I stopped to scratch his head behind the ears or between nose and forehead, a delightful spot for dogs, and his silent delight was my reward. When I found the welcoming shade of a special thorn tree, I lay there, my head on his strong healthy body. Through the canopy of branches filigreed with feathery leaves, the unblinking blue sky of Africa looked impassive. I took out my little book and wrote my poems in perfect peace.

Although the choice of living in Laikipia was one I never regretted, it was not easy at first to adapt to such a total change of scenery, routine, habits, background and people. Paolo had to be out most of the day, learning his part in the new venture.

Always an early riser, he was gone before first light every morning, and frequently he did not return before sunset. I had much time left to myself, with our house still unbuilt, the garden still unformed, to think and to come to terms with my irrevocable choice.

Gordon was my constant companion in those early days. It was he who uncannily made familiar the foreign, the alien acceptable. He guarded me with loyalty and generosity, courage and total devotion. At night he slept across the door of my bedroom, and his deep breathing was reassuring. Often he would wake, alerted by a strange noise or a wild smell brought by the wind. I heard him, then, barking at the shadows of animals among gusts of wind which swayed the newly-planted pepper trees and disturbed the pink-legged plovers into waves of laments. He was the first of a dynasty of many dogs.

As day followed day, the landscape and smells became familiar. I could recognize tracks left by different animals in the dust and twigs of the bush trails. I could distinguish the cough of the leopard from the roar of the lion, the barking of the zebra from the high-strung voice of the impala; I knew the call of the go-away bird, the cry of the fish eagle, and the sharp breathy noise of the rhino which seems to blend with the silvery stillness of the leleshwa. In the thickness of Laikipia, rhino were as elusive as the invisible aardvark, whose holes, dug in the middle of beaten tracks, were as much a threat to the car tyres as those of the warthogs, and the only proof of the aardvark's existence and of his unrelenting quest for termites. I learnt about acacias and succulents, the edible berries and the poisonous ones, and Swahili flowed easily. I walked every day, either with Paolo and Luka, or with Gordon. Often, I walked with Mirimuk.

Mirimuk was a thin Turkana of indefinable age. To a European eye he looked to be in his middle sixties, skin burned black by the sun, discoloured teeth, gaunt cheeks, slightly protruding eyes; but his stick-like, indefatigable legs had a much younger spring, and, as I discovered years later, he was then in his early forties.

In Africa age is equated with wisdom, since the original culture was the accumulated knowledge and skills which come only with experience and time. Old people were respected and honoured. Young people listened to them, and their advice was sought to solve quarrels and to pass judgement in all aspects of village life. Having gone through many seasons and listened to their fathers and grandfathers, they could foresee patterns in the rains and recognize early signs of drought. They knew the secrets of the animals and of the plants, the traditional herbal remedies, and the rituals to keep gods happy or to prevent their wrath. The elders were the library in which was stored all the knowledge the tribe needed to survive and to thrive. As in the herds of elephant, where it is the old matriarchs who lead the younger animals to the waterholes and the feeding grounds, the old people steered the village on to the right path.

Mirimuk was skilled, silent as his own shadow on the yellow rocks and red murram paths where he led me, following rhino tracks tirelessly, up hills and down gorges and cliffs. He would put his hand on fresh rhino scrape to feel the heat, and by this, and the evaporation and fading colour, he would know exactly how fresh it was, how far away the rhino. We climbed and walked steadily, making no noise, until the tracks became sharper, the footprints more definite; then, quietly parting the leaves of sage and euclea, he would point a bony finger — his wrist circled by a blue bead bracelet — at the stolid grey mass a few metres from us up-wind. Usually the rhino was sleeping, as still and massive as the dead trunks of the twisted olive trees, and as bleached: totally camouflaged. Sometimes it would be alert, sensing a disturbance, nose to the wind, sniffing high. Or the wind changed for a moment and our smell immediately alarmed some invisible eland; their trot would wake the rhino and they would disappear together, in a crashing noise of rolling stones and broken bushes.

We walked through dry *luggas*, scaring away reluctant troops of feeding baboons, whose cries of alarm echoed on the gorge, and disturbed hornbills and brown parrots from the tops of the yellow fever and fig trees. In the heat of noon we came across stagnant waters, and Mirimuk sometimes drank from frothy puddles, cupping his hands and grinning at my dismay. We stopped in the shade for a few moments, and sat on a rock talking about what we had seen or missed, and I shared with him whatever I had brought: usually just a lemon to quench my thirst. He would lick it tentatively, shaking his head at the sharp acidity, eyes laughing in the gaunt face. He spoke little and only if prompted. Chatting is not becoming to trackers, whose ears must be always alert to any noise which might mean danger; but his bushcraft was extraordinary, our mutual understanding perfect, and I could never repay him for all he taught me.

We shared great moments. Often we almost trod on a sleeping buffalo, or surprised the first of a large group of elephant crossing the path just a few metres from us: in no time we were surrounded by the rest of them, their stomach rumbles nearer than I cared for, soft-padded feet stepping on twigs, and a sudden trumpeting to blow away my heart. Yet I felt safe with Mirimuk, as I felt safe with Luka. They knew the wind and they knew how to think like the animals they stalked. They could anticipate the next move, they knew when to go close and when to withdraw quickly and silently. Once we found an enormous bloated python which had been suffocated by the bushbuck he had wanted to eat. The long sharp horns had perforated the mottled skin, and bluebottles made new patterns on the large flat head.

I remember one night with Paolo and Mirimuk at Ngobitu Dam, waiting for buffalo. It was a hot November night, dry and windy like most. We had put our blankets on a small promontory which stood higher than the surrounding ground on the eastern shore, sheltered by sparse carissa bushes and mukignei. First came a small herd of eland, white-grey shapes barely discernible in the twilight, the sound of their kneecaps clicking like castanets between gusts of wind. Later, a lone elephant followed. We sat looking at his large silent shadow playing with water, feet in the mud a few yards away, the strong unmistakable smell all round us. Straight trunk sucking away gallons and gallons like a gigantic straw dipped in a bowl of juice.

Then the moon rose, the wind stopped, and we heard the buffalo. A few snorts and the characteristic noise of rolling stones of the heavy, if agile, trot of these huge creatures; and there they were, three black adult males knee-deep in the water, grunting and drinking. Paolo took his binoculars, focused, precise and quiet as hunters must be. One of the buffaloes had wide-spaced horns, and looked really old, the perfect target. The gun was ready. In the night which magnifies all noises, out in the open, the shadows black in the moonlight, I felt small and inadequate.

The air was still with suspense. The frogs fell silent. Paolo lifted his gun; aimed. I saw the finger curl on the trigger ... and Mirimuk's hand, as fast and as silent as a striking snake, darted out and landed on his shoulder in warning. I saw the tension melting away in Paolo's neck. Mirimuk moved his head just slightly to the right, and on his lips we read 'Simba.' We froze. Only our eyes swivelled, and even this felt noisy: a few metres to our right, on a large old termite hill slightly up-wind, sat two mature lions, a male with an enormous mane and his mate. Nose to the wind, yellow eyes still, they looked totally in control, powerful and uncaringly dangerous, owners of the night. If they had seen us they could not smell us, and they gave no sign: it was clear they were stalking the same prey as we.

After drinking, the buffalo were moving along the shore towards us; in a few seconds they would have passed between us and the lions. Paolo and Mirimuk had their guns ready, although I knew they could not afford to fire. At the same time, the male lion turned. For a moment his yellow eyes looked straight at me, the tail flickered, and he jumped. My heart stopped, but it was the last buffalo which collapsed under the weight with furious, agonized snorts, and then took off towards the thick bush, the lion hanging from its back. The other buffaloes fled with wild bellows through the night, leaving their companion to die alone in a small thicket. For a while we listened to the lions feeding, before the whining jackals and the hyena came.

There were the nights when I joined Paolo in the hide made of branches, waiting for the marauding lions to return to the steer they had killed the previous night. Silence, the cry of the hyena, the rhythmic call of the eagle owl . . . nightjars and crickets, tree frogs and bull toads. Then, that moment of stillness when the lion approaches: our silence joined the silence of the night and all its creatures. Sometimes a far-away aeroplane — two small red lights above — crossed the sky, full of strangers, bound for Europe, unaware of us. Since those times, when I fly I always think about the unknown dramas developing below, unseen.

The crunch of a bone, a deep breathing, and Paolo was on his feet, gun pointed towards the bait. The wind brought us a feral whiff, the rotten meat and blood stench of carnivores. A second passed. The white torchlight outlined the massive shape, eyes like reflecting red coals lifted from the carcass, staring straight at the glowing darkness. A single shot. The lion jumped up high in the air, forepaws extended, as a rampant lion in a gilded crest . . . a roar split the silence.

The frogs resumed their singing.

It was not just the beauty and wildness of the landscape. It was not just the smells, intense of dust and elephant, of jasmine and moonflower, nor the incredible concert of birds singing with liquid voices in the golden afternoons. It was not just the profile of the hills and the short purple sunsets, nor the vivid colours of the hibiscus and of the sky and of the yellow grass, nor the emotions of a sudden rustle of leaves or a scared francolin while I was walking alone in the bush, nor the surprise of the leopard, still as a statue in the full moon.

It was also the extraordinary difference in the daily routine and the daily chores. In 1975, it was — and still is now, at the time of writing — much the same, with a few improvements, as it must have been in the early settlers' days.

Electricity was provided by a Lister generator, which pumped away at night like an old heart. Candles and hurricane lamps supplemented the electric light. There was no telephone. Communication with the outside world came through radio-call, and a characteristic and useful radio link known as 'the Laikipia Security network'. All farms and ranches in Laikipia subscribed to this, a police frequency established for mutual support in isolated areas at the time of the Emergency in Kenya before Independence. There were several calls a day at fixed times and Rocky regularly performed as control. We all had code call numbers. Ours was Delta 28, and eventually I acquired a radio for Kuti, with the number Delta 16. Voices of strangers or friends came punctually to life through the crackling of static, messages were exchanged, and I often thought how difficult our life would have been without this essential service. It was a relief to know that one could communicate in case of emergency and receive news and messages. Many times over the years we relied on the Laikipia Security network to call doctors or aeroplanes, to announce incidents, and receive urgent information which would have otherwise taken days to reach us. It was faintly unreal to talk regularly to people one had never met, to know what went on in their lives, be familiar with the sound of their voices, without knowing what they looked like.

There was no refrigerator at Kuti, and no gas stove, no electric iron and none of the appliances that we take for granted in Europe, no washing-machine, no vacuum cleaner. Everything was done by hand. Bread was baked daily, butter was made from cream, firewood had to be gathered in the bush and chopped with an axe. To press a shirt, a fire had to be lit in advance so that the red coal could be put in the old black iron. To have a hot bath, a fire had to be built below the rudimentary drums from which the boiling water was piped to the tub. To cook, the chopped wood had to be put in the stove. Brooms and mops were used to clean the floors, and vegetables were chopped with knives.

As everywhere in Africa there were people in abundance to help us, but they had to be trained, and my Swahili was still fairly basic. From the outset I was in the right mood for this sort of life, and enjoyed the challenge of reverting to the pace and the chores which possibly were no longer familiar in Italy, even to my great-grandmother. It was fun and it was rewarding, and although in time we made many improvements, the old-fashioned flavour of life remained unchanged. Many times I was to bless my mother, who always felt that, irrespective of the privilege of having domestic help, a girl should learn how to cook and look after a house. Instinctively I knew how to teach the staff, and people willing to help were easy to find, but what was needed to reach the standards I had set was eagerness, intelligence and a capacity to learn a totally foreign approach to cooking and housekeeping, and to remember. Nairobi offered a wide choice of trained people. It was not so easy in the depths of Laikipia. I went through a number of not particularly satisfying experiences, until a lucky day brought Simon.

He had heard of the new *Wasungu* (Europeans) at Ol Ari Nyiro and came to ask for work. A long-limbed Turkana man of perhaps eighteen, handsome and lean, with Nilotic features and a natural grace and elegance of movement, and attentive and serious black eyes, he was recommended by Paolo.

'Try him,' he said, 'I know you will get on. He is keen and has good manners. His father was a chief.'

As usual, Paolo was right. I liked him at first sight.

'I hear you want to be my cook. Can you cook?'

'I can bake bread. If you teach me, I will learn your sort of food.'

'I can teach you. If you want to learn, you can learn anything.' Simon was eager to learn.

The Turkana are a wild tribe of herders who keep their cattle and goats up round the lake which bears their name. It is an immense lake of purples and golds, with mysterious slate-grey depths where huge fish live, relics of prehistoric times. Sudden storms disturb its mirror-like surface, brought by the fiercest winds. Turkana are handsome and tall, built to move long distances; Simon always walked with unhurried long strides, as if barefooted on sandy tracks up north. They love milk and meat, and one of their greatest delicacies is a goat buried, unskinned, in hot coals until the fur burns off and the meat is roasted. To spend so much time cooking different and extravagant food, like our complicated, fussy cuisine, was totally alien to Simon. Yet he brought all his energy and a polite curiosity to his new task. It was a pleasure for me to see how eager he was and how soon he learnt to cook and present the plates gracefully, lending to his new task the African gift for decoration and colour. 'You *Wasungu*,' he told me once, 'are never hungry. You would not touch a half-cooked, half-burnt and not gutted goat. Your food must look beautiful. You must eat with your eyes first.'

I had taught him to garnish plates with leaves, lemon wedges, flowers. Soon he was excellent at this, and my table, thanks to him, became quite renowned for its delicacies and its flair in presentation.

Simon Itot was proud but willing, polite but never servile. He was soft-spoken, and commanded respect from the other staff. Although he was the youngest, the position of cook gave him senior status. After only a day it was clear that he was in charge.

15

Kuti

Über den Himmel Wolken ziehen,
Über die Felder geht der Wind,
. . . Irgendwo über den Bergen
*Muss meine ferne Heimat sein.**
  Hermann Hesse, *Poems* (1902)

Few things give me such a sense of fulfilment as building from nothing, with whatever natural materials are available, a space to live in, in harmony with the untouched landscape of Africa. It must be a work of love and understanding, and of humbleness for intruding with our presence in the silence and dignity of nature. That unquantifiable and elusive factor which is the beauty of the land, and our duty to respect it, is the aesthetic and spiritual principle foremost in my mind whenever I create anything.

When we moved to Laikipia, Paolo and I originally decided to take our time and to look around the ranch for some extraordinary spot on which to build our permanent home. The views from above the Mukutan Gorge to every hill on the ranch, from Mlima

* 'Across the sky the clouds move,
Across the fields, the wind,
. . . Across the mountain, far away
My home must be.'

ya Kissu to Kurmakini, from Nagirir to Kutua, across valleys and towards the sheer cliffs of the Great Rift Valley, were so pure and majestic that it was hard to choose. The hill of Mugongo ya Ngurue, with my favourite old tree dominating the gorge, was especially tempting, as the feeling of freedom, space and height always took my breath away. I am glad I resisted that temptation, and decided eventually to add to the original dwellings at Kuti which had already been altered by the people who had preceded us. There was a generator and a system of pumping the water from Ol Ari Nyiro Springs; otherwise the house and facilities were no more than basic, and an enormous amount of work needed to be done.

The house had been built on a rise with far views of rolling hills and I liked this feeling of space. We fenced off about ten acres out of the bush for a garden, and I kept all the acacias and the other indigenous trees.

Much thought, discussion and care went into every single step of the building, mainly over the proportions, which are the essential part of any construction. Decoration can come after, but one must start with the right, balanced, shell. We utilized what we found on the land: murram blocks and stones, wood from our forest and grass for the roof. It was a simple house, but it had harmony and a special positive atmosphere, and it conveyed to all who visited that it had been built with love. It was a place where people felt at ease. At the same time I learnt to make a garden. Gardening in Africa is most rewarding; given water and a minimum amount of care, everything grows so fast that one can sit under the shade of the trees one has planted in a matter of only a few years.

For all the new plants, more water was needed than the trickle pumped up all the way from the springs, over ten kilometres away, and Paolo decided to dam part of a valley above Kuti. It was an area elephants loved, as in it they found shade, food and moisture. *Olea africana, Acacia gerardia* and *Euclea divinorum* were the prominent trees. These provided the ideal habitat for olive pigeons, owls and genet cats, and, of course, leopard. The dam was within walking distance from the house, through an enchanted shaded track where I used to go with Gordon.

Once the dam was finished it attracted even more animals, and the valley and its surroundings remained one of the favourite places for elephants. Eventually I built a look-out on one of the tallest acacias overlooking the water tank which supplied the house. This allowed us to watch the animals without being discovered, a wonderful feeling of being part of the landscape. I felt rather less happy when the elephants came into the garden which I had begun to carve out of the bush.

I learnt about the most attractive indigenous trees, and enthusiastically set out to plant masses of flowers and shrubs: I soon discovered, however, that elephants loved to eat a wide variety of plants. Many mornings I woke up to find entire trees had been uprooted, and spiky cactus plucked as if they had been tender artichoke sprouts. What the elephants did not like, dik-dik and hares or impala did. Gradually I learnt what species were unpalatable to these visitors, and concentrated on planting them. I did not want, however, to eliminate certain trees, like acacias, which were elephant favourites, and after we put in a swimming-pool it became practically impossible to keep the elephants out of the garden. A herd of fifty of them elected to raid the garden and the newly-planted orchard every night. After one of them trod on and fell into the septic tank, we decided to electrify the fence around the compound. That worked well with the elephant, but not with many other strangers.

I began to keep a diary again in Italian, and its pages remind me of many details of our new life I might otherwise have forgotten.

30 July 1976
Ngobithu comes to announce that seven lions have killed a kongoni, and four more have killed an eland and a cow. Carletto flew in and with Paolo and Emanuele they went to wait for the lions. Heavy rain.

24 August 1976

New lawn planted and kitchen block completed. An elephant came into the garden last night and I tracked him with the gardener Seronera. He crossed the fence on the side of the horses' *boma*. He uprooted and ate three young pepper trees, made havoc in the new rock garden, eating all the blue yuccas, destroyed an acacia by the side of the swimming-pool hole, and went out from the south end of the garden.

28 August 1976

A hippo has killed a child at Antonietta's dam at Colobus. Game scouts have come to shoot it. That would be Rastus, Antonietta's old lone hippo. What a shame this had to happen. Elephant trumpeting in the garden at Kuti all night and no one sleeps.

31 August

Elephants in the garden again. Gordon chased them, before two palms were eaten. Dik-dik love the new buds of the coral bougainvillea.

2 September

Dozens of dik-dik eyes in the light of my torch last night, and this morning the new hibiscus are eaten. We have planted today an avenue of euphorbia along the main drive: one day they should be imposing, but all the staff warn me that elephant love them.

4 September

Our lorry returns from Colcheccio with sand for the swimming-pool, and the news that at Carletto's lightning has killed two bulls and four cows!! Paolo goes to wait for the lions which have been killing calves. A large male lion has killed a bull close to Kuti *boma*. Cold and humid.

5 September

In the pouring rain Paolo came back, having killed three of

the marauding lions. Yellow and muscular in the back of his pick-up, they look like large cats, sleeping.

6 September
Full moon. Exciting night for Paolo and Emanuele at the Big Dam last night. On the lion kill they first see two jackals, a rhino and a herd of buffalo. Then come a honey-badger and a leopard. Paolo shoots two male lions. At sunrise, he spares the third one. In the meantime at Kuti I cannot sleep, as Gordon never stops barking. Elephant all round.

16 September
Last night a pride of six lions round the garden all night. Paolo out for a wounded buffalo.

3 October
With Mirimuk and Luka to find two large rocks for the new bird-bath.

7 October
Three giraffe in my garden at dawn gazing curiously into the swimming-pool hole. Waiting for leopard on my own this evening at the bait above the house. Hundreds of birds are coming to the bird-bath, and I marvel at their beauty and strangeness. Mirimuk brings me an ostrich egg.

15 November
Elephant came again last night and destroyed eight acacia, drank at the pool and uprooted two pepper trees. Dung everywhere. Tubby and Aino flew in from Nairobi.

9 January 1977
The elephant came quietly in the night as close as the passage to the bedrooms. They ate all the hibiscus, and all the succulents. They finished the traveller's palms and demolished the acacia with the base of sanseveria. I think they want to let us know that we are intruding in their territory. If during the day they are invisible, the night belongs to them.

When the house was finally completed, the *makuti* roof thatched, the beams of red cedar from the forest polished to a shine, and the carpets and furniture we had brought from Europe arranged as if they always belonged there, we decided, as a housewarming party, to call an *ngoma*.

Teams representing all the tribes we employed on the ranch, dressed in their traditional costumes, came to dance in our garden and to wish us luck. There were the Meru with Garisha, in coloured *shukas* and headdresses, the Tharaka with Luka, in skirts of dried bog-grass, ankle-rattles and painted shields. Luka showed another unexpected skill as head dancer and mime. Covered in monkey skins, he danced for us — and mostly for Paolo — an acrobatic pantomine of the lion hunt. The Turkana came with Mirimuk. The women, wearing bright blue and red bead necklaces, wore long, richly gathered skin skirts, shorter in front and with trains which undulated gracefully, almost like tails, in the ostrich-like beat of the dance, and their men, heads covered in oblong blue decorations of feathers, sang raucous songs and jumped high.

I was touched by the transformation which had occurred in the people we employed, who normally wore European clothes. Now dressed — or undressed — in their traditional style, they had emerged from their everyday working rags and deformed shoes as butterflies hatch from caterpillars. Slim and agile, proud and handsome, colourful and noble, free and nimble in the rhythm of the dance, I wondered at their resemblance to a flock of birds in the glory of their metallic courting plumage, flying and singing in unison.

Unexpectedly, at high noon, in the middle of the celebrations, we thought we heard a noise of distant thunder. The earth almost seemed to tremble as before a quake. A haunting rumble of stamping feet advancing, and a song like the wind, coming in gusts: the deep-throated safari song of the Pokot people.

On the west side, Ol Ari Nyiro bordered with the Pokot reserve. The Pokot had been remarkable in keeping their traditions for longer than many other tribes. Unlike the Kikuyu, the Meru and the Kamba, the Pokot traditionally are not agriculturalists, but a pastoral people, hunters and gatherers. They had known Ol Ari Nyiro since time immemorial. They were familiar with the water sources, the shortcuts through the hills, and the game paths.

Their women were dressed in long skirts of soft hide, greased with a mixture of goat fat and red ochre like their faces and hair. They looked like terracotta statues, agile and feminine with their rows of brass bangles clasping thin wrists and ankles, and with brass rings hung from pendulous ears. Even their necklaces were the same rusty colour: made of leather and wooden or bone beads, they were piled one on to the other to circle a high, proud head like starched brown collars. Their breasts were greased and bare. Their heads were shaven at the sides, but reddish ringlets sprouted on top, like the crests of exotic birds or manes of wild animals, which gave a surprisingly feminine effect. The men were dressed sombrely in black *shukas*, knee-length, and sported long ostrich feathers on their small bird-like heads which were plastered with a mixture of dried dung and earth and painted blue and white. They always carried long spears, the oblong, razor-sharp blades protected with a sheath of tight skin.

They snaked their way through the garden and sang as they danced. Their beauty and wildness silenced my European guests, and long into the night the guttural cries mixed, without interfering, with the whooping cry of the hyena calling to the moon from the hills.

The house was now ready, and we started inviting the neighbours. There were not many left in 1975. Ol Ari Nyiro had been one of the last ranches to be settled: marginal land such as this was not considered suitable for cattle, and certainly not for agriculture. Only wildlife, it was thought, could ever dwell there. Ol Ari Nyiro bordered with the Buonajuti farm, Colobus, to the south, and with the Tugen and Pokot reserve from south-west to north-west on the Rift Valley side; with Lwonyek, a government ranch, to the north-east, and with Ol Morani on the eastern border.

Ol Morani had belonged to Gilbert Colvile, an extremely wealthy, eccentric landowner of the early days, who lived on horseback, never had a proper house, befriended the Maasai, and was nicknamed by them *Nyasore*, 'the Thin One'. Colvile surprised all when, in the forties, he married the young and beautiful Diana Broughton. She who had been involved in a notorious scandal following the murder of her lover, Lord Erroll, probably by her older husband, Sir Jock Delves Broughton, who later committed suicide. After a few years, Diana and Colvile were divorced amicably, and she married Lord Delamere. At his death, Colvile left Diana all his properties, including Ol Morani, and although she never lived there — there was never a suitable house on the ranch — at the time we acquired Ol Ari Nyiro she was still our neighbour.

Ol Morani, which in Maasai means 'the young warrior' but is still known today by the old people as Nyasore, was eventually sold to a local co-operative, and many Turkana bought *shambas* there. Ol Morani was flatter, without the dramatic geographical features of Ol Ari Nyiro, like the Mukutan gorge, but it was lovely land, with acacia groves and open plains teeming with eland, zebra and giraffe. The children loved to go riding there, and often I would join them at noon with a picnic lunch.

Further inland, there were the Rumuruti settlers. One could meet them on Saturday at the Rumuruti Club. I have been always impressed by the British tradition of creating a club wherever they are, often in the most unlikely places. Rumuruti Club was a rambling group of wooden cottages, rather primitively built, in a clump of gum trees. It had a tennis court and a bar, and the liveliness and loud good spirits of the patrons made up for the shabbiness, which, after a few drinks, no one noticed. All the members contributed to support it in various ways — I think we paid the barman — and everyone brought some special dish for the parties. Old Land-Rovers arrived from nowhere and everywhere on Saturday afternoons, dusty or muddy depending on the season, children already fed and in pyjamas set to sleep on mattresses in the back. After some games of tennis and a few drinks, both settlers and their wives changed for the evening party. Long trousers — sometimes dinner-jackets — and long evening skirts substituted for the dusty khakis.

Some of the people we met there were unusual and extremely interesting, and with those it was easier to make friends.

One was Jasper Evans. He owned Ol Maisor ranch, where he ran cattle and many camels, and some inventive agricultural experiments, ahead of their time, were carried out on his land. I liked his quiet manners, unruffled gentle ways, and his philosophy of life. His house contained rare collections of books and beautiful old objects, although there were often tortoises or frogs in the bathtub, and a variety of wild pets surprised you by poking their noses in your bag. He was one of those people you do not need to meet often to feel easy and in tune with, and I like to think that we became — and still are — good friends.

Then there were the Coles. The family had come to Kenya in the very early days, and Lord Delamere's first wife had been Florence Cole, sister of Berkeley, Karen Blixen's best friend. Hugh Cole used to come over often with Tubby Block's son Jeremy, to join Paolo for a buffalo hunt. Then they remained for dinner, for the night and a couple more days, perhaps, in Kenya style. You never asked your guests how long they were going to stay; every visitor in the Highlands had travelled for uncomfortable hours or days to reach your home, and he could count on your hospitality — and you on his — for as long as happened to be the case, one night or one week did not make much difference.

And there was, of course, Carletto. Our homes in Italy had been only a few miles apart, and here his ranch, Colcheccio, was about forty miles from Ol Ari Nyiro; by Kenya standards we were close neighbours. He had brought to Kenya the same conception of life which characterized his earlier days in Italy: his Pantagruelian passion for good food and drink, and his unparalleled hospitality. Carletto was a childhood memory and a link with the past, and it was uncanny that, in totally unconnected circumstances, we had ended up living so close in Africa with all the world to choose from.

Soon, another event created an even stronger bond between us. It was at about that time that the telephone rang in Nairobi very early one morning, and I was told that Carletto's wife, Chiara, had been killed in a car crash in Italy. She had been alone in the car, and had been suddenly blinded by black smoke drifting from tyres burning by the side of the highway: her car had been hit in the back by a lorry, and sandwiched against another invisible vehicle ahead of hers. It was one of those tragic chain-incidents: sixteen people were killed.

Her death affected me deeply. Not only had I known Chiara for years and she had been a close friend, but Carletto's had been the vehicle following ours that fatal night in Italy when Paolo's wife had died. I shall not forget her slim bare feet coming towards me while I lay on the grass in the field where I had been flung from our crashed car. She had sat with me waiting for the ambulance, quiet and gentle, and in the months that followed, her constant presence at my bedside was a comfort in a time of bewilderment and soul-searching.

She left three daughters, all of a tender age. The oldest was, at that time, at school with my stepdaughter Livia at Greensteds, in Nakuru. I offered to go and fetch her, so that she could travel back to Italy in the company of some friends due to leave that night. I was so distressed that I could not trust my driving, and went in a taxi. Just before the turn-off to the school, a grey lorry, coming at full speed, lurched from the opposite side of the road and headed straight for us. My driver swerved to the right, and missed it by a few inches. The solid grey mass slid past me as in a nightmare, and we ended up in a ditch on the wrong side of the road. I turned my head: Ugandan registration, the driver probably asleep or drunk, the lorry never stopped and hopped away in a mad zigzag through the pot-holes, like a sinister ghost. Sweat soaked my driver's shirt. Drained, he put his head on the steering-wheel in silence. If I had been driving in my upset state, I would by now be dead.

My heart still pounding, adrenalin flowing, I found Luisa waiting for me in the dormitory, dressed in her best school uniform. She did not know that her mother had died. Mute, Livia stood by her, and she offered me a little posy of flowers. When I bent to kiss her, her large brown eyes bore deeply into mine, and I could see she knew. Livia had the uncanny gift of seeing things before they happened. Holding Luisa's hand and my flowers, I walked out in the afternoon sun shivering, and it took all my self-control not to crumble. Carletto was totally heartbroken by Chiara's death, and despite his cheerful ways he never truly recovered.

16

Buffalo's Revenge

... buffalo ... he found to be ... vicious when wounded, always seeking to kill a wounded man.

Bartle Bull, *Safari*

The early days in Laikipia are studded with adventures. On 6 February 1977, I entered in my diary:

Today at Enghelesha a buffalo killed one of our people. His name was Malinge, and he belonged to the tribe of Tharaka. He was a good friend of Emanuele and the day of the *ngoma* he had guarded our house. He was a kind man, hardly older than a boy. There were three walking in the bush. He and Cypriano and another man of the Security. The buffalo went straight for them. His horns perforated Malinge's throat and lungs. He pushed him for over fifty metres and then he vanished in the bush. Luka came to tell us at the time when we were going in for dinner, and Paolo went out immediately with Colin to look for the buffalo.

He was a large male with horns still red with blood, a leg wounded by one of the snares made by the new settlers at Colobus: hence the blind fury and aggressiveness. Malinge lay in a pond of blood, his eyes already dry which Paolo could not manage to close. Colin sat on a rock next to him, addressing him gently in Swahili. A side of Colin which I shall not forget. Paolo said Malinge's face was serene, as if he were smiling. Our Fundis went today to make his coffin.

But tonight he is still there, outside, covered with a blanket, surrounded by fires to keep away the hyena, until the police arrive tomorrow to check, as demanded by law.

There is an ominous feeling about the telephone ringing at unexpected times, too early in the morning or too late at night, as if it could only forecast tragedies.

Shortly after settling in Ol Ari Nyiro, one early morning in Nairobi I received a radio-call. It was an extremely bad line. The only words I could understand, above the crackling of static, made enough dramatic sense: 'Paolo . . . accident . . . buffalo . . . Nairobi Hospital.'

I rushed to the hospital and with the help of Renato Ruberti, a well-known neurosurgeon who, as a friend, was always our hospital contact, we organized everything and set to wait. It is so draining, waiting without knowing, speculating about the worst, that when finally Paolo arrived I was almost surprised to see him alive. Under his usual tan he was pale from loss of blood, his eyes looked bluer in his dirty unshaven face, but he grinned up at me and lit a cigarette. Colin, who had driven him down, uncovered his thigh: an ugly gash, caked with blood, gaped in his slim leg, where the buffalo horn had penetrated deeply, missing the vital femoral artery by less than an inch.

The wounded buffalo had come for Paolo before he could manage to fire. He had thrown his useless gun away and had hung on to the buffalo horns to try to divert them from goring him. Realizing he would not be able to hold on for long, he had loosed his grip and had run for cover. But he had tripped on a dry branch, and had fallen face first on the dust. The buffalo had come for him from behind, and had tossed him up in the air before Mirimuk the tracker could manage to shoot.

In the several weeks he had to spend in hospital, Paolo's room became a sort of meeting-place. A few rooms from Paolo's, there was Peter Faull, a professional hunter who had been mauled by a lion. His face was covered in bandages, but he could walk, and often he joined the other visitors for a drink.

Among the first to come was Philip Leakey, who brought Paolo a pile of rare Africana books, some old first editions, to read in bed. A nice thought, and I remember taking Meinerzhagen's *Diary* home to read. It described a Kenya which had disappeared, when rhino were so common they were considered pests, and people were still few. In the very beginning, to fill the time while looking for the place he was dreaming of, Paolo had met Phil, and they had become partners in a cattle venture in the Nguruman. The Nguruman was in Masai territory, north of Lake Magadi, and a fantastic wild place of great beauty.

The youngest of the three Leakey brothers, Philip was very creative, with uncommon ideas. Once, in our early explorations, we went to Nguruman with the children, and stayed in a camp Phil had pitched close to a river, where huge fig trees grew. He had built a guest-house on the top of these enormous trees, and he showed it to us. It was a fascinating series of passages and rooms at different levels, from tree to tree, as in a child's dream of an enchanted tree-house, and it said more about Philip than words could. He knew and loved plants and things growing, and had a way with them. Very tall and still slim like all the young Leakeys, he had a peculiar, intent way of looking you straight in the eye, and a faint rakishness which made him quite attractive. He became one of the few Kenyans of European origin to become a Member of Parliament. He was the first of the Leakeys I met.

The Leakeys were one of those families whose members were all exceptional, one way or another. Louis and his wife Mary, Philip's parents, were world-famous palaeontologists. Their discoveries of early man in Tanzania and northern Kenya are historical and immortal. To my regret I never met Louis as he died in 1972, but it was through Philip that we met Mary, and later Richard.

In 1976 Philip invited us to join him in Tanzania at his mother's camp, close to Olduvai Gorge, and I spent with Paolo and

Emanuele some intriguing days visiting her digs as guests of Philip. She had just discovered footprints belonging to a remote ancestor, embedded in stone by the side of a stream, little wandering tracks which I found unbelievably touching. Mary shared her tent with thirteen dalmatians, her favourite dogs, a fact which made me like her immediately as it reminded me so much of all the dogs which always filled our house in my childhood. She was a person of great character, strong-willed, and with the irresistible charm and attractiveness of a versatile intelligence and ready wit. I liked her immediately and have never forgotten that first encounter.

I had met the eldest brother, Jonathan Leakey, the first time I had travelled to Kenya, when Paolo and I were visiting Lake Baringo. We had gone to the snake park which belonged to Jonathan, where he extracted poison from snakes for serums. There was a small commotion at the gate and a group of people came forward carrying a large bag in which something heavy moved, and Jonathan was there. 'Do you want to see?' he asked me, and opened the bag a bit, enough to expose the hugest snake I had ever — yet — seen in my life: a python. It was thicker than an arm, and looked powerful. It was possibly one of the first snakes outside a cage I had ever seen, and even though snakes were to become so familiar to me later, I always remembered that first incident.

Paolo was not a good patient. Being confined to bed made him restless, and it was only the company of our new friends, and the entertainment provided by their stories, which made those weeks bearable. On that occasion I discovered for the first time the strength and value of the bond of solidarity which links people in Africa, where dramas and unusual accidents are taken for granted; flocking to an unfortunate friend's bedside with books and flowers, smuggling in good old whisky, is an established habit.

In Africa most of the time is spent outside, and Laikipia was the ideal background for walking, running and riding. After he recovered Paolo began to develop a passion for archery. He pursued it as one would a philosophical doctrine, as what was needed was the capacity to free the mind from any interference and to concentrate on the target. Aloof and isolated in a world of silence, it was no longer important — Paolo used to tell me — that the tension should be released with the arrow. It was in curving the bow, focusing all senses, that he found its meaning, and I realized years later that this was Paolo's meditation in those days. He ran through the bush, a bow slung across his shoulder like an ancient warrior, an image of freedom moving in my memory; looking back now, I can see that those early days in Laikipia were possibly the happiest of my life. Yet if I had had the awareness which years and sorrows have given me now, I would have appreciated even more the unusual privilege of discovering Africa from the inside in a place so spectacular as Ol Ari Nyiro.

17

Emanuele's Two Fathers

Wer reitet so spät durch Nacht und Wind?
Es ist der Vater mit seinem Kind.*
J. W. Goethe, *Erlkönig*

One day in Nairobi a dusty Land-Rover appeared on my drive. It was covered in parcels and assorted luggage and camping gear. From it emerged Mario. He had a beard and shoulder-long hair; nothing was left of the smart playboy I had married, who drove a Ferrari and dressed in the Via Borgognona. He wore battered jeans and a T-shirt, and he had driven his way through Africa in that car with a girlfriend and her child. He spoke of Buddhism and philosophy, of sailing, and he was going through a period of spiritual awakening. He had crossed the Atlantic Ocean on his own, and now spent most of his time in Antigua and the Caribbean. I liked the change, as it was a growing.

Paolo and Mario had known each other from the old days in Italy. Although totally different, they enjoyed each other's wit. There had never been any strain between them, as when my relationship with Paolo had begun, Mario and I had been separated for years. Occasionally, after that first time, and always un-

---

* 'Who rides so late through the night and storm?
It is the father with his child.'

expectedly, Mario started to materialize at our doorstep, on his way from, or to, some exotic destination. He brought special and original presents for all, and had many stories to tell. Paolo's daughters were naturally particularly fascinated by him, mainly the elder, Valeria, who was developing into a beautiful woman.

For Emanuele, Mario was more like a friend he liked but saw rarely. Paolo was definitely the father-figure in his life, the constant presence he could count upon, and his support and love were the structure around which he grew. Paolo's mind was agile and original, and the many facets of his personality and interests made of him an irresistible model adventurer who appealed to the mas-culine instinct latent in any growing boy. Paolo was certainly Emanuele's best friend in his early days. He taught him to stalk buffalo in the bush, to aim and to shoot straight. He taught him to cast and to fish, and satisfied the unspoken longing for a hero-figure every boy nurses inside himself. Many times during the holidays Emanuele joined Paolo in the lion hide, and they always went fishing together.

Emanuele shared with Paolo some of his favourite books of adventure. Lately they had picked a recurrent phrase from a story by Wilbur Smith, *The Sunbird*, which had appealed to their imagin-ation and which they had taken to using jokingly and affectionately to each other: 'Fly for me, bird of the sun.' A singular quote which was to be repeated again and again in the years to come, and which became symbolic and unforgettable.

Like true companions, Paolo and Emanuele benefited from each other's company. Paolo respected Emanuele; he admired his calm and determined way of coping with life, his wisdom and know-ledge, and his peculiar capacity to get on with people, not by overacting, but simply by the sheer intrinsic value of who he was, which was evident in his quiet and self-assured countenance.

When Paolo decided to build a simple look-out overlooking Ol Ari Nyiro Springs, with a *makuti* shelter to observe wildlife coming to the water and to the salt lick in the evening, he asked Emanuele to record, when he was there, the animals sighted. Emanuele met this task precisely and with great pleasure, and he kept a book in the little hut with all his notes. Often, during the full moon, we went to spend the night there, and watched leopard coming to the bait we hung on a tall yellow fever tree. There was an old rhino, very light in colour, which regularly came to the salt below the hut, which Paolo had named 'Bianco' ('White'). It was fascinating to sit silently in the dimming light, listening to the noises of nightfall, frogs and francolin, guinea fowls and baboons, trying to distinguish the shadows of the animals coming to drink. To see Bianco walking slowly along the river, massive and ancient, was an awesome sight. We held our breath and focused our binoculars on the advancing mysterious shape.

Emanuele was a born collector. He had started with minerals and assorted shells. Later he used to spend days cataloguing and updating his extraordinary cowrie collection. When he travelled to exotic seas like those around the Seychelles, the British West Indies and Madagascar, his specific aim was to find a particular variety of cowrie. Over the years, Paolo, Emanuele and I went a few times to visit Mario, who was living in Antigua in an exquisite old yacht, moored in the English Harbour, in which he had crossed the Atlantic many times on his own. We sailed down to the Grenadines and up to the Virgin Islands. I remember on one occasion searching with Emanuele the chilly waters of the Atlantic for the cowrie-related *Ciphoma gibbosa*, whose peculiar habitat is the sea fans growing in the shallows around an islet south of Virgin Gorda. When he finally found the first one, small as a smooth pebble and half-covered with the slimy orange snail-like mantle, stuck to a lacy purple gorgonian, his triumphant grin, even through the goggles, was unforgettable. He had read all the books worth reading on the subject, including some very rare ones which had taken years to locate, and knew absolutely all there was to know about cowries.

When he was twelve, I brought him to London for a small nose operation intended to clear his sinuses, and for a week or so after it he was not allowed to fly. To occupy his days, he chose to go to the Natural History Museum Shells Department – where he spent hours and hours looking at the exhibits. He finally asked to be left there in the morning, with some pocket money for a snack, and picked up in the afternoon at a prearranged spot. One day I found him with a sort of curious glint in his eye: he had discovered one cowrie which had been wrongly labelled – some varieties were easy to confuse with almost identical ones – and he had managed to find one of the curators and had pointed it out to him: he was right! His bonus had been to be allowed to inspect boxes of cowries of all sorts waiting to be identified and labelled.

With the money he had received as a gift for his operation, he decided to buy shells. A friend suggested a place close to Foyles, the bookshop. I was somehow disappointed to find what looked to me like a seedy little shop, crammed with cabinets and accumulated boxes. Emanuele cast an expert look around, asked the shop assistant some key questions, establishing an immediate link with him, and, turning to me, said in the quiet, determined voice I had grown to respect, 'That's fine, Pep. You can leave me here for the day. I'll help around. This is just paradise.' He went every day and managed to pick up fantastic bargains and to acquire some rare specimens of shells, particularly the famed Aurantium, the Golden Cowrie he had coveted for years.

Emanuele had kept a diary since he was nine. Infallibly, every single day, he wrote about whatever event had taken place. In his diary he noted that day, 29 September 1978, in his typical dry style:

> I bought Cypraea Schilderorum, Spurca, Decipiens, Edentula, Acicularis, Pulchra, Eburnea, Humphreysi, Irrorata, Nebrites, Xanthodon, Comptoni, Ursellus, AND an Aurantium for 300 dollars. Decipiens and Pulchra were a gift. I spent all the 500 dollars I had got from Mario. I have now over 87 different species of cowries in my collection. Pep went for dinner at Mirella [Ricciardi]. Today the Pope has died.

The same year, on 10 December, Emanuele noted:

> . . . we went with Livia and Paolo to fish black bass at the Big Dam. We got a very large one and several small ones which we let go. Later, we were about to go buffalo hunting, also with Colin, but Robin Hollister arrived in his aeroplane, and we went to meet him. On taking off the engine stopped and the plane crashed. Robin was unharmed, but the aeroplane is a total wreck.

Robin was an attractive young man we had known for years and whom we liked, but saw rarely. Surviving an accident of that sort — the aeroplane was totally written-off — without as much as a scratch was very weird indeed. This odd incident singled Robin out for us: little did we know, in that December of 1978, what the strange ways of destiny had planned for us, and for him.

18

Pembroke House

I have had playmates, I have had companions,
In my days of childhood, in my joyful school-days, —
All, all are gone, the old familiar faces.

Charles Lamb, *The Old Familiar Faces*

To be able to be with Paolo and to learn to look after the place, I had to do something which is alien and extremely painful for an Italian mother: I had to send Emanuele to boarding-school. He was only nine years old, and this was one of the most difficult decisions of my life. Emanuele was an unusually private little boy with a fertile intelligence and hobbies which involved collections, books, papers, typewriter, and took a lot of space and time. His room was his kingdom, and he spent a great deal of his time there reading and rearranging his cowrie shells collection. The idea of his having to sleep in a dormitory, with no privacy and only a small locker for storing all his things, was a painful one. The knowledge that there would be nobody to answer his questions and to nourish the natural curiosity of his fertile mind kept me awake at night, yet there was no other solution. My stepdaughters were a few years older; Livia was already at a boarding-school in Nakuru with Carletto's daughter Luisa, and Valeria, the elder, stayed with a friend in Nairobi during the week and came up to the ranch with me for weekends. Emanuele was too young to be left alone in the house: he had to go.

The school was at Gilgil, at the foot of the escarpment climbing up to the Kinangop. It was made up of a series of grey stone buildings in spacious grounds close to a river and crossed by the railway. Generations of settlers had sent their boys there since the early twenties, when it was established. The logo was a red pigeon in a blue field. Homing pigeons had been the passion of the founder, a Mr Pembroke, and in past days they were used by the school team to send the results of matches back to Gilgil. The motto in Emanuele's days was still the outrageously arrogant original one: *Anglus, in Africa sto.*

There Emanuele lived for over three years, perhaps the last years of his childhood. Gone was the freedom to choose what to do with his time, what to wear, what to eat. Clad in a dull, uninspired grey uniform, his blond hair cut unbecomingly short, I will never forget my feeling of loss and despair, of failure and guilt, when I left him there for the first time in the care of strangers, a sad little boy trying to be brave, lost in an identical crowd of unhappy little boys, waving to me from the dark door-way of the chapel to which a bell had been peremptorily summoning them.

Back home that same night, sitting in his room empty of his presence, I wrote in Italian in my diary:

> And then, I left. The engine had an acrid smell of burnt petrol. The sun had already set. A bell rang imperiously, calling the children. You had gone, you, my little one, trussed in your new grey blazer, too big, your hair too short, your too-wide eyes full still of little boy's dreams . . . by what right did I abandon you in that anonymous garden . . . in your bed, where I shall sleep tonight, your child's smell lingers, and I love you . . .

Yet, seen finally in perspective, Pembroke probably gave Emanuele something which, as an only boy, he could never possibly have achieved in the sheltered protection of our home and presence: the independence, the ability to cope, the sense of leadership and survival in a strange, indifferent and perhaps hostile world, and certainly the self-assurance which comes from managing alone and from being able to win friends and to make a mark in a totally new environment, on his own. At the end of the first term, I asked Emanuele how he had coped and promised him that, if he had really been too unhappy, I would seek some other solution. Emanuele admitted he had not been happy, and had felt homesick often. 'But,' he added with typical fairness and generosity, 'the first term is always the most difficult. I did not have any real friend and, you know, everything was so different from home. I would prefer to try another term to see how it goes.'

I have always felt that you can guess a person's quality from the quality of his friends: Emanuele was always surrounded by the older, quieter, nicer boys. Charlie Mason, who later became Pembroke's head boy, was one of these. His parents lived in Kilifi and, since it was often impossible for them to fetch him for half-term, he usually came to spend it in Laikipia with us. Emanuele and he got on extremely well together, sharing the same passions, like riding and sailing and fishing. Kind, polite, loyal and good-natured, Charlie was the perfect guest, and it was a pleasure to have him to stay. Now an officer in the Royal Navy, he keeps in touch; and postcards arrive from him from the strangest places, or photographs in which the same young, pleasant face, little changed over the years, though the body has grown to almost seven foot, grins cheerfully below the cap of his naval uniform.

To allow Emanuele more freedom, I sent his grey horse Cinders down from the ranch. Although this meant that other children rode him during the lessons, Emanuele did not mind, and he could then gallop round the grounds in his free time. Rules were very strict at Pembroke in those days, and parents were never allowed to visit, apart from Parents Day once every two months or so. This was particularly painful as I drove past the school whenever I went up to Laikipia, and it was sheer torture to pass in front of the building, especially on a Saturday or Sunday afternoon when I knew he had no lessons, and not to be allowed to see him. We devised an innocent trick to make life happier. One of the horses' paddocks was along the Gilgil road, next to the railway bridge, and it had a wooden gate. Although he was not allowed to go out, Emanuele could ride as far as that gate, and we decided that I would put messages or small presents under a stone by the left-hand post. I found, however, that there were no stones of any decent size, in that area, and finally brought one from Nairobi, a grey stone which appeared to me totally out of place and terribly conspicuous compared with the reddish-golden sandy soil of Gilgil. Sometimes there were other people about and I had to wait for a while before I could safely hide my small parcels. All in all the scheme worked, however, and to have this little secret added some excitement to Ema's monotonous life and partly relieved my anguish.

Emanuele's success at school gave him some privileges, of which the most treasured one was writing home in Italian, to maintain the excellent command he had of the language. This allowed him the freedom to explain, in uncensored letters, exactly what went on. Although Emanuele was generally too polite to become involved in petty mischief, he often wrote about having been given 'tackies', the mild physical punishment still much in vogue in all such schools. The reasons for this were almost invariably 'for having kept snakes in the locker'. Yet, when they once discovered a nest of puff-adders in the roof, the teachers themselves asked Emanuele to get them out, and soon he became the acknowledged 'expert' in anything to do with reptiles.

Later, recalling the days at Pembroke, under the heading 'My First Snakes', Emanuele wrote:

At the time I was at Pembroke, a boarding-school at Gilgil, a small town 150 km northwest of Nairobi. There were quite a few snakes there, but I could only capture a few, which I was forcibly persuaded to release by the teachers. One of the first of these was a striped skaapstaker, a common grassland species, which I caught in my hat on the games pitch. Skaapstakers were quite plentiful around Pembroke and I saw many more ... I also caught a slugeater, a small docile snake which unfortunately escaped from my locker, and a few of the lesser snakes, such as house snakes and juvenile grass snakes ... I remember that one sunny morning the Headmaster had taken my class out on to the golf course during a lesson. On crossing a patch of long grass, he did a most spectacular jump of about three feet up in the air, as did the long brown snake he had trodden upon ... A lot of puff-adders were killed at Pembroke, including one which disrupted a cricket match passing between the legs of the referee ... there wasn't much left after the cricket bats were through with it ...

After the third term, in fact, Emanuele proudly brought me back a special present: a cured, perfectly patterned puff-adder skin, which is still nailed to the bookshelf in my bedroom in Laikipia.

Pembroke House was, all in all, a positive experience in Emanuele's life, and years later he recalled that time, with typical equilibrium and a glint of amusement, as 'not bad at all for a prison'.

19

The First Snake

'One day, Pep, you too will understand the hidden beauty of snakes.'

We used to go to the coast for the school holidays. It was a needed change from the dry windswept climate of the Highlands, and Paolo was extremely keen on fishing. With his little rubber dinghy he managed to accomplish unusual feats of sportsmanship which, having survived an attack by a Bull Shark when diving out of Vuma, culminated in his decision to try deep-sea fishing. In his first season he caught several marlins, and won the trophy for the largest billfish fished out of Mnarani Club. Deep-sea fishing became his new passion.

We liked Kilifi. The hot balsamic air, humid and ripe like fruit and jasmine, was a pleasant contrast to the chilly nights with a log fire and blankets in Laikipia. I enjoyed the smell of coconut, of seaweed, the breeze from the ocean, the long walks at low tide, peering into pools for shells and strange surprises from the sea. In the evenings I sat, back to the largest baobab in the garden, looking out at the evening tide and at the fish jumping, and for Paolo's boat 'Umeme' to come back. I always tried to guess from a distance, by the colours of the flags, what fish they had caught, and to recognize their figures, waving at me from the deck, wind in their hair, my men returning from the sea.

Paolo had started making friends with the fishing community of the Kenya coast. They were mostly retired farmers who had sold their properties to satisfy the advancing settlement and land hunger, bought a house and a boat, and spent their days pursuing the dream of persuading the largest fish in the ocean to come to their bait. Some of them were passionate sailors, like the Masons in Kilifi, Emanuele's friend Charlie's family. Some of them had unusual hobbies, like the Jessops in Shimoni, who had accumulated a world-famous collection of shells, Emanuele's delight. Others drowned their 'good old days' nostalgia in seas of pink gin. Some, like Diana Delamere and her entourage, brought with them the grander aura of long-gone times, when the privileged of the so-called 'Happy Valley' lived a gilded life between the large estates in the Highlands or on the shores of Lake Naivasha, the racecourse meetings, and the parties in the Muthaiga Club.

I liked Diana. There was an unbending style and strength in her ways, in the deep arrogant voice and the ice-cold blue eyes, in the perfection of her grooming and flawless hair and skin even after a long day of fishing out in the rough high seas. When her boat, 'White Bear', moored, invariably with many flags, she appeared fresh and straight, unaffected by her many seasons and by the curiosity she always stirred, wrapped in the charisma of her mysterious life, and one could not help falling under the spell of her legend. For the two fishing weeks in Shimoni at the end of February and the beginning of March, when the season was at its peak, she moved to the Pemba Channel Fishing Club in room number one, and in the evening changed into flowing chiffon caftans to hold court through round after round of vodka and lime, tabasco and oysters, gracefully and regally devoting most of her attention to all the men present, irrespective of their age. Stories of past fishing adventures, of people long dead, favourite horses and memorable parties, unfolded as in an old photograph album.

The small Shimoni Fishing Club, a few cottages in a garden of baobab and bougainvillea overlooking the channel of Pemba, was a favourite cove of local fishermen. Shimoni was dear to Paolo as the fishing was excellent. He spent much of the months of February and March there, and often I went too. Personally I am not fond of deep-sea fishing, and I used my time in Shimoni reading and writing poems, walking on the beach looking for shells, and waiting for Paolo and Emanuele to come back in the evening. Maia Hemphill, the wife of the owner, sat by the radio in the garden of creamy frangipane, day after day, listening to the news from the fishing-boats, and knitting unending little sweaters for her grandchildren. It seemed that time had stopped in Shimoni, or was of no consequence. The waves shimmered on the coral reef, every new day had the colours and rhythms of the tides coming in from, and receding to, the high seas. Fishermen went at sunrise and came back before sunset with large fish, which were weighed and carried away in soggy pick-ups. In the evening I walked barefoot in the coarse grass, looking up at the first stars blinking over the mysterious baobabs of silver. At night I slept under mosquito nets in damp beds whose linen had been washed in salty water. Days slid into weeks and life went on, almost without me noticing, towards the moment of truth which I would have to face, and which perhaps coincided with the end of my youth.

Since he was a little boy, Emanuele had been attracted by reptiles. He had collected chameleons, captured the odd house snake. At Pembroke his passion began to develop. And when he was ten, it was I who gave him his first legal snake.

It was a hot afternoon of January, like many others in Kilifi. The little Snake Park, down at the jetty, is a ramshackle affair of bamboo, rotten slabs, and *makuti* thatch. In the dark cages, miraculously intact despite the many patches, strange reptiles sleep away their life, occasionally waking up to be fed rats or birds, goats or rabbits, depending on their size. There are a couple of tame pythons, which visitors can handle for a fee while photographs are taken. It was the day before Emanuele's birthday, and we had delayed our return to Nairobi for a few days. There was nowhere to buy a present in Kilifi. The only *duka* was a dark cave selling flour with weevils, sugar, kimbo, onions, beans, orange squash,

spices and little else. At the market on the north side of the creek
you could get limes, eggs and mango, dried fish, coconut and
chillies — hardly what a ten-year-old boy would want for a birthday
present.

'You must wait for your present,' I told him, 'unless you can
find something here you would like.'

We had visited the Snake Park many times over the years. The
attendant, Mohammed, greeted us like long-lost friends: time flows
slowly in Africa and memories reach further. When Emanuele
took Ali, the smallest of the two pythons, and let him crawl
over him and round his neck, I had a first premonition, so strong
that in the evening I wrote this in my diary: '... my stomach
contracted as if I had looked down into a obscure and threatening
depth ...'

The snake had coiled sleekly around Emanuele's thin neck,
sliding down the shoulder to rest his head easily on his hand.
Emanuele looked up at me, a moment frozen in the timelessness of
memory. In his velvet brown eyes a question, and the serious
determination I had grown to respect.

'Pep. I know what I want for my birthday.'

Dry mouth. 'Not a snake.'

'Why not? You promised.'

Any escape. 'They are not for sale.'

'No harm in asking.'

Buying time. 'No. Of course not.'

Peter Bromwell owned the Snake Park. Better known as Bwana
Nyoka, he lived in a strange house, once grand and now dilapi-
dated, on the creek at Taka-Ungu, just next to the one which had
belonged to Denys Finch-Hatton, and later to the Coles. They
were built on opposite sides of an old Muslim cemetery, at the
mouth of the creek. The area, like many along the coast, had a
reputation for being haunted. It was said that ghosts were seen at
night, wailing amidst a clangour of chains, or silently drifting in
mid-air and gathering, in the nights of full moon, below special
baobab trees which local people regarded with awe and fear. The

coast was the place where Arabs came to get slaves to carry off to the Gulf. They kept them hidden in the natural caves on the creeks along the shore, and bore them away at high tide in the holds of their dhows, together with spices, ivory, coconuts, skins and rhino horn, sliding out in dark waters bathed by the moon.

Bwana Nyoka's house had been built by his father-in-law, a man of refinement. It was made of coral blocks, and had a garden of flowers, terraced down to the creek, planted with frangipane, jasmine, and purple-pink bougainvillea. In the old days, servants in white *kanzus*, red fezzes and embroidered waistcoats used to serve drinks on the patio from silver and brass trays, or in rooms decorated with exquisite Lamu furniture, precious carvings and unexpected authentic Chinese vases. Long narrow mirrors of all sizes were placed at strategically unpredictable angles along the walls of every room, as in certain supermarkets today: they served the same purpose, as the man was deaf and was haunted by the fear of being robbed and murdered. The mirrors gave him a kaleidoscopic view of every corner of his rooms. The house was veiled in mystery and cobwebs, and very few people visited it in my day. I had only been there once, to fetch my younger stepdaughter Livia who had been invited to spend the night with the daughter of the house, a blonde fey girl called Winkle, who lived alone with her ageing parents and never went to school, but knew all secrets of the tides and of the reef. The house, an incredible mixture of extraordinarily beautiful objects and shoddy neglect, exceeded the expectations of my curiosity. Sand blown by numberless monsoons carpeted the floors, where tortoises and snakes nested. Bats and swallows roosted on the carved beams, and scrawny kittens peered from the delicate Ming dynasty vases, whose patterns were obscured by dust and guano. Impeccably pedigreed goats bivouacked on the threadbare Arab carpets. A large rusty refrigerator stood open and useless in the large dining-room, where the sand had been wiped from the corner — just — of the long table set for three with exquisite, if chipped, porcelain, and piled high with wonderful-smelling, exquisitely prepared food . . . a place unreal, like a film set, and of intriguing contrasts.

1. Ol Ari Nyiro: Paolo and Gordon at 'Paolo's Rocks'

2. Paolo

3. Emanuele and Cinders

4. The lion hunt: Emanuele and three marauding lions

5. Emanuele with an agama and a minute house snake

6. Emanuele and Kike

7

8

7. Paolo, Emanuele and Luka after a Tharaka dance

8. When the house was ready, we called a Ngoma and the Pokot came to dance

9. The buffalo hunt: Luka and three male buffalo

10. The first snake: Emanuele and Kaa

11. Waving goodbye: Emanuele, Paolo and Gordon at the Big Dam

12. Emanuele and Sveva

13. The last Easter: Emanuele, Sveva and green grass snakes

14. Sveva and the house staff at Kuti

15. Kuki and Simon Itot

Bwana Nyoka had been bitten many times by the poisonous snakes which he captured along the reptile-infested sand dunes of the coast, and it was rumoured that he would not survive another bite. He was a slim, bearded man with glasses, of undecipherable age, usually dressed in shorts and sandals, often with no shirt to cover his suntanned torso, unexpectedly muscular and younger than his face. A sure place to find him was at the bar in the Mnarani Club from 6 p.m. onwards, when with his wife, a faded fierce beauty, he always occupied the first two stools on the right, next to the entrance. To keep my word with Emanuele, I caught him there. I had hoped he would refuse, but even before I asked him, I felt it was written that he would agree.

'Of course,' he said, 'selling snakes is my job. I will not give you one of the tame ones, though. Those are for visitors. I have a new young one I have just caught. Should be easy to tame, with patience. About three feet, fifty shillings a foot. Quite a bargain.' Less than ten dollars for a python, less than cloth, I surprised myself thinking.

The small snake was handsome and sleek. I forced myself to touch it when it coiled defiantly around Peter's arm, guarded, ready to strike. The thought that it was probably more afraid than I was crossed my mind quickly: cold and dry, smooth, powerful and deadly. Non-poisonous. But the constrictor's strength, darting black tongue, expressionless glassy eyes, were a symbol of danger, and I was repelled and afraid. Emanuele was happy. When he looked at me, his first snake coiled around his fragile young boy's neck, an uncontrollable shiver shook me for a moment, and, for the second time that day, a dark premonition closed around my heart.

'Are you sure?' I whispered hopefully. 'Perhaps you should still . . .'

'I will call him Kaa,' was Emanuele's answer. He had always liked Kipling. 'You will help me to tame him, Pep? When I am back at school? You must handle him every day so he gets used to us. Please promise. See? It is easy. He is gentle.'

That night, sleep was hard to come by. I felt we had entered a new era with that first snake. I knew there would be more and I had agreed to look after that sinister, mute, sleek little horror. He had to be fed. To be cleaned, handled, exercised. Tamed. I had promised to do it for him. Emanuele's last words going back to school had been about Kaa.

'Don't you think he is beautiful? No? One day, Pep, you too will understand the hidden beauty of snakes.'

So many times over the years he was to repeat that phrase. For years I tried and tried to conquer my instinctive horror. I could finally handle harmless snakes without fear, but it was only at the very end that just once I saw the beauty.

Too late.

20

The Egg

The music, yearning like a God in pain.

John Keats, *Endymion*

Paolo and I had decided not to have children, as his girls and Emanuele got on well together and we did not want to break that fragile equilibrium. Furthermore, I was not particularly tempted to go through all the performance of having another baby. There was so much to do and to discover. Emanuele, Valeria and Livia were growing up and I was freer to join Paolo in his expeditions and travels.

In the early summer of 1979, however, Paolo was involved in an extraordinary adventure, which made us think again. He had just returned from Europe, and after one day with me in Nairobi he had decided to go back to the ranch. He left at night after dinner, although one should not travel after dark in Kenya where the traffic is extremely dangerous. But Paolo liked night-driving: it was more relaxing, and the road after Gilgil was, in fact, rather quiet. In the car, his Venetian music at full volume, Paolo drove fast towards Laikipia. There were many thoughts in his head. The ranch, problems to solve, the pleasure of being back in Africa. Past Gilgil, past the turning to Wanjohi, just before Ol Kalau, a car overtook him at full speed, spun around in front of him, and blocked the road. From the new blue Volvo a smiling young man, smartly dressed in a suit and tie, emerged and came towards him.

Not for a second — Paolo maintained later — did he have any suspicions. He thought of plain-clothes police or something of the sort. The man approached Paolo's door and greeted him politely. But an instant later, a gun was pointing at Paolo's head and the man was saying: 'Get out, this is a robbery.'

From the other car a barefooted gang now erupted: Paolo counted seven men, dressed in rags, looking wild, carrying pangas and simis. There was no choice: he got out into the night air, which felt and smelt good. It was a starry night, cold, in June.

They took his watch, his shoes, and all his clothes apart from his underpants and a turquoise silk scarf I had given him. One of them sat in his car at the wheel. It was the car they really wanted: the one they were driving had been stolen too long ago to be safe at road blocks (it had belonged to a university teacher who was found next day, tied to a tree in Langata). They opened the boot of the Volvo and tried to push him in, yelling in Kikuyu. Paolo refused . . . and then he noticed there was someone else in the boot, an African all curled up, half-covered with a blanket. He was not dead: the fingers moved slightly, as if pleading; on the spur of the moment Paolo entered, he was locked in and the car moved off.

Some music by Grieg was playing at full volume, and kept playing on and on with the auto-reverse no one had cared to or known how to stop; the boot of the moving car was flooded with the northern music of fjords and snowy valleys. The tune kept his courage high. Paolo attempted in vain to get out. Groping around in the darkness, he managed to find — stroke of luck — the tool box. With a spanner, he tried to force the lock open. The car by then had left the tarmac and was bouncing at a mad speed over the rough and bumpy road, skidding on the mud of recent rains, towards a black, unknown, sordid death. During that time, Paolo believed he was going to die, and prepared himself. He descended into the depth of his soul and the reason for life. While still attempting to open the lock, jolted and tossed in pitch darkness, in the company of a stranger who, paralysed by shock and terror, lay mute and motionless, Paolo tuned to the music of Grieg and the discovery of the secret of life, which is the discovery of the mystery of death. Blind in the night, Paolo's awareness grew in that car, as if he had lived many lives and died many deaths in a few hours.

The lack of a watch, the lack of sight, meant that time was measured only by the heartbeats of his emotion. Memories came and went, fears and regrets ... then the car, and the music, stopped abruptly, and time came to a halt. Doors opened. Steps approached the boot and he could feel the hostile closeness of the bandits through the thin, hard metal. The key was put in the lock, to get them out and kill them. The key was turned and turned, again and again, but nothing happened: in his desperate attempts to get out, Paolo had jammed the lock.

Voices consulting, talking; finally agreeing in Kikuyu to leave them there, where nobody would find them for weeks, to a certain death, the car abandoned on a deep forest track. The noise of his own car reversing, leaving, far, further, then silence.

Slowly, he worked with invisible tools for countless drops of time, unscrewing bolts, pushing, forcing, and at last he succeeded in getting out ... in being born again, like hatching from an egg ... and out was Paolo, 'a riveder le stelle'.

He looked up at the cold clean stars, breathing deep the balsamic forest air, seeing everything with fresh new eyes ... a true rebirth. Reassured, the man in the boot suddenly revived, and Paolo was shaken from his contemplative mood by a gigantic bear hug which made him lose balance; they both rolled in the wet grass, the man crying, 'Ndugu yangu!' ('My brother!'), his new-found voice exultant with relief. They walked together side by side, following the muddy tracks through the forest, and reached the main road at sunrise. The rare cars did not stop at the weird scene of two almost naked men standing at the side of the road, asking for a lift. When finally one car did, they managed to reach the police station at Ol Kalau.

After this incident, I often came home to find Paolo standing, his back against the brass wedding chest he had once given me, the room vibrating with that same music by Grieg, or with his favourite Albinoni Adagio or Boccherini Quintettino. A new light seemed to have sprung in his eyes, that hypnotic quality of depth of one who has gazed beyond death and has come back to life for a time. He spoke frequently afterwards, but not morbidly, about his own death. He gave instructions. He chose the music for his funeral. He told me again and again that he knew this was the last escape destiny had allowed him. 'I have run out of lives,' he used to tell our friends. And to me: 'I would like you to hold my hand when I die. But I know I will die alone. Remember the music. Promise you will remember the music of Venice.' He wanted to be buried on the ranch, under his head a small cushion I had once embroidered for him with the date of our wedding and his name. The choice of the place was mine, 'but from where one can see the hills'.

More and more frequently, after the accident, Paolo took to visiting the Pokot *wazee* down at Churo. The men sat around a large gnarled acacia, their wrinkled old torsos matching the tree's grey trunk; perhaps they were the same age. They smoked strange grasses, chewed strong tobacco and sniffed at an acrid sort of snuff which Paolo liked, and which made them sneeze. They drank a heady brew of herbs and fermented honey, and ritually ate strange seeds which they went to find in the bush. These came from the pod of a leguminous plant which grows after the rains. Only the old people have the right to partake of them, as they create hallucinations which can blow a young man's inexperienced mind, and give weird and prophetic dreams.

Their faces were like masks made of shiny old wood, darkened by the smoke of many fires. These old men all looked different. Only the shape of their headdresses was the same rounded brilliant blue. To obtain it, they used the azure blue powder which, diluted in hot water, is normally used to sparkle up the white in yellowed linen. Some of them sported crude earrings of glass beads or bones. One of them was blind, and his white eyes stared unseeing and aloof in a haggard face. One had painted a pair of bright yellow glasses across his nose and around the eyes: a true old wizard. Paolo went often to sit with these old Pokot people. They accepted him, and he gained from those times with them a different outlook which was part of the new awareness he had acquired.

Once he was offered one of their seeds, and he ate it. The flavour, he told me, was bitter and grassy, and in an odd way he felt sick; but soon his mind seemed to clear, as if a window had been opened suddenly on a weird landscape, and he felt lifted into another dimension in which a strong wind blew hard. The grass of the savannah around them seemed phosphorescent, and on it two sinewy leopards, glowing silver, advanced slowly side by side. He felt suddenly transported high and beyond his body, like a bird, soaring high like a vulture, and with his bird's eye he clearly saw my car driving up the road from Nyahururu, small down there on the red murram track, towards Ol Ari Nyiro. He had not expected me that day, and he drove slowly home to wait for me. The effect had not lasted for long and he told me the story. He showed me one of the seeds, silky and as large as a pea, covered in a white and lustrous skin. He gave it to me, cautioning me not to try, and although I was much tempted I obeyed him. I kept it for years, until it became frail and brittle, and I never managed to discover from which plant it came. The Pokot whom I asked pretended to know nothing about it: the seed was, after all, no medicine for women or outsiders, and I respected their privacy. Even Philip Leakey, to whom I once showed it, had never heard of it and could not recognize it. Eventually I planted it, but life had dried in it and the secret plant never sprouted.

Paolo's love for me became almost a worship. He started writing letters and poems for me more often, and asked me to write for him. I had always written poems. For our wedding anniversary he gave me an antique Zanzibar writing box, inlaid with brass. Inside, there were some ancient jewels, a fantastic old silver belt, and this note which I have kept:

This box is for your poetry, which I love so much. May life allow us never to distract our inner ear from the voice of the soul. Please go on talking to me.

It was at about that time that I arrived one afternoon up in Laikipia to find Paolo lying on our four-poster bed, staring at a large perfect ostrich egg which he had hung from the central beam with an invisible nylon thread.

'There is a message for you in this egg,' he said, looking straight into my eyes without blinking. 'But if you want to read it, you have to break the egg.' It was as if he wanted to test my curiosity. I did not want to break the egg. 'You can open it whenever you like. But you do not have to. I just want you to know that there is a message there for you. A very important one. One day you will have to find out.'

There was no smile in his deep blue eyes, and his hair, dark gold, made him look like a pagan god. The egg remained floating above our bed in the months to come, and I never thought of crushing the thick smooth shell to find out what the message was. Somehow I felt this had to be like an oracle, something you interrogate when there is a real need for an enlightened answer, not just out of curiosity. He did not reply to any of my questions. He just looked at me intensely as he had often done lately, unsmiling, as if he already knew more than he could tell me. In those moments he seemed unreachable, distantly and almost ethereally handsome, his blue eyes transparent like clear water, and I could only love him more. I sat at his side on the bed. He took my hand in his. There had always been something I found irresistible about the touch of his skin, an electric attraction, a dry goldness of hair over the dark tanned skin. He handed me a small book. It was *Illusions* by Richard Bach. On the first page he had written:

To the luminous egg, which made my illusions fly high, above death.

I did not open the egg. It hung there, year after year, until one morning, after the longest night of my life, I suddenly understood what it meant. Then, I no longer needed to open it.

It was immediately after the kidnapping episode that Paolo

asked me to have his baby. It became a fixation, an absolute obsession. He felt his life was soon going to come to an end, and that we should have a child as a living proof of our love. More, as a way to go on living and still being with me. He became interested in reincarnation, and often had premonitions and dreams. One morning in Nairobi, when I opened my eyes, I found him peering at me with an indescribable thoughtful and loving expression. 'I was waiting for you to wake up to tell you about my dream.' He had dreamed of his father, who had died a few years before in 1973, and to whom Paolo was much attached; of his brother Franco, who had been killed by the elephant in Kenya; of Mariangela, his first wife, who had been killed in that fateful car crash; and of Chiara Ancilotto, who had died in 1975, also in a car crash. He had seen them standing on a staircase in front of a large carved door which looked like the one in the house at Kipipiri, where he had lived for over a year with Mariangela, during his first time in Kenya. He used to tell me about Kipipiri, a rather splendid house at the foot of the Aberdares on the Kinangop, and how it had a reputation for bringing its owners bad luck. Most former owners had in fact died prematurely in accidents. I had gone to see the place with him once: but an eerie feeling of gloom hanging over it, the dark unhappily hovering mountain, were more overwhelming to me than the magnificent garden with formally cut yew hedges which formed an intricate maze, and I refused to go inside. At that time, as on the few other occasions when these uncanny premonitions occurred to me, Paolo humoured me. He knew I had very strong forebodings at times, and he respected them since he knew they were not dictated by whims. In his dream these people were silently waiting for him, and his father opened the door and beckoned Paolo to enter.

Soon this dream was followed by another: we had had a baby, and everyone was there to celebrate. There were both his daughters, Emanuele, and of course me. And Paolo? 'I was there, but at the same time I was not. I could see and hear, and I was my own self, but not as I am now. It was as if I were the baby.' A still formless premonition quickly crossed my mind: 'If we had a baby, would you trust me to bring him up on my own?'

'Absolutely. I have often wished I had a mother like you.'

Paolo kept dreaming and talking about the baby, and it had to be a girl. In a letter he wrote me at the end of June 1979, before flying up to Laikipia with his new aeroplane, named 'KUK' after me, he noted uncannily: 'I am going to fly with that little girl of ours: don't forget to plait her hair.' At the time, I was not even pregnant.

Paolo's daughters had long been back in Italy and Switzerland to complete their studies. The elder, Valeria, then seventeen, had bloomed into a beautiful and sunny young woman, gifted with captivating manners, successful at school and popular with her friends. Just at that time, however, to everyone's surprise and to Paolo's consternation, she decided to abandon her studies to elope with Mario — my first husband and Emanuele's father — with whom, we learned, she had been madly in love since her early teens. Mario was going through a spiritual and religious stage, and they went to live in an ashram in India. Although they were not blood relations, and although Mario appeared to be genuinely fond of Valeria, Paolo had been shocked and had felt betrayed at the discovery.

This episode made me decide to agree to Paolo's desire. Furthermore, if I wanted another child I could not afford to wait too long. I was thirty-six years old. It was a major decision, but I loved Paolo. I agreed, and in a few weeks our child was on its way. Paolo was beside himself with joy, and I looked forward to having such a 'wanted' baby.

Preparations were started, and Paolo decided that he wanted a crib made in the shape of a canoe, 'for the baby to sail the sea of life'. He loved the sea and he loved boats. He ordered one in Shimoni, where he was going fishing in his boat 'Umeme' for the high season of March.

Fetching the crib for the baby was the reason why he drove down to the coast instead of flying, in that March 1980. The small canoe, carved out of a mango tree trunk, was too long to fit in the aeroplane.

21

The Premonition

There are more things in heavens and earth, Horatio, than are dreamt of in your philosophy.

Shakespeare, *Hamlet*

It was a lorry which suddenly crossed into his lane at the petrol station in front of Hunter's Lodge, on the Mombasa road. It happened so fast, a screech of brakes, a crunching noise of metal against metal, a silence, people running towards the wrecked vehicle: it occurs every day. Trapped between the dashboard and the contorted seat, his face crushed against the steering-wheel, in the tremendous impact his neck snapped and broke.

Paolo was dead.

The crib remained intact. Only a tiny crack, almost invisible, on the prow. What were his last thoughts, I will never know in this life. Did he see who stole his money, frantic hands fumbling through his pockets, tearing away his watch, robbing his defence-less body of all they could, even before the police came, like a swarm of hungry careless safari ants? Only the wedding ring I had given him remained hidden by his cracked Greek god's head, reclining on the slim tanned hands with the fine blond hair I had loved to touch, covered in blood. Did it really matter? He was no longer there.

Back at home in Nairobi, at the very same moment, with a pang of anguish I saw the accident in my mind and felt his overpowering presence, as tangible as the hot sun of March on my tear-stained cheeks.

I had been thinking that the bougainvillea seemed to be the only flower which did not suffer from the drought. In the garden I sat, waiting for Paolo. He was coming back from Shimoni with the crib for the baby. We were due to go out to dinner. The vision came suddenly, and I could not dismiss it. With the eyes of my mind, and with bewildering clarity, I saw Paolo's car as a twisted wreck, people gathering, running, and I knew he was dead. The vision changed to a sunny scene of scalding heat, faces of mourning friends, an open grave surrounded by banana leaves, a coffin. To the ears of my memory his deep voice said again: 'I would like you to hold my hand when I die. But I know I will die alone. Remember the music. Promise you will remember the music of Venice.' How could I ever forget?

Tears swelled my eyes, my throat ached with choking pain. In a dream I walked back to the house. With slow movements, as if performing a ritual many times rehearsed, I chose the cassette, inserted it in the tape-recorder. Soon the waves of music filled the room, louder and louder, as I sat dazed, my heart heavy with unbearable agony. I kept putting back the music until the garden darkened with the shadows of the evening, and, as on all evenings, the house servant brought the ice, and started pulling the curtains. Paolo's presence was hovering, closer than he had ever been, yet I felt and knew he had forever gone from my life. I acted as if guided by an invisible force. When the room became dark and Bitu came in to light the candles, I slowly stood up and went up to my room to put on a dark maternity dress. Soon, I knew, they would come to tell me Paolo had died, and I had to be ready.

When the first car arrived, I was waiting.

It was Tubby Block, the friend of happier days. The distress lining his face changed to bewilderment when I told him in a voice which did not sound like mine: 'I know. Paolo has gone. He told me.' I touched my stomach. 'But, really, he is not born yet.'

22

The First Funeral

A farewell is necessary before you can meet again.

Richard Bach, *Illusions*

I will not forget the smell of gardenia, and the feel of the fleshy petals on my clutching fingers, the day we flew Paolo's body back home, to bury him.

It was a hot, dry late morning. I left the house knowing that I would be very different when I came back. That nothing I had so far known would ever be the same again. I was acutely aware that my perceptions were accentuated, my senses heightened, and every detail of what I felt and saw was going to be forever engraved in the depth of my being, as if I were born anew.

I wore a white cotton maternity dress, and for a time I stood alone on the doorstep, looking up from the door at the cascade of purple bougainvillea, and at the many cars parked out in the sun — so unusually . . . The dense perfume of gardenia came strong to me from the large bush, almost run to tree, which grew close, and I felt dizzy with memories and grief. With the heat, and the baby.

Never again would Paolo pick a gardenia for me, holding it out in a sweeping gesture, as if gently attacking with his fioretto. Paolo was as supple as a dancer of flamenco, elegant and handsome in an unusual way. I used to think he looked like one of the apostles — but without the beard — or a Roman emperor with his head of curls, or a Renaissance prince. He could have been a warrior of any tribe in the world, a fisherman in any sea. There were many persons in Paolo. He was one of those rare people who are at ease and make an impression wherever they happen to be. There had been around him an aura of intense liveliness and awareness. An unforgettable depth. Our life together had been full, and I knew I had been luckier than most just in being able to accumulate all the memories, to share in all the adventures, to walk with him to the end of his road: yet I felt the agony of not having been there when he died, as if, unwillingly, I had let him down. I picked a gardenia, and stepped out in the sun. A silence descended on all the people as they turned to look at me. They moved towards me, and in the serious faces, in the puffy eyes which had not slept, I read my grief reflected.

Somebody held my elbow: a young, hot hand which, giving me support, was also trying to steady his own bewildering agony. I turned and looked into my son Emanuele's eyes. They were red and they were dry, they were as deep and as sad as they had always been, but they now contained new shadows, a new solitary determination to hide his pain with dignity. Even if he was just fourteen, I knew Paolo's death had already made a man of him.

I did not know yet what it had done to me. In my agonizing sense of loss, of 'never again', I too felt as if a new strength had descended over me during the night he died. The knowledge that I was not alone. I had been Paolo's friend, lover, companion, wife: now there was still the baby I was carrying. It all made sense: I would now be his mother.

'Let's go,' I said squeezing hard the brown hand which offered and asked help. *'Andiamo a seppellire Paolo.'*

Golden particles of dust were suspended in the still air. It must have been hot, but my hands felt cold and clammy.

In his coffin Paolo lay, long-muscled legs in short khaki trousers, a clean striped shirt rolled at the elbows, bare slim feet in sandals. Somebody had composed his hands on the stomach as if he were asleep, his curly rich hair stuck out in a halo, as still as a statue's, and I could not see his wasted face, as a scarf had been placed on it. In the aseptic room nothing moved. It was unnaturally cool, and the strong smell of disinfectant could not cover the smell of death.

There was a fly, one only, which buzzed around unsettled, and I concentrated on it, staring at it, following its flight to the high ceiling, almost landing on Paolo's hands, almost out in the sun again. Nobody said a word while I walked to the coffin, and for the longest minutes I looked for the last time at the body of the man I loved. Slowly I ran my hand, like an uncertain butterfly, lightly over his legs, his hair. I held on to the red scarf, winning the urge to uncover his face, but somebody — was it our friend Amedeo? — shook his head in warning. Before bringing me there, they had all begged me not to look at it now, to remember the baby: Paolo's face was no longer his face. I wanted to keep the memory of the handsome face I knew, yet I felt I could have coped, I could have coped with anything. I forced our wedding ring back on to the rigid finger, and put there gently one of the two gardenias. For timeless moments I held his hand, then I bent to kiss it. The fingers were ice-cold, and dry like snakeskin.

Somebody sobbed, somebody left the place. Again, a last time, I let my hand touch him, I caressed his arms, his legs, I squeezed once the foot, as cold as metal.

Even last times must end.

I tried to talk to him with no words, to communicate beyond that squalid, bare room where he did not belong. Where was he gone? Was he looking at me? Could he feel how much I loved him? Could he? I looked at him, and around and up, and everywhere: the fly had disappeared.

Wherever Paolo was, he was not in that room at the mortuary. The stronger me took over. I let her talk. 'He is here no longer. Let's bring him home.'

The friends looked at me, mute, and followed me out.

The sun hit me as if I had surfaced from an old tomb.

*

Flying up to Laikipia on a sunny day, leaving the Nairobi skyscrapers behind, is always an extraordinary experience. The air was blue, with golden clouds, and a flock of pelicans joined us at Naivasha and flew with us as far as Ol Bolossal. Paolo would have loved that.

The Aberdare Mountains and the deep forests of bamboo and cedar gave way to yellow plains dotted with acacias and small *shambas* with mud huts; tin roofs gave way to thatched roofs, little herds of scrawny cows and goats, waterfalls, brown fields waiting for rain, and the shimmering of Lake Nakuru with all the pink flamingoes.

The tarmac road to Nyahururu and to Kinamba, silver-grey, with toy cars and trucks, rare, more rare, dwindled into nothing. Lake Baringo appeared like a magic vision behind the green hills of the Mukutan Gorge.

The plane was a Cherokee 6, and the pilot who was a friend, cried all the way. I clutched the gardenia to my face. Its perfume could not hide the smell of death.

The stifling sweetish scent of the bunches of dying flowers filled the air. It was hot in the aeroplane, and my stomach felt swollen, my mouth very dry: when was the last time I had drunk anything? Everything practical was pervaded by the ethereal unreality of a bad dream which never seemed to end. I was confused, yet well aware that nothing could ever again be as before. Paolo was dead. Paolo was dead and his body was dissolving inside that coffin, made of shiny wood by some uncaring stranger. It lay on the skin of a large eland, memento of a long-gone hunting adventure.

Almost abruptly the fields were giving way to the thick leleshwa country. We were descending now. I could see the big dam, and there were elephants drinking; I recognized the red tracks, the labour lines, Colin Francombe's garden with the tall gum tree. A herd of eland kicked up the dust, jumping in scattered leaps. The shadow of the plane, like a large bird, scared away families of warthogs, while Egyptian geese and herons took off from the Nyukundu Dam.

We were there. The other aeroplanes had all landed. They were parked on the airstrip in a neat row of twelve or more. The people were out, and they were all looking up at us. I had flown with Paolo many times before. Now I was flying him home to bury him.

I could not bear it that there was nothing left for us to do together.

Before landing, once more, one last time, I decided to fly with him over the land he had loved. I looked out at the beloved hills of Ol Ari Nyiro, bathed in the gold of noon, waiting for Paolo. I reached back and put my hand on the coffin as if to touch his hand. I looked at the pilot's devastated face and moved my finger in a slow circle. He understood instantly, as if he too was thinking of how to postpone the landing. We were descending. He now flew over the upturned, surprised faces, out off the runway, and we were up on the hills.

We flew almost touching the treetops, low down to the Mukutan stream, up to Mugongo ya Ngurue, Ol Donyo Orio, Nagirir, Kuti, Enghelesha with the grass leys dotted with trees, down to bomas and dams. We circled down all over the ranch, over and over again. The painful finality of last times. After a while I nodded.

We landed, and before the dust had settled, someone opened the door of the plane; I found myself engulfed in the embrace of Garisha the cattleman, who wore the same old torn green pullover of every day, and, as usual, smelt faintly of cattle yard. Most people were crying, some uncontrollably, some silently, and no one talked. Everyone was dressed formally: the men wore suits and ties, but all the women wore white.

Without a word the coffin was put in a Toyota pick-up. The silence and the large crowd were unreal.

Paolo's younger and only surviving brother, who wore a dark suit strangely out of place in the afternoon sun of the African bush, and who had not slept during the flight from Europe, took the wheel. I could sense what he thought. Paolo was the only brother he had left, and the second to die in Africa. They helped me in; they were all treating me as if I had suddenly become fragile and weak, and yet somehow, in a strange way, I had never felt stronger, untouchable, carrying my living Paolo inside me, and going to bury my dead one.

The engine broke the silence, and I turned my head: Emanuele had jumped in the back, with the coffin, and was holding on to it with one hand, a gesture of love and despair and longing, his eyes clouded with pain, but dry. It was this which broke the knot which closed my throat, and for the first time that day, I, too, finally cried.

The dogs came to greet the car as usual, wagging their tails and jumping, but before the car came to a halt they started whining, laid back their ears, and sat dejectedly, looking up at me, trembling. I put my face in Gordon's fur, to dry my tears unseen.

The house was full of flowers, the servants wore fezzes and their best white uniforms, the table was laid for a banquet. They all came to shake my hands and Emanuele's, murmuring 'Pole', the antique acceptance of death painting their faces, like wooden masks. Simon held my hand for a long time.

The garden was ablaze with bougainvillea and hibiscus, as always in the dry last weeks of March before the long rains. In the hot still air, a thousand birds sang their song of life. They concentrated here from the surrounding bush or stopped to rest during their short migrations, attracted by the small oasis of green and water and shade and food. Blue starlings crowded the bird-baths with metallic gleams, doves, weavers, parrots with green feathers, picking at the seeds that, even today, a faithful hand had laid. Extraordinary how, in my dazed state, I noticed all the familiar things, all the smallest details. Bumblebees circled the petria, and the querulous croak of the go-away bird called from the treetops.

They put the coffin out, in the shade of the acocantera, and I sat there with the dogs, to wait.

I do not know how long I waited, and I do not know why. I sat with Paolo for the last time in the garden we had carved out of the bush during the long years, when our dream of Africa had materialized and every day we learned more about this wild, beautiful land on the edge of the Rift Valley, which had become our home.

I thought of the sense of adventure that had never left our life together. The magic of Paolo was the alertness with which he could create excitement and interest in all around him. There never had been a dull moment; boredom was unknown to both of us. Gone was the poet which was in Paolo, and the romantic squire, the ardent lover and Emanuele's hero. Absurd though it seemed, our road together had come to its end. Yet, uncannily, I felt his presence more than if he were visible. Hovering and protecting, his love cloaked me with light.

I walked again with Paolo for the last time, the coffin carried by his friends, Emanuele at my side in his white trousers. I turned to look at him, and felt an unbearable pity: his beloved father-companion had left him, and his world was shattered. Yet he walked straight, in control of his emotions. His red-rimmed eyes had shadows I could not read, but the slim arm he offered me was no longer a child's. We were going to bury his dreams also.

In front of the grave a kind hand had erected a green tent to shelter me from the sun. The earth which had been dug stood in a mound ready to be thrown back, and was covered with flowers. Exactly as in my premonition, the hole was surrounded with banana leaves.

In the shade of a large bush, a silent group of women clad in their colourful *shukas* and many bead necklaces, babies at their breasts or strapped to their backs, sat still, watching with liquid eyes, like sad gazelles. The crowd drew close. I saw Oria, Carol, Aino, all dressed in long white skirts like guardian angels.

For the last time, before he was buried, I talked to Paolo.

Over the years, we had made a special habit of writing to each other, even — especially — when we shared the same house, the same bed. We exchanged letters, poems, or little curious notes. Paolo's often came with unusual presents which never ceased to amaze me with his thoughtfulness or perfect timing. He sent me once a huge flowered bush, the first day of spring; a wedding chest of brass for a wedding anniversary; a writing-box of ebony from Zanzibar when he had asked me for a poem for his birthday; a pair of antique ice skates the day I had begun to walk again.

The night he died, I wrote to him until morning. I chose to say now the simplest words. I did not have much voice.

I tuoi occhi eran colore d'acqua:
Si, tu sei acqua.

Avevano trasparenze d'aria:
Si, tu sei questo cielo adesso.

La tua pelle era cotta dal sole
come la terra del Kenya:
Si, tu sei questa rossa polvere.

Per sempre
Per sempre
Per sempre, Paolo,
Sei diventato tutto.

('Your eyes were the colour of water:
yes, you are water.

They had transparencies of air:
yes, you are this sky now.

Your skin was baked by the sun
like Kenya's earth:
yes, you are this red dry dust.

Forever, forever, forever, Paolo,
you have become everything.')

These were my words of requiem, and I crumpled the sheet of paper and threw it in the open grave, together with what was left of that gardenia. It fell gently and noiselessly, like a feather.

Colin passed me the spade. With an overwhelming feeling of unreality, I dug it into the red earth, and threw the first soil on the coffin. It landed with a dumb thud, and I passed the spade to my son. He was the man left to me.

A last-minute thought: I murmured to Colin, and he nodded: Luka and Mirimuk and all the Security men in their green uniforms stood in a line and fired a salute in the air, aiming towards the sky. The last gunshot in Paolo the Hunter's life echoed on the hills, doubling the silence.

Boccherini's Quintettino filled the air in liquid waves, the music written in Venice by which Paolo had been haunted, which he loved and had chosen for his burial. The sun shone on the music. I had kept my promise.

On the grave I now planted a little yellow fever tree which would one day grow out of his body, tall and lean as he had been, for us to touch and see.

Elephant screamed at the water tank, so close that everyone was startled. A white eagle flew high above the grave in great slow circles. Soon all faces were upturned to watch it. It was a rare sight, an omen. Paolo's words came back to me, and I said silently:

'Fly for me, bird of the sun. Fly high.'

I loved him.

Hot was the night, and the ostrich egg hung from the four-poster with its secret message.

The egg hung over my head the night after I buried Paolo, with its silent wisdom and the answer perhaps to my bewildered pain, yet I had the sense to resist the desire to listen to Paolo's message. The time was not right for an act of violence.

In the bed, close to me, I felt a presence, a familiar breathing, something gentle seemed to caress my face with infinite love. A flutter in my womb. A knot closed my throat with emotion. Paolo was dead, but Paolo was now moving alive for the first time inside me. The egg could wait. The baby had to be born. Then perhaps I could read the message.

I closed my eyes and let the memories and the pain come and take me. Alone with the unborn baby he had so much wanted, surrounded by the music I had promised I would play for him at his death, I surrendered to the design of destiny and to the agony of his loss, knowing fully that Africa had just begun to claim her price, and I could only accept it, pay it and try to learn from it. A letter he had written me on the first day of January of that year, soon after he had learnt the baby had been conceived, was still in the Zanzibar writing-box he had given me. That night, after I had talked to him for hours as if he could still listen, I read again that letter:

In this golden morning the pollen of abundance lifts from the dust of years of drought: It will be the year of our baby. I wish for one thing: That you may give her a soul like yours. That you may bring her always through forests, treasures, battles, loves to the centre of an horizon from which one can dominate the world. That you may let her fly lightly following the track of your butterfly wing, like a golden powder on the leaves which may guide her through the thickets. I love you both. P.

PART III

Emanuele

23

The Time of Waiting

*Je me souviens de jours anciens, et je pleure.**
Charles Baudelaire, *Les Violons de l'automne*

The afternoon after the funeral, Emanuele rode out on his horse to the hut on the Mukutan. He returned sooner than I expected, and came straight to my room. He was holding the book in which, at Paolo's request, he had recorded the animals sighted at the salt lick.

'I saw Bianco there and a herd of twelve elands. Then came two male buffaloes. There were elephant breaking trees on the hill behind Marati Ine. I found a white-lip snake in the thatch. And this. It was in the book.' He handed me a fragile leaf of paper folded in four.

I felt as if the wind of memory had blown it from the past. The handwriting was Paolo's. There was no date.

Dear Emanuele, [the note said]
I miss you. This place without you is different. When I am gone, look after it for me. Remember. Fly for me, bird of the sun. Fly high. I see you, Ema.

Paolo

* 'I remember the old days, and I weep.'

We looked at each other. His lost eyes stared back, shadowed in misery. Still holding the note, I embraced him. His head barely reached my shoulder. He was just fourteen. 'Yes, Ema. You will look after us all.'

His voice was changing. 'My life, you know, my life is no more worth living.'

I felt too weary to comment. Emanuele never said anything he did not truly mean.

From then on he slid into his new role as the man in the household. He now sat at the head of the table, and took responsibility for the day-to-day problems. The staff started referring to him about the matters of maintenance which had been Paolo's task. He learnt to carve the meat. He served the drinks in the evening. He concentrated on practising driving with Arap Rono, Karanja, or Colin. As a child he had always been reliable. As a young man, he could be in charge. I found great comfort in his presence and wisdom.

Friends took turns in keeping me company, but the house and the garden, the hills and the gorges, echoed with Paolo's absence. '. . . and Love is immortal and death is only a horizon, and a horizon is the limit of our eyes,' had quoted Jack Block in his letter of condolence. I tried to remember this.

Paolo's presence had been so vibrant that now the world seemed to be suddenly silent. Days passed in a haze of solitude and expectation. I found refuge in my poems, and in my journal I wrote daily as if I were still talking to him. I began walking with the dogs in the evening. My favourite hour in Laikipia is that time before sunset when everything seems covered in golden dust and yellow light lines the silhouette of the hills. The silvery-green of the leleshwa blends with the shiny dark of the euclea as in a subtle tapestry of brilliant sage green. The water in the dams reflects the sky, families of Egyptian geese float smoothly, drawing darker ripples in the mirror-like surface, and pelican fish in small co-ordinated groups, like dancers. I loved walking with the dogs. I called their names, and they came, pushing their warm muzzles against my legs, hoping for a pat, and each got a scratch on the nose or behind the ears. We met buffalo sometimes, and often elephant, feeding silently from the upper branches of an acacia, betrayed only by the sudden cracking of snapped wood. It was a matter of staying quiet, hoping the dogs would resist the urge to bark or rush in a playful attack. This always resulted in a mock charge by the elephant, and in my blood chilling for a few still moments. I came back when the last shadows before darkness created new shapes in the bush, and they all looked like buffalo.

Emanuele was quieter than usual. He had made a large poster for his room with snapshots of happy days, and had concentrated on completing a 'Study of Kenya's Billfish', with drawings, text and photographs, which he had been secretly working on at the time of Paolo's death and which he had intended to present to him. When he finished it, he wrote on the first page:

For my father, Paolo, who taught me to appreciate the skills and crafts of Deep-Sea Fishing, and the challenge that this magnificent, yet unpredictable sport presents. Emanuele.
28.3.1980

In the meantime my belly swelled, and the birth of the baby was imminent. Every day I tended Paolo's grave at the edge of my garden. A large oblong rock had been brought from a favourite spot of Paolo's, below a gigantic euphorbia which he had liked to use as a meeting-place, and which, because of this, had been named Bobonghi ya Paulo. It was his tombstone, and weighed more than two tons. With Emanuele's help, Colin had engraved just simply: PAOLO and, underneath, the date of his death: 19.3.1980.

One day I was sitting cross-legged, my back to the stone on Paolo's grave, plucking off the weeds which grew between the small portulaca I had planted, lost in thoughts and in a monologue with him which did not need words. I was trying to communicate with Paolo, and I was thinking that there are things, like music, like perfumes or light, which are so evocative of moods or places

135

or people, and which, being shapeless, are timeless. I remembered the phrase Catholics apply to saints: 'He died in the odour of sanctity', and recalled many stories I had heard about people dying and fragrances strangely filling the air. There was the account of my grandmother's death; she was a particularly pious woman, who was also a medium. When my mother walked to her bedroom where she had been laid to rest before the funeral, the perfume of gardenia – her favourite flower – was overpowering. Yet there were no flowers at all.

Concentrating on this thought, I wished for a sign, any sign. There was not a particular scent which I could associate with Paolo: he had used no lotion nor after-shave. Yet suddenly the air was filled with a very strong smell. It was not a perfume, but a disinfectant or deodorant, sweetish and vaguely medicinal, not particularly nice and definitely artificial, and it was coming from the fingers which I was using to weed the grave. It was so strong and sudden, and so recognizable, that my mouth felt dry with emotion.

For this was the smell which had pervaded the mortuary the day I had gone to see Paolo for the last time, before we flew him up to Laikipia to bury him. Cradling my hand like a fragile nestling, I went to look for my mother, who had come from Italy for the birth of the baby. I wanted a witness to this strange happening.

'Do you smell anything?' I asked hopefully, as if it had all been the fruit of my imagination. She wrinkled her nose: 'Yes, very strong . . . a disinfectant or something . . . what is it?'

When I told her what happened and my only association with that smell, she did not look surprised. 'I have always known you are a bit fey, Kuki,' she said calmly, 'like your grandmother. Nothing about you would surprise me.'

And that was it. That strange odour persisted a long time before fading. Only once again, three years later, did it come back to me, and in such a way that I knew this first time could not possibly have been a coincidence.

24

Sveva

... a little while, a moment of rest upon the wind, and another woman shall bear me ...

Kahlil Gibran, *The Prophet*

'Have you ever seen eyes so blue?' The doctor was holding out the baby for me to see. 'A beautiful baby girl. Well done.'

I had been waiting for this moment during the long months, listening to the baby kicking in my enlarged belly, resting in the afternoons, embroidering a cushion in needlepoint with the words: FOR PAOLO'S BABY. Eating the right food, going through exercises, check-ups, scans: nothing should go wrong for the birth of Paolo's child. Always I listened to the music of Boccherini, which had a soothing effect on me.

In view of the problems I had gone through, and my age, the doctor had suggested that, if the baby was late, they would induce it. I had chosen a prospective date, which sounded like a good omen: 18.8.80.

On the chosen date, the baby was born naturally. It was 4.35 a.m. She weighed eight pounds and was fifty-one centimetres long.

I had arrived at Nairobi Hospital feeling well, with a great sense of expectation, an unbearable curiosity. The nurse kept coming back to check, a puzzled look on her face. I was in labour. From the headphones around my head, from the ones around my belly, the music flew, taking away the pain, submerging us both in waves of pure harmony. The music Paolo had loved and chosen for his funeral was going to be the music of this re-birth. The baby was born with the music as the only medicine. And she was not crying.

It is a unique moment, that first meeting of a mother and her new-born baby, the first glance at the mysterious creature that for months has been carried and nursed in the secret of the womb, and now has become a different, forever independent human being, with features inherited from generations of ancestors.

I held out my hands. Perfect head, tanned skin, dark golden fuzz of hair, and, extraordinary for a new-born baby, open, direct, intense and knowing blue eyes.

'A sign, just give me a sign.'

Slowly, almost deliberately, while the deep-blue eyes never left mine, the index finger of the left hand curled up tightly, and she grabbed my hand with the other fingers. Weakness, relief, joy at the pit of my stomach.

'Welcome back,' I whispered, before I finally slept.

I had felt sure the baby had to be a replica of Paolo, and, therefore, a boy. Paolo knew better than I. I called her Sveva, the name Paolo had chosen, with Paolo as a middle name. The Svevi were a noble tribe which had invaded Italy from the north in the early tenth century, and had settled in Sicily. Their blond hair and blue eyes can still be found today in some Sicilians, normally very dark. It was a rare, beautiful name which suited her looks perfectly.

Within a day, my room at the hospital became a conservatory overflowing with all sorts of flowers and plants, which filled every vase and shelf and spread into the corridor. A procession of people came to visit. Friends brought champagne, and letters and telegrams kept arriving from everywhere. I had engaged a nurse for the baby. She was a Kikuyu woman by the name of Wanjiru, intelligent, pleasant and well educated, responsible, large and with a sense of humour, who already had six children of her own. She came to the hospital with Emanuele, marched into my room and went straight to the crib. She took the baby in her arms and lifted her high, cooing delightedly: '*A musijana!*' ('A little girl!'). '*Mutoto yangu!*' ('My own child!'). Sveva smiled a toothless bright grin. '*Makena!*' ('The happy one!') Wanjiru exclaimed in Kikuyu. I could see from the first moment that the relationship between those two would be one of great affection. It became in fact a deep mutual love and Wanjiru will forever be another mother to Sveva.

When after a few days I returned to the house at Gigiri, I found it full of flowers. Oria had brought a basket of special heart-shaped biscuits, baked by her old cook Kimuyu. In an elegant pot stood a young yellow fever tree, with a note addressed to Miss Sveva Gallmann and the words: 'Welcome home, Sveva. This tree, which your father loved so much, will bring you luck and happiness.'

Paolo's favourite bird had been the seagull, which reminded him of the sea. Entering Sveva's nursery I found that while I was in hospital one of the pale blue walls had been painted with a delightful flight of seagulls and drifting clouds. It was the gift of Davina Dobie, an artist and a close friend of ours. She had left a note: '. . . love you and baby Paolo, always, even from far away'.

A few days after Sveva's birth, we flew up to Ol Ari Nyiro. It was a very strange feeling, to go back to Laikipia with Paolo's baby in my arms. The dogs ran down to meet the car as usual. They sniffed her tiny feet, shyly, tentatively nuzzling them.

My room was waiting, with the egg. I climbed on the bed and touched it, holding it in my hand and shaking it gently to let the message inside know I was there. I moved Sveva's tiny hand, already with tapering fingers, to the shell, smooth as cream. In the night, by the light of my candle and fire, I watched the egg yet again, as if it were some mysterious face with a concealed secret to tell, and the egg stared back at me like an enigma. The point of the game was perhaps to keep guessing, trying to see the reasons and the symbol behind the egg. I was not ready yet. I could not yet break the egg.

As a sign of celebration, sheep were slaughtered and roasted, and I cancelled all the outstanding debts of my staff. Our people came to greet Sveva and wish her well, as is the custom. They looked at her, touched her pink fingers, giggled at the colours of her eyes and hair – just like her father – and brought her gifts of eggs, a cockerel, a bead charm.

In time, they gave her names. Kainda was her Tharaka name, which Luka gave her, and which means 'the hunter's daughter'. Kaweria was her Meru name, given by Garisha, which means 'the loving one'. The one which stuck was her Kikuyu name, Makena, 'The happy one', chosen by Wanjiru, for her sunny character. Mirimuk came and looked at her gravely and closely for long moments. 'Paulo has returned. His seed was not lost. He is this girl now, and we are happy, as he will look after this *shamba* again.' He put his hand on her head, and spat on her a drizzly spray of saliva in the traditional Turkana blessing. '*Jambo Paulo*,' he said in his husky voice. '*Asante wa kurudi*' ('Thank you for coming back').

I had grown to feel a deep affection for Mirimuk, his acute eyes, his good-natured reserved moods, his endurance on a diet of *posho* and milk, his independent pride mixed with respect and eagerness. He cared for Sveva, Emanuele and me, and this was apparent. We returned this care. His chosen name for Sveva touched a deep chord in me.

25

The Drought

In the Highlands you woke up in the morning and thought: Here I am, where I ought to be, because here I belong . . .

Karen Blixen, *Out of Africa*

We had buried Paolo on 22 March.

March had ended in gusts of wind, and the extraordinary galloping clouds of Africa, which forever move and change in fantastic patterns, were not yet visible in the pure blue sky. We started looking up for signs of rain; but the nights brought only ceaseless wind which bent the fragile new pepper trees I had planted, and the young yellow fever tree on Paolo's grave had to be staked with a bamboo post to prevent it from breaking. Dust devils arose in the hot plains in swirls of sticks and thorns, and a fine film of dust dulled the *crotons* and the evergreens.

The Pokot burned their pastures, and in the night chains of fires garlanded the hills like ceremonial lights: but the rains seemed to have receded. A few times the sky became grey and heavy, and we looked hopefully to the east from where the rains used to come to Laikipia, but we could only hear the noise of the howling winds playing new notes through the hollows and branches of the tallest trees. The pastures grew drier and poorer by the day; the cattle started losing condition. Now ribs could be seen sticking out below the patterned skins. The humps hung flabby. The waterholes dried out and the level of the dams reached the lowest ever.

One night I was woken up by furious snarling noises, dogs barking and growling. Someone was also knocking frantically at my door. *'Chui!'* the askari was shouting urgently, *'chui nakula mbwa!'* ('The leopard is eating the dogs!'). The commotion was extraordinary, and seemed to be coming from the lawn outside the sitting-room.

The generator is switched off at night, and it is not the easiest thing, for one shortsighted like me, to light the paraffin lamp, find and load the gun in darkness, get a torch and creep out, barefoot in the dewy cold grass, towards an invisible prowling beast. Nothing I had learnt in Italy had prepared me for this.

The leopard, attracted certainly by the dogs' scent, had discovered he had to reckon with seven of them. He had repaired up one of the young yellow fever trees, where he hung tenaciously, snarling and lashing out with his paws like any cat. In the flash of my torch, his yellow eyes and bare fangs looked wild and breathtaking. Sensing me, the dogs redoubled their brave efforts. The barking grew louder, and one of them tried to jump up the tree. The leopard caught him swiftly with its claws, and in the screaming which followed, I fired in the air and my torch fell. The leopard took advantage of the darkness to jump away – which was what I wanted – and my dogs took off in hot pursuit, their fierce barking, mixed with plaintive whines, silencing the shy creatures of the night. There was no major casualty which mercurocrome and antiseptic powder could not cure that time, but several other leopard attacks, on one or the other of the dogs, became a fairly normal occurrence. Many times Colin Francombe had to come up to Kuti with his specialized surgeon's kit to attend to serious wounds.

In mid June, Colin left with his family for England for his overseas biennial leave of two months. For the first time since we had come to Africa, I was alone.

Soon, the cattle started dying. At first it was two or three a day, and John Mangicho, the assistant manager, with the headmen Ngobitu and Tunkuri could cope with this. But when different symptoms that they were not familiar with began to appear, and the number of deaths grew to ten or more animals a day, I sent for Jasper Evans. He was the neighbour Colin had suggested I should contact in case of emergency, and he came immediately. Jasper was one of those people you cannot imagine ever losing their temper. He was phlegmatic and balanced, and just seeing him standing on my verandah, a warm pink vodka in one hand and his khaki hat in the other, discussing the problem with absolute calm, reassured me. He gave logical instructions which made sense, and suggested certain cures. His last remark when leaving was typical of his fatalistic attitude: 'You have six thousand head of cattle. Do not worry about losing a hundred.'

I did worry, however. I still knew practically nothing at all about cattle, but I could see that, in their debilitated state, they were prone to any disease they would otherwise have been resistant to. In this case it was east coast fever, a tick-borne infection brought by buffalo, for which there was still no cure. Over four hundred head died before Colin came back, and this taught me a lesson I shall never forget. I decided to start planting again, and to grow fodder which could become silage to keep ready for an emergency such as this. The grass leys at Enghelesha needed to be rejuvenated, and I felt we should grow the maize that we had otherwise to buy to feed our labour force. Part of the maize and the green stalks could be used for silage. Never again should a drought find us unprepared.

In the meantime, reports of poaching began to disturb me more and more often. A certain amount of 'healthy' poaching is unavoidable in a property teeming with wildlife and surrounded by a settlement where nothing wild has been left. The Pokot on our north-east boundary were extremely poor. They knew Ol Ari Nyiro from time immemorial, as it had once been their territory where they had run cattle and goats. Occasionally they speared an eland for meat, and I could never find it in my heart to condemn this. However, small-scale poaching had never been a problem until the very late seventies, when a new factor changed the entire scene.

Gangs of Somali infiltrated the Pokot, and provided a market for ivory and rhino horn. The price they offered for a horn represented over a year's income, and was a temptation the Pokot people could not resist.

We had at that time sixteen people employed in our private Security on the ranch. Their task was to patrol the place on foot and make sure no trespassing went undiscovered. They were responsible for the safety both of domestic stock and wildlife. Thanks to them we had a zero record of cattle rustling, quite an achievement for a territory so close to the land of the Samburus, whose young warriors stole cattle on full-moon nights as an accepted tradition. Our Security were armed mostly with bows and arrows. The majority of them belonged to the Tharaka, a tribe of hunters living on the rim of the Meru National Park, and they knew all the secrets of poaching and hunting, having once been poachers themselves. They were small and muscular, built to track unending hours and to hide quickly. They were resilient and courageous, and Luka was their chief. In the Security there were Turkana, taller, long-limbed, wilder, tireless walkers: Mirimuk was their leader. There were also a few Somali, cunning and more sophisticated, and immensely brave, led by Hussein Omar. Only these three men had guns. It was soon apparent that sixteen people armed with bows and arrows were no longer enough to patrol the entire ranch efficiently, as well as fighting an organized and well-armed poaching offensive.

There were many new things I had to learn to cope with, apart from my personal solitude. The first of these was to adopt the right attitude to the land I was suddenly responsible for, as on this would depend its future.

Many of my old friends from Italy were horrified at the thought of me alone in the heart of Africa, with only a very young son and a small baby for company, no telephone, no proper roads, surrounded by thousands of acres of bush where it was not just the wildlife that was dangerous, but also people determined to kill whoever came between them and their quarry. Many came or wrote begging me to reconsider my decisions, to sell the place for a profit and go back 'home'. The idea of leaving, however, never once crossed my mind. Not in the darkest moments of loneliness when the tasks ahead seemed beyond my own power, and the things which I had to face on my own too complicated and alien. Even if Paolo was no longer there, the reasons for our choice still were.

My first symbolic decision had been the one to bury Paolo in Laikipia, rather than send him back to Italy as had been expected. I knew that burying him in the land he had loved and chosen was not only following his instructions, which in itself would have been reason enough. It was an essential statement confirming my position and my choice: Laikipia, Ol Ari Nyiro, were 'home'.

In Africa, great importance is attached to laying to rest the dead in their own land. The homestead is where your ancestors have been buried and where you one day will be. I felt that if one cannot choose the place of one's birth, one should at least choose the place where, once dead, the body will rest. For this very reason I had planted the acacia, the African tree *par excellence*, and the one Paolo loved most. The roots would one day reach and feed on his body, which would grow out of the grave again and become part of the landscape he had loved so well. Because of this I had decided to resist the pressure to go to Europe to give birth to Paolo's baby. In the space of a few months, Paolo would have died, he would have been buried and he would have again been born in Africa.

I had chosen to stay in this country. Emanuele was showing every sign of being well able one day to run the ranch in the enlightened way that Paolo would have wished. His passion for natural sciences was obviously not a passing fancy. After his university studies he would have come back with all the new ideas and tools to develop the place on the lines Paolo and I had believed in: keeping a careful balance between the development of the natural resources and the protection of the environment. I felt strongly about the guardianship of the land. Going away would mean renouncing this responsibility and declaring defeat. I could not let Paolo down. I should hold on a few years for Emanuele, and I was lucky to have in Colin a competent and loyal supporter whom I respected and trusted. The first step, however, was the policy I wanted to adopt, and I was conscious that this was ultimately up to me. In the surrounding ranches in the Laikipia, rhino were being poached rapidly, and soon none would be left, apart from those in the few fenced and protected sanctuaries belonging to a handful of dedicated people. Most landowners felt that the responsibility for the survival of the wildlife was no longer theirs. Since the ban on hunting in 1977, wildlife belonged to the government. Ranchers were allowed to control whatever they felt was dangerous to them or their property, but the protection of wildlife on private land was no longer strictly their concern. It was also an extremely expensive operation, which guaranteed no return.

I had found Ol Ari Nyiro teeming with wildlife. I wanted to protect it, even if theoretically this was not my task and nobody expected me to do it. I wanted to protect it because of Paolo, because of Emanuele and because of my own self-respect; because all around us I could see what would happen if I let go. Across the hill of Enghelesha, Colobus farm was being chopped up into small *shambas* where wildlife had no place. The forest of cedars and podo, the old black acacias, had been cut and made into charcoal. No more magic refuge for the Colobus monkeys and the rare birds was left along the bare slope of the hills once thick with wildflowers and liana. Maize was planted everywhere. Tin roofs dotted the ploughed fields where buffalo and antelope had been abundant.

If I went, the same would happen here: where would the animals go? The forest of Enghelesha was the only large piece of indigenous forest remaining in that part of Laikipia. The variety of flora was exceptional on the ranch because of its varied terrain. I could not bear the thought that all this would inevitably be destroyed by settlement, never to return. The idea of selling that beauty for money not only appeared to me ugly and pointlessly greedy. It would be an act of cowardice which would show that the privilege of being there was wasted on me. More than anything, I wanted to prove that I deserved my guardianship.

Sitting on the top of the hill at Mugongo ya Ngurue, looking down at Baringo through the intact cliffs of the Mukutan Gorge, I touched the rough trunk of the old twisted acacia growing there at the edge of the world, as a sentinel to the silent, vast, majestic scenario. That landscape had been there long before our advent. It would still be there after I left. Not only had I no right to spoil it, but I had to be actively involved in protecting it. Special privileges come at a price: and this was my inheritance.

With my daughter's birth my life had changed again completely. The gap of over fourteen years between her and Emanuele was a large one to bridge, and all this had happened at a time when, as a result of Paolo's death, so many new demands on my time and energy had arisen which I could neither avoid nor postpone. All the many tasks of a housewife and a mother were still there, and in addition there was the baby to nurse and to look after. She was of course my priority, and as I did not want to leave her alone, I got myself one of those kangaroo-like baby carriers and took her with me wherever I went, as all African mothers do. I also decided to breastfeed her for as long as the pediatrician suggested. He advised two years, and, having overcome the initial shock, I set about it without a second thought; thinking about it now, this was one of the most sensible decisions I ever took. Also, I had employed Wanjiru to take care of all the practical details of caring for a baby. She became part of our family immediately and for good. She eventually learned Italian, and travelled with us, while Sveva adored her as a second mother.

Colin came back from leave, and I then set out to tackle what could not be postponed. With his help I began to understand about cattle and the problems of a ranch. I learnt to talk business, and to cope with those alien things which are balance sheets and legal or financial language. Mostly, I learnt to take decisions which could affect many people and have far-reaching results without relying on Paolo's judgement and experienced help. But a plan of action to protect the wildlife was needed: however much it cost, I was determined to succeed.

26

Death of a Rhino

The immense longing not just to protect, but to rehabilitate the Earth.

Laurens van der Post, *A Walk with a White Bushman*

One day, Luka found the corpse of another rhino down the
Mukutan. It was Bianco. He was the huge male who used to come
regularly to drink at the springs below the little hut on the
Mukutan, and Paolo had called him Bianco because of his very
pale powdery coat. His death meant more to me than all the
others' because I knew that rhino: it was now time to do something
consistent and effective, and I consulted with Colin.

Including Bianco, nine rhinos were killed on the ranch between
the end of 1979 and 1980. If no action was immediately taken, all
would go. To make the anti-poaching Security effective, we needed
to double their numbers and to equip them properly. We needed
guns, radios, uniforms and adequate means of transport. Colin
could provide the training and leadership. I could renounce my
profits, and invest them in maintaining and paying the salaries of
all the extra personnel. With the drought and the resulting effect
on the breeding of cattle which affected our sales, it was a gigantic
burden. I felt, however, that I was a trustee to the land. Paolo and
I had found the place teeming with wildlife. I could not give up.
My task was to protect it, and to do that the first step was to
improve our Security. I gave Colin *carte blanche* to employ as
many people as he felt were needed. The Security was now

149

doubled to thirty-two men. I could not, however, afford to equip them.

To my rescue came Richard Leakey. I had not yet met him, but I had known his brother Philip since the early days. Richard was then Vice-Chairman of the East African Wildlife Society, and Director of Museums. He was young for that task and had a reputation for being ruthless, ambitious, and not suffering fools gladly. Philip, who knew Colin well and was aware of our problems, suggested that Richard might be able to help. He organized a meeting and I went to Richard's office at the Museum.

The first feature I notice in a person is always the eyes. Richard's brown eyes radiated intelligence, wit and curiosity. There was a restlessness about him as if he could not bear to waste time, but he could concentrate on an issue deeply and competently, and deal with it with flair. If he chooses, he can be charming. He greeted me with: 'I have heard a lot of things about you.' He grinned. 'All good.'

'I have also. Not all good.' I grinned back. 'But I like to make up my own mind about people.'

We discussed the ranch, its wildlife, the Security and my commitment to curb the poaching and to protect the animals which happened to be on the land. He understood the problem immediately, sympathized, and promised to help. I could see he would never support me if he did not believe that what I was trying to achieve was worth it.

Ol Ari Nyiro was home to the largest known population of indigenous black rhino remaining on private land in Kenya: this was a known fact, and invaluable from the point of view of conservation and research. They needed to be protected, as their loss would be irreparable.

Before I left, Richard said, 'I am very interested in your circles. Perhaps one day you will let me investigate them.'

I did not have the faintest idea what he was talking about. I looked puzzled, and at myself, as if I feared I might have grown some strange spots. Richard explained that flying over the ranch on his way to Koobi-Fora he had noticed unusual formations, in a circle shape, of darker and thicker vegetation, which defined the perimeter of very large areas on the ranch, and he was curious to discover what they were. The idea was most exciting to me who, as a little girl, had followed my father on his archaeological expeditions in Veneto, searching for fossils and ancient artefacts.

It took Richard only a few weeks to organize radios and old .303 guns for the Security: our anti-poaching campaign was born. From that first encounter, a relationship destined to last, based on mutual respect and trust, was established between us, and over the years we became true friends.

Richard pursued his goals with clear-minded determination and great intelligence. He was a workaholic. He worked like one who cannot bear to waste precious time. Waking up long before sunrise and going to bed early, refusing social commitments at night, he produced a tremendous amount of work. He had no patience with people who were slow or inconsistent or stupid, but he was very fair, and was worshipped by his staff. His achievements were staggering, and it was difficult, when he made one of his speeches on anthropology or on anything else, not to fall under his spell. I imagine that Richard had learnt the value of time when he thought he had none left, when his kidneys became infected and he had to undergo a kidney transplant. It was his brother Philip who had then given him one of his kidneys, and another chance of life. Richard was a gourmet and loved good food and wine, and sailing north of Lamu where he had a house. He was an excellent and safe pilot, but he regarded flying as a means of getting somewhere quickly, not as a pleasure in itself: he valued his life too much to take risks, and during the rainy season he avoided the sky. Like all Leakeys he loved dogs, and some of Gordon's progeny became his lucky pets. Richard had an exceptional family, and I became fond of his wife Meave and of their daughters, Samira and Louise, bright lively girls who often came to Laikipia to stay, and who loved riding camels, racing them up and down my airstrip with mad screams.

*

The challenges were enormous, and more difficult than I had ever imagined. My solitude was beginning to become a burden to me, and my friends and my small child could not really fill it. These were the toughest years of my life, but as I had decided to stay and make a success of it, I cried my tears unseen in the night, and during the day I got on with the job.

Paolo's daughters were away. The elder, Valeria, in India with Mario at the time of the accident, only discovered what had happened months later through a chance phone call to her maternal grandmother in Italy. When I heard about this, I was happy that Mario was there to take care of her, which he did and has done since, as they are still happily together. The younger, Livia, was sixteen, and Paolo's death affected her badly. Artistic and bright, original, unpredictable and highly-strung, Livia had never been an easy child. Her mother's death when she was only five years old had created an emotional gap no amount of love and care could ever truly fill. She had been Paolo's favourite daughter, and his disappearance added to her misery.

I had Emanuele with me. He was fourteen, and coped as I expected: deep in his school work, he drowned his sorrow at Paolo's absence in his books, and in the passion which could somehow substitute for the excitement of those forever lost adventures after a buffalo or a lion. It was an odd and unusual passion, which he had had since he was small, but which I felt I should not restrain.

Snakes.

27

A Dangerous Passion

The serpent, subtlest beast of all the field.

John Milton, *Paradise Lost*

There lived in Ol Ari Nyiro an old Turkana herdsman with a long curly grey beard – very uncommon for Turkana – which made him look like St Joseph in the Crib, and this is what Paolo and I called him. He had a noble countenance, a proud and handsome profile, like the saints painted on church ceilings. They brought him to me at Kuti one day, one leg hideously swollen by the bite of a snake which had escaped unseen, and which could have been a burrowing viper or a small puff-adder. It was my first experience of snakes in Laikipia.

Simon, who took any Turkana cause much to heart, came to announce this event, and gravely brought me to inspect the man. He lay on the back lawn, mute, with closed eyes, wrapped in a threadbare blanket, looking more than ever like a dying saint in a fresco. Ngobithu stood by, waiting to see what action I would take.

I was used to treating all sorts of illness at the ranch, from children's coughs to septic wounds, from dehydration to female problems. I even set a couple of broken bones, and dealt with twisted ligaments, and I had found that there was a touching, unending faith in our people in my ability to perform miracles on their minor illnesses: I had never yet had to deal with a snake bite, and although I had learnt the theory I was not quite sure of what the practical results would be. This time, luckily, the God of Turkana was keeping an eye on his son, and on me.

I injected the serum, administered cortisone, painkillers and a tranquillizer, and I gave him some weak sweet tea to sip. The man lay on my lawn all day, attended by an old woman, and I went to check on him at regular intervals. His heart-beat was regular, and he slept most of the time. By the evening the swelling seemed much reduced and he looked better. In time he recovered completely, but felt, with a certain logic, that, as I had given him another chance to life, he was now my responsibility, and refused to work. He hung around the Centre wrapped in his blanket, the ostrich feather of his skullcap beckoning in the breeze. Then one day he was gone, as often with Turkana, and I never saw him again.

Paolo had disliked snakes, and was repelled by them. Once, in the early days in Laikipia, Paolo was driven home by Arap Rhono, and I was surprised to see him getting out of the car holding his head with both hands. His left eye was swollen to almost twice its normal size, bloodshot and swimming with ugly yellow tears. He had been fishing black bass at the Engelesha Dam when he heard, very close to him in the tall grass of the shore, the agonized cry of a yellow-neck francolin. Curious, he stooped to look: a quick movement through the papyrus stems, a silver spray aimed at his naked eye, and a burning pain blinded him. He never saw the spitting cobra. The francolin limped away dishevelled, cackling aloud his outrage. I washed the eye with cold boiled milk, rinsing away the cloying poison and shutting my mind to the unease I felt, and in a few days Paolo was fine again, although he complained he had lost some of his eagle sight in that eye. This episode made him dislike snakes even more, and he never much sympathized with Emanuele's interest, or encouraged it.

Emanuele and Paolo had adored each other. Theirs had been a full friendship. They had shared the same passion for the outdoor life, hunting, fishing, nature, safaris. They had been so close in many adventures. I remember a time shortly before Paolo's final accident. They had both gone out with Luka after an old wounded buffalo bull. Paolo came back limping, holding on to Ema's shoulders. They were both dirty, caked with blood, with the same mischievous grin on their faces. 'Emanuele saved my life today,' Paolo had said, looking affectionately into Emanuele's eyes. They had found the buffalo after hours of tracking in very thick bush, and it had charged them. Paolo had waited to shoot until the last moment, only to realize that he had no more ammunition left in the gun. There was nothing to be done, as the buffalo was already on him. He fell backwards, the snorting animal trampling his body with his heavy hooves, head down, vast horns ready to gore. Emanuele stood paralysed just behind Paolo, holding his own gun ready. 'I was sure Paolo was being killed,' he told me calmly in his boy's voice, 'and I decided to fire my last bullet and to run. I was afraid of shooting Paolo instead. It was so close I could touch it. It was so big. I shot, and ran. I turned to look: I had killed it . . . Paolo had jumped away in time, just avoiding being crushed. It was . . . quite exciting.'

Unavoidably, after Paolo's death, Emanuele's passion bloomed. In the many hours now empty of the company and excitement which Paolo's presence had provided, he chose to numb the pain of this irreparable loss with his dangerous and unusual interest, which he could pursue alone and in Laikipia, and which fulfilled his innate disposition for analytical and scientific work.

As with the shells, Emanuele now gave the same meticulous care and precision, seriousness and determination, to this passion. During the Pembroke days his interest had become so well known that his prize when he excelled in the Common Entrance exams for Senior English, Latin, Biology and French was a book on snakes. Now he set himself to learn about snakes thoroughly and methodically, and bought, ordered and asked for every possible book on African reptiles.

As I had expected, many other snakes succeeded Kaa. Emanuele developed a sixth sense which allowed him to find snakes in the way others would find mushrooms, or edelweiss, or fossils. He knew where to look, and what to look for. He used to ride out in the early golden mornings on his grey horse Cinders, the world lay ahead of him, and it was full of snakes. When he came back the bags hanging at his saddle were heavy with his alarming catch, and in his eyes were depths of unexplored passions.

He took over one of the stables and filled it with assorted cages of all sizes. The snakes were measured, weighed, photographed. For days or weeks they were observed, fed, cleaned. He carefully entered all relevant details in his new 'Snake Diaries' which he updated daily. Curiously, while his personal diary was written in Italian, the 'Snake Diaries' were in English. After he had collected all the information he thought he needed from an individual snake, he usually let it go, but often only after months or, in some cases, years. He later recalled this period:

> I started snake-catching in earnest after my father's death, in March 1980. Those were my learning days, and I began with harmless and semi-harmless snakes, but soon, inevitably, I moved on to more poisonous species.

When the stable became inadequate for the number of snakes he had accumulated, I called up our *fundi*, Arap Langat, and he built a proper snake pit at the bottom of the garden. It was round, rather like a water tank, lined with stones, with a pond full of water, rocks small and large, sand and gravel. Emanuele planted grass, succulents, shrubs, papyrus. Frogs, lizards, agamas, all sorts of insects, two tortoises and snakes inhabited this small ecosystem.

Certain snakes feed on mice, and he started to breed these. If a snake died, he performed a post-mortem, entering all the details in his diary, then skinned it and cured and dried the skin. Some unusual specimens he preserved with formalin in jars, and used to raid the kitchen for empty jam pots. When in Nairobi, he started visiting the Snake Park, and the Herpetology Department of the Museum, where he became a very popular figure. He donated many specimens which still today line the Museum shelves, white and blue labels where, in his young precise handwriting, details are noted such as:

WHITE-LIPPED SNAKE
(*Crotaphopeltis Mutamboeia*)
25.4.80 – 4.6.80
Length: 22 cm 5 mm – 30 cm
Laikipia
E.P.-G.

Emanuele entered into correspondence with herpetologists in various parts of Africa, and most of his time was spent in pursuing his passion. It became well known in the country, even outside the circle of our friends, and in Laikipia well beyond the ranch boundary. He became known to outsiders as Kijana wa Nyoka ('the young man of the snakes'). Our people, however, kept calling him affectionately Muenda, Meru for 'the one who cares for others'.

His passion for riding gave place to the almost inevitable love of the teenager for motorbikes. In Laikipia he took off each morning on his shiny new Yamaha – a present for his last birthday – and came back with bags and bags full of assorted snakes. He developed a snake network and rewarded people who brought him snakes: radio messages started coming from all over the ranch, on the internal radio network, of snake findings in the most unexpected places: the game ditch between us and Ol Morani, termite hills, warthogs' holes, hollow trees, cracks in rocks, and cattle *bomas*.

Sooner or later some of the snakes caught were poisonous ones, as I had always feared, and which I had originally forbidden. At this stage I decided to consult Mario and to share with him – as Paolo had gone – the responsibility of letting Emanuele pursue this dangerous development of his unusual hobby.

One day in October 1980, when Sveva was about two months old, the telephone rang in Nairobi and a familiar voice said, 'It's Valeria. I am in Nairobi to meet my sister. Mario is with me, and he would like to see Ema.' In this way, Mario entered our lives again. Behind his long beard he was as young and attractive as ever. Valeria looked older and happy. They each wore the maroon and red colours of their Guru, and his photograph hanging from a wooden bead necklace. They cried with us and they brought presents. After some resistance because of his loyalty to Paolo, who had not approved of this match, Emanuele surrendered to the pleasure of seeing again the old friend who was after all his father. They played chess, shared books, flew kites, rode horses, joined in short safaris, and in time Emanuele went sailing regularly with Mario and Valeria in the Greek Islands. Their rapport had changed subtly as Emanuele had grown up, and I could see how Mario rejoiced in their reunion.

When I consulted him about the reptiles, both Mario and I agreed that Emanuele was mature and competent enough to be trusted, as he knew what he wanted and what he was doing, and his serious interest in reptiles was clearly not a passing fancy.

I feel one should never discourage a true abiding interest in a child. So rarely are sparkles of interest pursued with such intense dedication as to bloom into a passion that we as parents ought to be grateful and let it flourish, helping as we can. After all, there were lots of other creeping dangers for a teenage boy. This was Africa, and snakes were not a totally alien passion for children brought up here, like Jonathan Leakey, or Ionides. Emanuele had made his choice, and we agreed that he was responsible enough to be allowed to get on with it.

About then, the first accident happened.

A day like many days in Laikipia: September and birds singing from the treetops, the light of the sunny morning slanting shadows on the lawn, the bright pinks and reds of the bougainvillea, the euphorbia candelabra's arms outstretched to the sky. Sveva a few months old, still nursing as she would be for two more years ... he came towards me holding one of his hands, self-control barely disguising what must have been an excruciating pain.

'Pep,' he said simply, 'I have been bitten by a burrowing viper. I think I ought to see a doctor.' His hand was hideously swollen, the skin tight and purplish.

On his instructions, I immediately gave Emanuele anti-histamine and painkillers, but he was so allergic to many things that I did not dare to inject him with anti-venom for fear of a negative reaction. We made an immediate radio-call and sent him down to Dr Lowi in Nyahururu, the closest village, then still called Thompson's Falls. Dr Lowi was like a man in a story. An old Jew of Czech origin, he had come to Kenya like many other Jews after the Second World War. Old and bent, but with direct unbending manners, he had set up a practice in Thompson's Falls, where neither hygiene nor modern medical methods were much observed, but where he managed to help numberless people and to save many lives. My mother, who was still staying with us, and a driver went with Emanuele. The shock and horror made my milk go sour. That day Sveva refused the curdled yoghurt I managed to produce.

By the time they reached Thompson's Falls, the hand was twice its normal size and the pain running up his arm was excruciating. Dr Lowi injected Emanuele with cortisone and serum and he observed him for an hour in case there was any reaction. This time, there was none.

Alone at home with my baby I waited in agony. The only hope was that at least this scare would cure him of snakes forever. I waited until the shadows grew long and the dogs came around me, waiting for the evening walk. The car arrived back finally, and the Emanuele who got out was paler and taller — it seemed to me — than he had been before, and the sun was setting red on the bandaged arm. In his free hand he held . . . a snake bag. Full.

'It's a hissing sand snake, Pep. I got it at the gate. It is huge and blind in one eye.' He grinned. 'I'll call him Loyamuk.' Loyamuk was an elderly Turkana herder in charge of a *boma*. One eye was blind and filmed with glaucoma.

My anxious questions about his treatment and how he felt were answered with casual acceptance. 'Yes, damn painful . . . still now . . . I will be all right. Don't worry. I must put Loyamuk in the pit.'

He walked towards the snake pit in the darkening garden, a

new way of walking, it seemed, balancing his brown slim legs in long effortless strides. The short trousers, the khaki shirt sleeves rolled at the elbows, the straight shoulders . . . I knew that, whatever happened, he would always like snakes. He was no longer a boy. He looked like Paolo.

This accident, and the number of snakes he had by now accumulated, made me realize Emanuele needed someone to help him. It was Emanuele who chose him from among the handful of ranch employees who liked snakes and were not afraid of them. The accepted rule for Africans is that the 'best snake is a dead snake'. Liking snakes is exceptional. He was a young Turkana by the name of Joseph Ekai. He had been employed as a casual labourer, but in his spare time he volunteered to go out with Emanuele and to help him to catch snakes. Emanuele had been impressed with him, and they got on extremely well together. Now he was allotted, full time, the task of being Emanuele's 'snake man', a job he enjoyed, and in which, consequently, he excelled. He helped him not just to catch the snakes, but to clean the cages and the snake pit, and generally assisted him in looking after this ever-growing snake kingdom. The snake pit had become a place of fascination for guests, who spent much time sitting around it, looking down at the reptile world wriggling at the bottom. Frogs inhabited the pond, surrounded with papyrus and arum lilies, and snakes of all sorts swam in it, sliding along a sandy slope. Green snakes, egg-eaters, sand snakes, white-lips and blue and orange agama sunned themselves on rocks or on the small carissa bush and euphorbia Emanuele had planted in the middle. Insects were attracted to the short succulents blooming with brown fleshy flowers which stank of putrid meat. Birds came for the insects. Snakes started out of their apathy to snap at them. There was a lot going on in that pit.

Eventually Emanuele decided to move the puff-adders into it, and the pit became strangely quiet. Of all snakes, puff-adders are the ones I most disliked. They are sluggish and thick, with none of the sleek grace of the green grass snakes, or the eerie mystical aura of the cobra. There is a dangerous, evil vulgarity about these vipers, and I was revolted by them. Emanuele describes them like this in his 'A Field Guide to some Common Snakes of East Africa' which he was compiling at that time, and never quite completed:

COMMON PUFF-ADDER (*Bitis Arietans Arietans*)
CLASSIFICATION:
Family: Viperidae
Genus: Bitis
Species: *Bitis Arietans Arietans (Merrem)*

DESCRIPTION:
Shade: Yellow, brownish or grey.
Pattern: Pale stripe on top of head between eyes and a series of pale-edged black chevrons down the back. The tail has cross bands, and the underparts are white with regularly spaced blotches.

The description proceeds in detail for two pages, and continues:

HABITS:
Occasionally basks in the sun during the day, and can often be found crossing roads. Reluctance to move away when approached and excellent camouflage in grass result in large numbers of people and livestock being bitten. Puff-adders responsible for more human deaths than any other African snake, 75% serious snake bites in Africa inflicted by puff-adders. Will usually hiss in warning just before a strike, and are extremely fast, the average striking speed being put at 2.36 m/sec. Puff-adders frequently lie in wait along rat-paths. The prey is bitten, then released, and the snake follows the rat's trail and when dead animal found, is swallowed head first.

TREATMENT OF BITES:
Poison = haematoxis or cytolitis – destroys blood cells in body and attacks tissues. If lethal dose is injected, and

treatment unsuccessful, death occurs within a few days. In case of puff-adders' bites, rest and immobilization are essential and shock symptoms may be treated with aspirin and codeine painkillers. Tourniquets must NEVER be used in adders' bites. If symptoms of poisoning occur serum should be administered according to instructions, preferably by somebody with medical knowledge.

E.P.-G. bitten + 3, no symptoms.

I had not known until I read this that Emanuele had been bitten by puff-adders before.

Ekai was not afraid to descend into the snake pit to cut the grass or prune the bushes. He was tall and muscular, strongly built, not lanky and lean as Turkana usually are. Unlike Turkana, who have narrow faces and thin noses, Joseph Ekai had widely spaced cheekbones, which gave his face a rounded appearance. There was a certain roguishness in his eyes and countenance, which I did not find unpleasant, as it was tempered by great natural kindness. When he smiled, which was often, one was startled to see that all his front upper teeth were missing – knocked out in a fight or in a fall, I was never quite sure which – leaving only the two pointed canines, very white, to guard the wide gap. It was quite a shocking sight the first time one noticed, as the large naked gums and the filed fangs gave him the appearance of a spitting cobra.

It is a habit in Africa to give people nicknames. They are usually based on their appearance or characteristic behaviour. They are sometimes dictated by affection, occasionally by irony or contempt: whatever the reason, they are always appropriate and shine with an infallible sense of humour. Predictably, Joseph Ekai was known as Mapengo, which in Swahili means 'a wide open gap'. He was brave and very loyal, and he really loved adventure. He took off with Ema, sitting on the back of his bike rather as Luka used to do with Paolo, and made use of the skills he had acquired during his free childhood.

African children still living in wild surroundings, where there are no schools or missions, have any amount of time to learn directly from the book of Nature what urban children must attempt to learn from the poor surrogate of badly-printed books. From sunrise to sunset they spend their days roaming the forest and the savannah, often tending small herds of goats or camels. In the hot, lazy hours of the day, when they must repair from the unforgiving sun to the shade of the thorn trees, they naturally observe, and absorb, with the curiosity and receptivity common to every child everywhere, the unending lessons of the rich world around them. They see the weaver birds build their intricate nests on the safe thin branches downwind, which snakes and predators cannot reach. They watch the minute, intense insect life which goes on all around them, the industrious dung beetles and the busy harvester ants, the termites and the feared siafu which leave death and clean skeletons in their wake, the stick or leaf insects camouflaged to perfection among the dry twigs. They follow the call of the honeyguide birds to the beehives, and learn to steal the precious honey, smoking the bees away without killing them. Their eyes become attuned to every movement of grass and leaves, their ears to every noise. The song of birds and wind, the screeches and shuffles, the roars and trumpetings, the grunts and snorts and whistles, the barks and cries: all sounds in the orchestra and choir of nature hold for them no secret. They witness mating and kills, and learn early the secrets of life and the unemotional acceptance of the necessity of death as part of the whole. They learn survival through the habits of the wildlife, and recognize the edible parts of plants, the ones they can use for medicine. This is the background to their harmonious growth in balance with the laws of Nature.

These are the people who can use their unique, instinctive skills to protect − or to kill − the animals they are so familiar with.

But now in the times we call modern, like the large herds of animals which once roamed the Highlands, like the forests and the indigenous plants of Africa, these people are endangered because their space and their way of life are disappearing fast and for ever. Since the mission came, with the school and the church, and the shop full of strange things which one needs money to buy, life has changed for the worse for the free pastoral African people. They have been given seeds of alien plants to sow in the virgin forests and of alien beliefs to confuse the innocence of their minds. They wear the discarded garish nylon rags of the white man, which cost money they do not have, rather than the traditional *shukas* made of animal hides, camouflaged and resistant to the wear-and-tear of bush life, which need not be washed with the chemical soap they cannot afford and which offends their pure streams of clear water.

Their culture endangered, their minds filled with notions and rules they do not need and cannot understand, the new generation is forgetting — no time to sit under the thorn tree now — what allowed their immediate ancestors to survive and thrive in their unspoilt surroundings. In the recent past, when life was still as in their forebears' days, African children grew up with the extraordinary privilege of learning instinctively through experience and mastering the secrets of their land, which, in turn, survived intact because they existed and cared.

Such still were Luka, Mirimuk, Hussein, Silas, Ekiru, Lother, Cypriano, Sabino, and such was Emanuele's snake man, Mapengo.

One of Emanuele's — and Mapengo's — favourite haunts were the steep cliffs down the Mukutan Gorge. This is the most spectacular feature of Ol Ari Nyiro, just at the edge of the Great Rift Valley. It is formed from a series of converging canyons thick with vegetation, and precipitous rock surfaces favoured by eagles and griffons, meeting in a larger and deeper gorge which zigzags all the way down to Lake Baringo. Appropriately, Mukutan means in fact 'the meeting'. The Mukutan stream, fed by Ol Ari Nyiro Springs, runs at the bottom. The abundance of water, the shelter from the winds and the difference in altitude and climate allow for a tremendous variety of vegetation and bird life, and snakes abound there.

Emanuele loved walking down to the waterfalls, a dramatic drop of about a hundred metres of granite boulders, hung with liana and wild aloe, where he could find masses of green grass snakes. Mapengo was particularly good at catching them. One needed to be fast, and ready to dive into the water and through the tall undergrowth where they tended to disappear like green wriggling darts, these handsome, harmless, jewel-like creatures with beady, alert black eyes.

Another favourite place was Maji ya Nyoka ('the water of the snakes'), also known as Python Pool. This was an idyllic large pond, surrounded by date palms and papyrus, with a smaller waterfall running into it from massive grey stones to which fig trees clung tenaciously, growing out of every crevice. Rare aloes, alight with orange clusters of flowers, and spidery orchids hanging from the tallest trees, made Maji ya Nyoka a place of magic. A few boulders emerged from the water, and, if one managed to approach it very quietly, one could often surprise pythons sunning themselves there. Unless they had been made heavy and torpid by a recent meal, they usually slid down into the water, disappearing almost without a ripple. Emanuele and Mapengo captured many, thicker than a man's leg, almost all of them over twelve feet in length, and immensely strong, and managed to bring them home to measure them. For this purpose they always carried bags of assorted sizes, as, curiously, once the head is covered and the eyes cannot see, snakes quietly slide inside a bag of their own accord, and succumb to a torpor until the light wakes them again. For smaller snakes the technique is to cover one's right forearm with the bag, like an inside-out glove, and, having grabbed the snake's head with the free hand, reverse the bag gently and let the snake slide inside: in Kaa's days I myself had become quite adept at this trick.

One day in 1981 news came of an unusually large snake seen in the *lugga* between the Nyukundu Dam and Lwogwagipi. Emanuele describes the episode in Italian in his diary:

31 January

Ndegwa told me he saw an enormous python close to the Nyukundu Dam. When approached, he did not move, as he had just eaten a gazelle or a sheep. We'll go and check tomorrow as tonight is too late . . .

1 February

We woke at five and went to look for the python, with Ndegwa and four other people. Colin came too. We walked about ten minutes before we found him asleep, behind the dam wall, bloated and coiled under the *leleshwa* . . . We took lots of photographs while he tried to strike . . . it took us half-an-hour to catch him, and six people to carry him to the car. I noticed a long quill skewered through the skin, so what he has in his stomach must be a porcupine . . . I held his head, but when we reached the car he darted towards Mapengo, and sunk his teeth in his coat, luckily without reaching the flesh . . . we measured him at the Centre (14'11"), weighed him (112 lbs), and let him go again in the same place . . .

Every evening now, when in Laikipia, Emanuele would come into the sitting-room after his shower, having changed into fashionable jeans and shirt, tall and serious, with a natural elegance and way of moving. Fitting gracefully into his task of host, he served drinks to everyone, exchanged a few words with all, and sat always in the same place to write his diaries. Mapengo now looked after his reptiles in Laikipia when Emanuele was away, but even in Nairobi he pursued this interest. He started a popular Snake Club at school.

After Paolo's death, Emanuele and I had agreed that, rather than going to England for the last two years as we had planned, so as not to split the family further he would continue attending school in Nairobi. He had passed his Common Entrance exams with flying colours, and after Pembroke he had gone straight to Hillcrest, where his step-sister Valeria had been before continuing her studies in Switzerland.

Dear Mrs Gallmann, [wrote his Headmaster from Hillcrest]

I would be grateful if you could persuade your son not to leave bags containing dangerous reptiles in the classrooms.

A typical example of his passion is an episode which occurred one Sunday spent in Nairobi, when we went to visit Carol Byrne at her house in Kitengela. While I chatted with Carol before lunch, Emanuele and her son Sam climbed down the slopes to explore the rocky shores of the Mbagathi River, obviously searching for snakes. Our conversation was interrupted by Emanuele's voice screaming from the bottom of the ridge: 'Come! Come quickly!' The urgency in his tone, and the fact that Emanuele never screamed, conveyed that there was no time to lose.

Carol and I dashed down the slope, loose stones rolling under our running feet. Deep in water up to his waist, Emanuele was fighting with some huge wriggling creature. Water splashed in all directions. A mottled tail, thicker than an arm, slashed the air, spraying us. Perched on a stone, Sam watched the scene with a mixture of admiration and worry. It was a python, of more than remarkable size, and it was clear that it was not going to surrender easily. Emanuele half-disappeared under water. I recalled the story of Philip Leakey, whose house was just a short distance down the same river. A few years back, he had been caught by a large python while swimming and had almost drowned. The strength of even a small constrictor is uncanny in proportion to its size: this one looked well over ten feet long.

'Quick!' Emanuele emerged spluttering. 'Carol, you take the middle. Pep, you take the tail. I have the head. I must measure it. Do you have a tape?'

Neither Carol nor I thought for a moment of disobeying. Emanuele had a way with him which made the most improbable things sound normal. We entered the water, and grabbed the snake as instructed. It was heavy, wet, slippery and immensely powerful. Quite rightly, it had no intention of letting us catch it.

'Our neighbours are closer than our house,' said Sam excitedly. 'They will certainly have a tape measure.'

He led the way up the twisting track and we followed, carrying the contorting snake – an odd procession, wet and dishevelled, panting up the steep rise. It was quite an ordeal. This python was a fighter, and we had nothing with which to cover its head and quieten it. Halfway up the slope, its cloaca contracted and opened and a foetid spurt missed us by inches.

'Never,' gasped Carol, bewildered, 'not even for my own children, would I have dreamed of doing such . . .'

We had arrived. The path ended, and we emerged on a flat platform planted as a lawn, where a group of people were assembled for a late Sunday brunch. I shall never forget the expression on their faces when they saw us. Eyes stared above the coffee cups. Mouths gaped speechlessly. They would never forget that scene either: led by a child, an unknown young man drenched in water, two soaking-wet women in a fit of giggles, holding a struggling serpent several feet longer than a man.

'Good morning,' Emanuele said with a straight face and a normal voice, while still trying to hold the snake down. 'Could we please have something to measure this snake? Quickly?'

The entire thing was so irresistibly absurd that no one demurred, and with amazing speed they all dashed into action. A girl ran to get a tape measure which she handed to Emanuele, keeping the greatest distance possible between them. Someone fetched a camera. We held the snake. Thirteen and a half feet. A female. Emanuele let her go and we all jumped back to a safe distance. He took some notes.

'I will call her Carol.' He bowed slightly, grinning his rare, charming smile. 'Thank you for helping.'

Carol the snake coiled, hissing defiantly, then sprang forward, trying to strike, several times – not unreasonably. She stood her ground, and Emanuele with spread arms, moving in front of her on light feet, looked like a toreador in a strange *corrida*. Finally, Carol slid away back down the slope to her river, the glimpse of this memory already fading in her reptilian brain. Carol my friend looked at me and at Emanuele, shaking her head, and everyone was laughing.

1981 evolved into a special year in Emanuele's life and growth. Although the agony of Paolo's loss had left a deep scar in him which would never heal, he started then to have more time for friends and parties, and he discovered girls.

28

A Young Man

... Though lovers be lost, Love shall not ...

Dylan Thomas, *And death shall have no dominion*

Emanuele's day-to-day diaries in 1981 and 1982 are full of notes on snakes, pieces of shed snakeskin, and drawings and photographs of snakes. His daily activities are described in detail, and his friends, boys and girls, appear more and more often. He was very popular. The unusual amount of knowledge he had accumulated, his rich and varied life, his gift for languages, the way in which he would tell a story, together with his quiet charm and a subtle sense of humour, were attractive enough. He was also developing into a very good-looking young man. From Mario he had inherited a natural way with girls. Names and photographs started to appear in his diary, and the telephone rang for him constantly. On 4 November 1981 he notes soberly: 'Went to disco with Ricky. Slept with Juliette.'

Although I have never met Juliette, I knew Ricky Mathews well. A few years older than Emanuele, he was the son of Terry, a well-known and dashing professional hunter of the old days, who, having been blinded in one eye by a client, had become a successful wildlife sculptor. He had four sons, and I can understand why Emanuele, who missed Paolo's masculine company, was attracted by the lively man's world of the Mathewses. Ricky was one of the few friends who shared Emanuele's interest in snakes, and he was already familiar with the world of teenage parties, cars, and a wider freedom. They were in the same class, and theirs became a deep and lasting friendship.

There is a tremendous bonus in bringing up children in Kenya. It is not just the climate, the freedom of having ample space, the opportunity to practise every sport all the year round, the healthy food and the still generally unpolluted surroundings. Kenya is a truly cosmopolitan country. Apart from the local African population, there is a large Asian and Arab community, and Nairobi, the capital and the place of residence of all foreign envoys and of many international organizations, is populated with people of all nationalities, races and colours. Children educated by parents with an open mind learn from a very early age that it is normal to look different, to dress in different ways, to eat different foods and worship different gods; and that all this is not just acceptable, but interesting, enriching, instructive and worthwhile.

The house in Nairobi was in those days alive with young people. There was Toon Hanegraff, a Dutch boy who, like Charlie Mason, had been at school with Emanuele from the very beginning. Their families both had houses in Kilifi and they had kept in close touch over the years, forming with Ema an almost inseparable trio. Toon was read-headed, with a strange crooked nose sprinkled with freckles, and — like Charlie — every time I saw him he seemed to have grown another couple of feet. They had come to Laikipia for half-term, and spent their days riding, a sport in which both Charlie and Emanuele naturally excelled, in shooting rabbits, exploring, swimming, fishing tilapia and black bass in the dams, and generally having a tremendous time. Emanuele loved riding bareback, and often they unsaddled their horses and rode through the dams, cavorting and splashing in the water, an image of youth, freedom and happy days.

There was Mukesh Pandit, a thin, quiet boy with black hair, glasses and compassionate ways, who came from a wealthy Indian family and who lived nearby. Emanuele was particularly fond of him, and attracted by oriental philosophy and customs; I never failed to notice, when they were together, a strange similarity in Emanuele's and Mukesh's eyes – a sad, deep wisdom beyond their years. There was Ray Matiba, whose father was a minister in the Kenya government. And Felipe Garcia-Banon, whose parents – his father was the Spanish Ambassador – were close friends of mine.

There was also a young man neither Emanuele nor I had actually met at the time, but with whom Emanuele corresponded and spoke on the phone occasionally, and by whom he was very impressed. His name was Michael Werikhe, and he lived in Mombasa, where he trained guard dogs for a firm which assembled vehicle parts. His passion, however, was wildlife, particularly rhino, and, unusually, snakes. At the end of 1982 he had spent his annual leave walking the 500 kilometres from Mombasa to Nairobi to raise awareness, and money, to alleviate the plight of the black rhino which were being heavily poached at that time. For company, he had carried a small python around his neck. A mutual friend had put him in contact with Emanuele, and I still remember Emanuele's comment after they had spoken on the phone the first time.

'You know, Pep,' he had said, 'Michael is extraordinary. He really knows and cares about snakes. But he has also walked all those miles for rhino: and he has never seen one yet in all his life! Of course I have invited him to come to Laikipia and see one. He will be able to come on his next leave, at the end of the year.'

There were the girls, but as they were usually younger and not allowed to drive, I saw less of them, although the telephone kept ringing and a variety of young girls' voices kept asking for Emanuele. Lately, there was Ferina. She was half British and half Indian, reddish-gold hair, feminine, a sunny disposition. She was very popular with the boys, and when I eventually met her, I could see why.

Although he was quiet and independent and perfectly happy to be on his own, Emanuele also enjoyed the newly discovered social life, and naturally loved parties.

It was at the beginning of 1983 that we had the idea of having a 'different' feast in Laikipia. Emanuele had never really given a proper party. This would be his special eighteenth birthday celebration. We thought of an occasion in which everyone on the ranch could participate in one way or another. To this he would invite his friends and I mine, the fellow ranchers of the neighbourhood who would all bring a team to join our ranch team and would participate in various competitions, some to do with cattle, horses, donkeys or camels, and in games of skill such as spear-throwing, climbing a greased pole, and target-shooting with bow and arrow. We thought of a sort of all-day-long fair, with food, drinks and traditional dances, prizes for the winners, and a disco to end it all at night. We could call it a 'rodeo'. We decided the date, close to his birthday, and made plans daily, adding details to the events, and much looking forward to organizing it and enjoying it with all the crowd.

The relationship between Emanuele and me had been always one of love, mutual trust and friendship. I had no secrets from him and often confided in him, knowing that I could count on his balanced advice. He was not emotional and rarely showed his feelings, but he was never aloof, and was capable of unexpected gestures of great charm. For my birthday, the first of June, a public holiday in Kenya when Laikipia is always green and in a glory of flowers, Emanuele went out with his horse or his motorbike and brought me back armfuls of *Gloriosa superba*, the magnificent wild red lily which he knew I loved.

I remember a late night one weekend in Nairobi, when I was in bed with flu. I heard him coming upstairs two steps at a time, and knocking at my door. He came in hugging a large knobbly elephant made of twisted and thatched banana leaves which he had garlanded with pink bougainvillea. 'When I went out this morning,' he said with a grin, 'I saw an old cripple on the corner of Kitisuru Road trying to sell this elephant. No one stopped. When I returned tonight he was still there with his elephant, and it was raining: so I bought it.' He looked critically at the elephant. 'It is rather ugly. Nobody would have wanted it. I just felt sorry for the man.' He

offered it to me with a flourish and a mock bow: 'For you, Pep.'
He put it in a corner of my room, and it is still there.

Emanuele had a compassion unusual for his age, a depth of
feeling, and a concern for others. Like all babies, Sveva often woke
up in the night in the grip of a nightmare, or because of a slight
cold or upset. I sleep very lightly; the faintest noise is enough to
wipe away my dreams instantly, and it takes me only a few
seconds to reach Sveva's room at the end of the corridor. But
most times I found that Emanuele had preceded me, and was
sitting on the side of her bed, her small hand in his, gently
soothing her back to sleep. 'She is fine, Pep,' he used to whisper
reassuringly. 'Why don't you go back to bed? I can take care of
her.'

Emanuele was fourteen years older than Sveva, and she worshipped him. He carried her around on his shoulders, sometimes dress-
ing her up for fun in his large shirts and sweaters. He taught her
new words, and told her stories as Paolo had done for him when
he was a child. She sat quietly for hours observing him skinning a
snake, rode out sitting in front of his motorbike, and often, looking
at Emanuele, strong and healthy, holding her in his arms on the
saddle of his horse and trotting around the sunny garden to her
delighted gurgles and squeals of joy, I felt how lucky we still were
as a family, and how privileged my children were to grow up in
the freedom and beauty of Ol Ari Nyiro. I am sure Sveva owes to
Emanuele her natural unaffected way with young people which
makes her delightful and charming.

From Paolo, Emanuele had inherited a passion for fishing and
from both Mario and Paolo his love of the sea. In Paolo's days
Emanuele had become a good fisherman and they had shared
many expeditions and successes. He had caught several sailfish
and his first marlin when he was eleven, a small striped one out
between Shimoni and Pemba. After Paolo died and Sveva was
born, I went back to the coast occasionally, usually to Kilifi, with
my children and Sveva's Kikuyu *ayah*, the adored Wanjiru. Emanuele went out with our boat 'Umeme' and brought me back fish

to cook: bonito, tuna, or cole-cole, barracuda or kingfish, once even a small shark.

Sitting with my back to the largest baobab in Kilifi, I still waited for that one solitary figure on deck to wave to me, and pointed out to Sveva her big brother on the boat. 'Umeme' hooted three times ... and it was gone behind the palms, inside the creek. Emanuele once surprised us all when, still physically very young, he boarded a large yellowfin tuna, a fierce fighter, the heaviest ever caught in the Tia Maria competition at Shimoni, and won the cup. He always entered – as Paolo had in the past – the Lady Delamere Cup, the prestigious fishing competition organized every February by Diana from the Mnarani Club. It was a sporting and social occasion which Emanuele thoroughly enjoyed, and all the fishing community converged there.

In memory of Paolo I presented an annual trophy for the largest blue marlin caught off the Kenya coast. It was a bronze sculpture of the jumping fish by which Paolo had been haunted and which had many times eluded him. For this occasion, Emanuele came to Mombasa with me and presented the trophy at a special dinner in the old Mombasa Club.

Once, in 1982, passing through Kilifi to go and present the prize, I heard that Diana was sick, and I went to visit her with Emanuele and Sveva in her elegant summer house on the north side of the creek. Built in large grounds and with manicured lawns landscaped beautifully down to the sea, exotic shrubs shadowed by tall whispering palms, the place was peaceful and patrician. She sat, half-reclining, in her wide four-poster bed in an open verandah room filled with flowers and potted plants, propped up on many cushions of silk and lace. She wore an embroidered négligée with silky scalloped edges, and was perfectly made up and manicured, her silver-blonde hair impeccable, as if expecting visitors. She looked beautiful in her peculiar ageless, cool, aloof way, playing the part of a living myth to perfection, and receiving our homage like a reclining queen. Sveva was just a baby, barely beginning to walk. She looked like a cherub with her halo of blonde curls, enamel-blue eyes and golden skin, and with her white lacy frock was a breathtaking picture of contrast in the arms of Wanjiru. Always appreciative of beauty, if not particularly fond of children, Diana said: 'Why don't you choose a bear, darling?'

The corner of the room and almost every couch and easy chair in sight were covered with teddy-bears of all sizes and all ages. Some looked as if they had been nursery favourites of long-dead Victorian children, their fur worn and shiny, a glass eye gone. Some were enormous silky creatures larger than a child. Sveva pointed to one of the smaller animals, a brown scruffy teddy-bear, partly moth-eaten, and with a dangling ear.

'How extraordinary you should choose that,' Diana said in surprise. 'It was Tom's favourite when he was a child.' I protested. 'No, of course she can keep it. Tom would like that. Teddy-bears are really for children.' Lord Delamere was rather sick at the time, and seldom appeared in public, or with Diana, preferring the cool climate of their house at Soysambu to the humid heat of the coast. He was to die a few months later. Amongst her dolls and puppets, Sveva still has today that funny teddy-bear who had kept a lonely little lord company at night in the nursery of Elmentaita, in the early days of the Kenya colony.

Certain friends adopted us and became naturally closer after Paolo's death, and among these were Oria and Iain Douglas-Hamilton, whom I had first met with Paolo in the early days, at the Roccos' house in Naivasha. Oria was warm as the earth, artistic and inventive, with a positive, motherly energy, and, like a true Rocco, she was always up to something out of the ordinary. An excellent photographer, her mischievous, restless brown eyes were always alert to catch the unusual. She loved Africa, the land and its animals, with a passion. Over the years she had become like a sister to me. Iain, in those days, had long fair hair to his shoulders, and an absent smile which could suddenly spread to transform his face. He was deceptively vague, animated as he was by an unwavering determination to succeed in his campaign to save the elephant, about which he knew more than possibly anyone in Africa. A professional zoologist and a scientist of vast expertise and intuition, Iain was idealistic and chivalrous, with the charisma of the gentlemen adventurers of days past, and although much of his work had now to do with computers and office tasks, he shone in the bush, and I loved walking with him up to elephant in Laikipia and trying to spot animals from his aeroplane. As a bush pilot he had the reputation of taking risks, but I adored flying with him. Iain flew gallantly, as the first aviators must have done in their sturdy little biplanes. Like them, he could take off and land practically anywhere, on a beach or a road or a clearing in the bush, and quite often he did, sometimes for fun and sometimes of necessity. He was such a natural pilot that I always felt secure with him, as I knew instinctively that he could cope with any emergency in the air with clear-minded competence.

Among Emanuele's favourite friends, although they were much younger — a few years' difference is a lot at that age — were Saba and Dudu Douglas-Hamilton, delightful, good-looking, vibrant girls whom I adored, and who often came to stay in Laikipia with their parents. A date they never missed was the anniversary of Paolo's death.

The anniversary had become a special occasion, and a time to be together in remembrance 'far from the madding crowd' for a small group of caring friends. It was soothing and healing for all, a different party, the reason for which was not mundane but dictated by concern and love.

Paolo had often said that he wished to be remembered by his close friends with a party, so I gave him a party every year. About a dozen people drove or flew up, Tubby and Aino, Carol and Sam, the Dobies, the Douglas-Hamiltons, some friends of Ema. Colin and Rocky drove up from the Centre with their children, and in the evening we walked to the grave at the edge of the garden. It was covered with flowers, and carpets and bright *kangas* surrounded it, on which people sat. There were candles and incense, and bonfires of mutamayo — the wild olive abundant in Laikipia — brightened the night. The dogs sat close, Emanuele was at my side, and small Sveva in my arms. My family, my friends, my memories: what more could I want?

I said a few words, a small poem which I had prepared to commemorate Paolo, then 'his' music, the Quintettino of Boccherini, filled the night up to the silent stars. Elephants trumpeted at the water tank. Champagne corks popped, cups were filled. Emanuele stood, an extra-full glass in his hand. This was his task. We toasted Paolo.

The glass exploded on the tombstone in tiny crystal fragments. More corks shot up and goblets were refilled. Emanuele's eyes were unreadable when he sat back, and unexpectedly he kissed my cheek with dry warm lips.

A year earlier, a few days before the 1982 anniversary, I had found one evening on my pillow a letter. It was from Emanuele and it was pervaded by a subtle pain and nostalgia. In his neat handwriting he had poured out his hope, his feeling of belonging, his love for Paolo whom he calls 'my father'. It was to me a terribly sad letter in a way, as it had been generated by a pain and a desperate longing for which I had no cure. Sitting on my bed with all my memories, I had read it with a sinking heart:

In Memory of Paolo

It is now one of the driest months of the year at Laikipia, and the hot wind blowing from the east dries out everything in its wake, turning the land from green pastureland to a hot, arid dustbowl. It is during this month that we burn the land. I do not like the burning, it destroys much of the abundant animal life that finds refuge in the tall golden grass, but it is necessary, for when the rains come they will turn this blackened wasteland into a green sea of life.

If the rains come.

Here in the north life depends on the water that falls from the sky, and if the rain does not come, the rivers and dams will dwindle and dry out, and the animals will die.

Sitting on a top of a hill watching the dust-devils racing

each other across a vast waterless plain, I marvel at the thought of the herds of elephant, buffalo and eland ambling through the early morning mist, at the rain bird who sings its song of a rain that may never come, at the golden majestic beauty of the sun setting behind the hills of the Mukutan, and at the vaster beauty of this land which belongs to us.

I wonder if our children will see this land as it is now, for can such beauty go unspoiled for long?

I hope that they may have the privilege of seeing it, that they in turn may tell their children the stories of the land of Laikipia and the tales of a beautiful garden of flowers on a small rise in the middle of the emptiness. A garden with a solitary thorn tree towering over it, whose roots dig deep into the earth, the same earth into which we lowered my father on his last safari, laying him down for ever in the land to which he belonged.

And with eyes that are the growing buds of the thorn tree, and with a voice that is the whispering of the wind in its branches, Paolo watches over his land, a land over which he shall reign for ever, and from which he shall never be separated.

His land – his home – LAIKIPIA . . .

FLY FOR ME, BIRD OF THE SUN. FLY HIGH.

Emanuele

29

Aidan

Round us was silence where only the winds played, and cleanness infinitely remote from the world of man.

Wilfred Thesiger, *Desert, Marsh and Mountain: The world of a nomad*

A life, like a concert, is made of high and low notes, of pauses in the elation and of peaks of reverberating, deafening heartbeats.

In my life, as in most, there have been emotions to fill gaps of solitude, voices I searched for to again chase the silence, and, once, a romantic flicker of flame which turned into a fresh temptation I did not try to resist. It was an encounter which for a time brought me back to the days of my earlier youth, to the fragile breathlessness of relations which cannot have any future.

There had been a walk on the beach at sunset, pink crabs teasing the waves, dancing on frail long legs like ghosts of spiders. There had been curtains of wind and the colours of twilight, whispering palms, salt spray on lips and eyes, water skiing in the silvery wake of a speedboat in a creek at the coast. There had been restless hippos screaming at night, and early-morning sun filtering green through the canvas of a tent in the Mara. There had been nights of music, lights playing golden gleams on blond hair, and the exciting feeling of living 'moment by moment' with the knowledge there could be no tomorrow. There had been another sunset, of vibrant reds and molten golds, the treasured memories and the knowledge that the river of life keeps flowing, carrying away for ever our dreams and our regrets.

Many patterns are embroidered on the canvas of my life, but the thread of my relationship with Paolo was never interrupted – not even by his death – as our love ran deep like those rivers fed by secret springs, which appear and disappear again into the deep soil, to flow hidden, but never lost.

The account of my life in Africa would not be complete, or sincere, if I omitted to talk of the first man I loved after Paolo died, for he left a mark in my life which will last for as long as I live.

One of Jasper's daughters was getting married, and I received an invitation to go to the wedding. Up to the last moment I was not sure I would attend, since it would mean driving back to Nairobi on my own with Wanjiru and little Sveva, and having to find from the sketchy map the place, somewhere near Gilgil.

Since Paolo's death, about two years earlier, I had not driven from the ranch down to Nairobi. I chose always to fly, as I used to do with Paolo, to begin with because I was pregnant, and after Sveva was born, because it was easier. I used to pick up Emanuele at school every Friday, go to Wilson airport, and with some of my pilot friends and Paolo's plane, which I had kept, I flew up to Ol Ari Nyiro. Occasionally Emanuele stayed with a friend for the weekend.

The road to Laikipia had been very rough, but it had recently been repaired and resurfaced. Sooner or later I would have to drive down again, and I suddenly decided in the morning that this festive occasion was as good as any. I felt well, and it was time for me to get out of my self-imposed exile and see people. Furthermore, I liked those country weddings, and I was fond of Jasper. Little did I know it was the plan of destiny that this decision should have an unexpected influence on my life. Because it was there that for the first time I met Aidan.

His name was often mentioned, but he was seldom seen. Although they actually never had the chance to meet, Paolo had described him with great respect as a model rancher who lived life as an adventure, a man whose property was so vast and scattered that he spent a great many hours in his aeroplane and socialized very little. Whenever he could – rumour said – he disappeared up north to the desert close to the Ethiopian border, where he walked for weeks with his camels, exploring new land, looking for rare plants and following the errant, solitary dreams of all nomads. They said he owed his name to an uncle who had been eaten by a lion in Iran; that he had for a time been a mercenary for the Sultan of Oman. There was about him a magnetic charisma, accentuated by his elusiveness.

He came from an unusual family of scholars and farmers, some members of which had come to Kenya in the early days, and had succeeded in establishing a large farming and ranching domain, at the same time managing to maintain a low public profile. After his studies in Europe and the freedom of an African unconfined youth, he had taken over work on the family estates, making such a success of this that he became a sort of living legend. After all I heard about him over the years, I had formed my own idea of what he must look like, and I was naturally curious to meet him one day. I guessed he would by now be in his early sixties, and imagined him as a weatherbeaten Kenya farmer, tall and lean, with a halo of white hair, eyes accustomed to look out at limitless distances of wilderness, and a discreet, solitary disposition.

At the farm where the wedding was to take place I found a crowd of people, mostly up-country landowners dressed in their festive clothes. As at all Kenya weddings, every age was represented: fair-haired and freckled children with their *ayahs*, women in flowered frocks, men used to khaki shorts now dressed in dark suits and ties, groups scattered on the lawn drinking, talking loudly, laughing.

I greeted friends here and there, stopped to chat with various people. Then someone said, 'Have you met Aidan yet?' There was a group of four or five men, holding mugs of beer. They turned to look at me, and I could not figure out which one he was: I already knew two of them, and the others seemed too young to be him.

'I am Aidan,' said the tallest, bowing slightly and tipping his wide-brimmed hat.

The sun caught a dark cornflower-blue gleam in his eyes, and I was taken totally by surprise. He seemed so much younger than I had imagined. Naive as it sounded, I could not help exclaiming: 'I have heard so much about you, I thought you were much older!'

He could not have been more than forty. He focused on me, excluding for a moment the crowd, the place. 'I have heard so much about you,' he replied gallantly, 'and I thought you were much older!' He laughed. I could see he did not laugh that often. A solemn note, with which he seemed familiar, shaded his deep voice: 'I admire you,' he said without smiling, 'for having held on to your land after your husband's death. You are a brave woman.' I felt he meant it. His face was still and thoughtful. 'We landowners should stick together.'

'Landowners?' I spoke from my heart. So often I had thought about that very point. 'I do not feel like a landowner. I cannot believe that we really *own* the land. It was there before us, and it will be there after we pass. I believe we can only take care of it, as well as possible, as trustees, for our lifetime. I was not even born here. It is for me a great privilege to be responsible for a chunk of Africa.'

There was a silence, and in that pause I knew something had happened. It was that sentence, possibly, which singled me out for him there and then. His eyes took an intent, concentrated gaze, and many wrinkles appeared at their corners and on his forehead. 'Yes. You are right,' he said slowly, looking straight, searchingly, at me. 'I had never thought about it in this way before. I like your philosophy. You have a lot to teach.' He was not teasing. In the sunburnt face his serious eyes shone with an intense light, which reminded me, almost painfully, of other deep blue eyes I had loved and lost.

I looked at him, trying to steady the sudden irrational quickening of my heart. The hair was tightly curled, almost like an African's, but golden brown. This and a handsome Etruscan nose and well-cut mouth over a chiselled chin, straight neck and proud head, gave him the classic appearance of a sunburnt living statue. He was a man of contrasts. The tallest person around, there was an air about him of easy aristocratic grace, a masculinity tempered with gentleness. A patrician quality, which intrigued me, emanated from his slender figure, broad shoulders, long legs, slight wrists, strong hands with tapered but calloused fingers used to hard work. His direct eyes bore deep into mine, and I felt my legs grow weak, and a crazy butterfly trapped in my stomach. Only one thought came to me to drown all the rest: 'He looks like Paolo.' I was caught. Nothing had changed, the crowd was still there, but I had his undivided attention as he had mine. The rest of the people no longer mattered.

For the first time in over two years, since Paolo had died, I felt attracted by another man. I had been unprepared for these sensations and instinctively I knew that I was going to fall seriously in love.

He seemed to have everything I find most attractive in a man: a presence, an aura of adventure and of times now past, of wild remote places where time still follows the sun and the seasons. I perceived him as one who could deal with the unexpected, and be fearless and in charge, fulfilled and happy far away from town or people, under the unending concave sky of the African night. He was a man who was used to taking responsibility and leadership. He had a curious way of talking in staccato sentences, as people do who speak little and are unaccustomed to social conversation; I found his low, grave voice stirring, the old-fashioned turn of phrase beguiling, and I felt that he meant every word he said. He was chivalrous, attentive, yet there was this elusive quality about him, a halo of mystery . . . a strength . . . a weakness? And immediately I wanted to know more, to explore the depths of this other human being, while his uncanny physical resemblance to Paolo made him totally irresistible. I did not resist.

When I said goodbye at the party, I heard myself inviting him to call by for a drink when he was next in Nairobi. He might never have come. A week later, he did.

After that he came often, always unexpectedly, for months and months. I loved him as the image of the man I had always looked for. He loved me as he loved his desert: with me he could be totally at ease, totally himself, and as relaxed as when he was alone up north with his favourite camels.

It was a secret relationship, as he was not free, and a difficult situation. He cared for his family, and I well understood that he was torn apart by his honesty and sense of duty. This was the only shadow in the harmony of our time together.

He came in the night, bringing with him the feeling of the open spaces, and whenever he came it was a reunion. I was fascinated by the intriguing combination of wildness and sophistication. He often carried a small, worn book of poetry. He read to me until the small hours of the morning in his deep masculine voice, verses of Tennyson, Kipling or Wordsworth which appealed to the romantic side of his adventurous nature, and which brought me back to the times of my youth and the poems I had shared with my father. Often, I read my own stories to him, and he liked to listen. I used to treasure those hours. The candle burned and a low music played in the background. The fire created new lines in the classic features I had grown to know so well, and time ceased to exist. When he went, quiet in the first light of the morning, it was as if he had been part of another dream, and going back to sleep I often asked myself how long this unusual situation would last, and how much would I suffer again when I woke up to reality.

I missed him when he went. I never knew and never asked when — even if — I would see him again. Days would go by and a book would arrive in the post for me, often a rare book out of print, or one with a special meaning. Weeks would go by and again he materialized at my door, bringing with him his magic, a Somali shawl which smelt of spices, the warmth of the desert wind. I had learnt not to expect anything from him, as I knew he gave me what he could. I accepted his presence as a gift, an unprecedented fact for my proud and independent nature. But he had touched in me a deep chord, a flicker of recognition which went far beyond the time and limit of our encounter, and its quality compensated for its rarity.

The only person who knew of Aidan's existence in my life was Emanuele. I had confided in him, and I could count on his discretion and quiet support. There was a certain similarity in their characters. The rapport between them was of mutual respect and instinctive liking, as from man to man. I could well imagine them walking together silently on some forgotten track up north.

One day, I loved to dream, one day this might well happen.

30

The Snake of Good Luck

I balanced all, brought all to mind,
The years to come seemed waste of breath,
A waste of breath the years behind
In balance with this life, this death.

W. B. Yeats, *An Irish Airman Foresees His Death*,
quoted in Emanuele's diary

We had a wonderful time at Easter, with all the Douglas-Hamiltons staying. We went for early-morning walks with Oria and Iain and Luka, rhino-tracking, and we watched elephants drinking at the treetop tank and at Paolo's Dam at Kuti.

The treetop was a simple look-out which I had built on the top of a large gerardia, in a favourite site for elephant. One could climb the tree and hide high among the branches like a bird in a nest, looking out unseen from the concealing leaves at the animals coming to drink at the water tank just below. So close were the elephants that one could smell them, and the sucking of their trunks in the silted water and the low stomach rumbles were the only noise in the high silence of noon.

Emanuele took off on his motorbike one morning to visit Ferina, who was staying with her family for a few days down at Baringo, and on his way back in the evening he ran out of petrol just inside the ranch. He called us on the hand-set radio, and I went to look for him with Saba, bringing a full jerrycan of fuel. We found the bike in the middle of a path, but no sign of Ema. I could not even find his tracks in the dust, as if he had vanished into the air. It was by now evening, and there were signs of elephant everywhere, and leopard spoor. We searched for him, calling, and just as I was beginning to get worried, a stifled giggle attracted our attention. Emanuele was perched on the very top of a large *Acacia gerardia* drinking a beer, laughing down at us. Saba jumped on the back of the bike and I drove behind them.

In the car lights, eyes of secret creatures shone phosphorescent. Hair windblown, talking and laughing to each other in the majestic African night with its shapes and shadows, they were a picture of youth, privilege and freedom which I shall not forget.

For lunch the next day I made a gigantic Easter egg for Sveva, and chocolate bunnies for everybody. Oria took photographs of Emanuele sitting at the head of the table in the place which had been Paolo's, Sveva on his lap and Saba and Dudu each holding an assorted handful of harmless green grass snakes and sand snakes, each girl with a snake or two coiled around her neck.

We went for a barbecue picnic down the river at Mukutan Spring. On our way we saw many vultures gathering at a spot just close to the road, where we found a young eland just killed by lion. Emanuele and Luka carved the fillet out for us and we left the rest to the lion. Emanuele had come with his blue-and-yellow Yamaha, and Oria took photographs of him overtaking the car. In the evening, I noticed the youngsters plotting something, and Kipiego and Rachel came in grinning and served me a round chocolate flan on a silver platter, which turned out to be a large elephant turd covered in cocoa and coloured sugar, and decorated with flowers.

The evening had ended with Emanuele and the girls, who looked beautiful in tight leopard- and tiger-patterned leotards, dancing on the cedar beams of the sitting-room roof to the music of 'Cat's People', and of Ema's favourite tape of the time, 'Heat of the Moment'. Iain, Oria and I, the older generation at floor level, dressed in ample caftans. laughed and took photographs of the sleek young ones dancing above. Moments of happiness forever frozen in memory.

14. Emanuele and green grass snakes

15. Emanuele with a puff adder in the snake pit at Kuti

16. Mapengo, Emanuele and a spitting cobra

17. Emanuele, Mapengo and a giant python

18. Emanuele, Mirimuk and security people at Maji ya Nyoka

16

19

19. Dudu, Emanuele and Saba dancing on the roof

20. The Longest Night

21. Luka at Emanuele's funeral

22

23

22. Friends at Emanuele's funeral:
Simon Evans and Saba

23. Mapengo at Emanuele's funeral

24. The snakes go

25. The last snake

24

25

26. Sveva and Mirimuk

27. Sveva at Mugongo ya Ngurue

The news came as a shock at breakfast on Easter Monday, passed on through the Laikipia Security network. Jack Block had died while trout-fishing in a river in Chile, where Jeremy now lived. The body had not been found, and it was not clear whether he had drowned, or whether he had had a stroke. Jack's brother Tubby and his wife Aino had been up in Laikipia only a few days before for Paolo's anniversary. Involved in wildlife conservation and in tourism, Jack was a popular figure in the country, respected and admired by African and European alike. Lively and interesting, compassionate and loyal, it was hard to believe he had met such an odd, dramatic death in a far-away country.

The news shocked us all and cast a shadow on our day. It made me reflect once again on the thin thread which separates us from disappearing into nothingness. I became pensive, and for the rest of the day we were all quiet. I decided to drive down next day to Nairobi to offer Tubby my condolences.

In the afternoon, Emanuele asked me to go fishing with him and he drove me to the Big Dam. The mood still hung on me, and I ended up sitting on the shore looking at him casting and swiftly getting one black bass after another.

Sitting there on the rocky red earth, I talked to him about the temporariness of our passage on earth, and about the import-ance of living in the here and now. I spoke of Paolo and of his feelings for this place, our commitment to keep the balance be-tween the wild and the tame. Again I told him about my last Will in case anything happened to me. He listened in silence, apparently absorbed in his fishing, and so quiet was he that I almost thought he had not paid attention. When I finished, he folded the rod, put it neatly aside, and came towards me. He sat on his haunches just in front of me, looked straight into my eyes and said seriously: 'Fine, Pep. I got all that. Now I would like to tell you what I would like you to do if I die first.'

The sun was setting behind the dam wall, and in the evening shadows I could not see his eyes. A flock of pelicans landed in the water feet first, balanced on wide white wings, with hardly a ripple.

'You cannot die. You are seventeen.' Even to me, the feeble denial sounded lame.

He did not note my interruption. 'I would like to be buried close to Paolo. I would like a yellow fever tree on my grave too. For the music, *Bolero*, by Ravel. That cushion you made for me, with NO, PEP embroidered on it, under my head. Champagne, for my anniversary. And, as you just said to me, I also would like you to go on with life and to take care of Sveva.'

In the fear which gripped my mind, I could only realize that he had thought about this before. On the mirror-like surface of the lake a fish jumped. A loud chattering of birds heralded the approaching silence of the night. My voice was hollow and out came only a whisper. 'Whatever could you die of, at your age?'

A sudden smile transformed his face for a second, and in that moment I knew what he was going to say. He squeezed my hand, as if to reassure me. His voice was quiet, patient, with just a touch of irony, as if explaining the obvious to a child. He chose Swahili, as if the exotic language was more appropriate to an exotic death: '*Nyoka tu*' ('Just a snake').

He stood up. I stared at his long bare legs, covered almost to the knee in the motorbike boots. I had not yet noticed how tall he had grown in recent months. In the stillness before night fell, darkness gathered fast, painting greys and blacks on what seconds before had been molten gold and vivid warmth. It was as if only he and I remained in all the world. I shivered. 'Please don't. If you died, it would be my end also.'

He collected the rod and the fish, and started walking towards the car. I could sense he was smiling, 'No, Pep. You are a survivor. You will make it. Let's go and clean this fish.'

A reply died on my lips. We drove home in silence.

After the intense weekend everyone seemed tired. Emanuele wrote his diary as usual, the slim muscular legs in tight jeans outstretched in front of him. The white shirt with a round open collar, and a blue waistcoat, set off his young, strong neck. Oria took a few more photographs at the table, catching his serious eyes in the flickering candlelight, and the dark halo of his hair.

The Douglas-Hamiltons left early next morning for the coast. Emanuele drove them to the airstrip, and they flew back to Kuti for the customary goodbye, flying low over Paolo's grave and down towards me. Having anticipated Iain's trick of making me go down flat on my stomach, I stood with my back to the tallest petria for protection, waving and sending kisses to their four smiling faces.

I drove straight to Nairobi to see Tubby. Jack's body had been finally found and it was discovered that he had died of a heart attack after all. Perhaps, to his fisherman's heart, the largest trout he had ever caught had brought too much joy. There would be a memorial service later in the month at Longonot Farm in Naivasha. I promised I would come down for it, and I drove back to Laikipia the same day. I was uneasy, with a sense of foreboding, and I wanted to be with my children.

All seemed fine there, but Emanuele told me next morning that his female cobra had escaped. He was worried because she had been sick with a sort of mouth rot, and he was determined to find her. I was playing with Sveva, a round fair little angel, when he approached us across the lawn, and I could see from the look on his face that something had happened to upset him. A snake was slung across his shoulder, looking limp and dead. It was larger and thicker than I had imagined, and it was the cobra.

'I killed her,' Emanuele announced in his matter-of-face voice, but with a tinge of regret. 'Mapengo and I smoked her out of the hole where she was hiding. We miscalculated the amount of smoke and she suffocated. Her heart has stopped. She's quite dead. It is my fault.'

It often happened that I could foresee what Emanuele was about to say. Now, I saw a thought dart through his mind, and I knew he was thinking of an episode which occurred a few days earlier, when Colin had revived a young calf by blowing down its lungs through a pipe. We had been very impressed, and Emanuele had asked many questions. Now he stood suddenly, a determined expression in his eyes, and started walking towards the house, the snake swinging around his neck like a thick wet towel, saying over his shoulder, 'I am getting one of those silver straws of yours from the bar. The ones you use for Pimm's. I'll try to revive her.'

I closed my eyes wearily. There seemed to be no end to this. Yet Emanuele had a way of making even something as absurd as trying to revive a spitting cobra through mouth-to-mouth resuscitation seem a perfectly normal exercise. Sensing my dismay, he stopped for a moment and came back a few paces to reassure me. 'She has no spit left anyway. She has just spat from the hole, at my goggles.' He pointed to the goggles hanging round his neck, smudged with grey, sticky saliva. I shuddered.

When he came back a little later, I could see he had succeeded. His face was alight, transformed as only his face could be. He explained to me how the heart had started beating again, and the elation he had felt at being able to resuscitate her. That night he described the story in his diary in great detail and ended: '. . . and if she lives, I shall call her Bahati, "the Snake of Good Luck", because she came back from the dead.'

It had worked for the snake.

31

The End of the World

'... Who is Mungu?' I asked.

'Mungu lives up there,' they answered, 'and if he wants you to live, you live and if he wants you to die, you die.'

Llewelyn Powys, *Confessions of Two Brothers*

It began like any other day with the tea brought after a knock at the door of my bedroom in Laikipia. Simon's smiling *'Jambo, Memsaab,'* and all the dogs coming in to greet me, cold noses against my cheek and tails wagging. Simon's tall frame was silhouetted against the windows as he pulled the curtains to let in a fierce sun. It was already hot. The rains were late. It was 12 April 1983, during the Easter holidays. Soon after, Sveva came in, hugging her favourite African doll. She was two-and-a-half years old, a blonde cherub with deep blue eyes and beautiful, easily tanned peach-bronze skin, like Paolo.

I was drinking my tea when Emanuele knocked and walked in, followed by his dog Angus, a large yellow Alsatian, the best-looking of Gordon's sons, and stopped at the foot of my bed. I observed how tall he had become, how broad were his shoulders, and how his shaven jaw was no longer a child's. He wore khaki shorts and a khaki shirt, sleeves rolled at the elbows. From the belt hung a knife, and the inevitable snake-tongs. He was seventeen. A handsome young man with quiet ways, a brilliant mind and an intriguing personality, which made him extremely attractive to girls.

'*Buongiorno*, Pep,' he said with his new husky man-voice, 'can I have a rubber band?'

I knew what he wanted the rubber band for. He used them regularly, to tighten a piece of plastic round the neck of a sterilized jar. He would push the glass against the fangs of a deadly puff-adder viper. The gland was squeezed against the rim of the glass, and the venom spurted out in a spray. Emanuele then crystallized it, using a chemical procedure. We found the band.

'I am going to milk the snakes.'

'I hate you doing that,' I could not help saying.

He looked at me in his peculiar way, straight in the eye, with just a glint of amusement. 'You always worry. I have done it dozens of times.' I knew he was right.

His face was suddenly transformed by one of his unexpected smiles, he touched Sveva's cheek affectionately, and he was gone, his dog following.

I stood looking at him from the door.

Off he went in the light of the early morning, with the shadow of the house on the lawn, as the sun rose behind it. His shadow was long on the grass and the sun on his back streaked his hair with a golden halo. He was young and strong and handsome . . . and no longer mine. He walked in long easy strides through the glory of the bushes in bloom, under the shade of the yellow fever trees, the snake-tongs swinging at his waist, past the swimming-pool, towards the snake pit.

He went away, and he never turned back.

I watched him with a strange feeling about me, like a cloud of premonition which closed round my stomach like a painful fist. When I could see him no longer the lawn looked suddenly empty. I sighed, and went to have my shower. Sveva followed me, with her doll. I was towelling my hair dry when I realized someone was knocking.

The urgency made the glass of the door rattle and my saliva dry out. I stopped drying my hair, and shouted in answer: '*Kitu gani?*' ('What happens?').

'Mama.' Only Mapengo, Emanuele's snake man, called me then 'Mama', the familiar respectful African way of addressing a married woman. His voice sent a chill down my spine. It was low and altered, unnaturally hesitant and unrecognizable. In the hollow stillness of doom, the only sound was the echo of my terror.

'Mama, *iko taabu kidogo . . .*' ('There is a small problem . . .').

'Emanuele? *Nyoka?*' ('A snake?').

'*Ndiyo*' ('Yes').

'*Terepupa?*' ('A puff-adder?').

'*Ndiyo.*'

'*Wapi?*' ('Where').

'*Gikoni*' ('In the kitchen').

I did not stop to think for a second. With a conscious effort which took everything out of me, I refused to indulge in useless despair. Not just yet. I knew I could not afford hysterics, and I knew I could not lose time. I was alone, far from help, twenty minutes' drive from our airstrip and eight kilometres from Colin's house. I was the only one who could drive, and the only one who could help. I also knew that if I lost my head nothing could be done to save him . . . Save him? I knew instinctively it was already too late, but that I had to try in every way I could.

That day and the night and the day which followed, I shed layers of my being as a snake sheds its skin. I kept coming in and out of myself, watching myself acting as from a great distance, and suddenly re-entering my body and the agony of my tormented soul.

Now I watched one part of me splitting from the other, and taking over.

The new Kuki grabbed yesterday's clothes from the laundry basket. Like an efficient, emotionless robot, she took the glasses without which she knew she could not see, and the hand-set radio. Before reaching the door in two strides she was already screaming into the set, trying to keep her voice steady and clear: 'Emanuele has been bitten by a puff-adder. A puff-adder. Very seriously. Call the flying doctors. Now. Immediately. I am driving him down.'

She repeated the message twice, in English and Swahili, while running towards the kitchen, ignoring Sveva's bewildered screams, and once she was sure the message had been received, threw the radio aside. The stones of the passage were cold under her running bare feet. She was there.

The kitchen walls were green and the silence hung like a shroud. They stood silent as only Africans can, and the eyes moved to her in unison, expressionless, then returned to the shape on the floor.

Emanuele sat rigid, legs spread out on the green cement, facing the window. With a feeling of overwhelming unreality, she crouched in front of him. From his open mouth, green saliva dribbled in ugly bubbles. The skin was grey, the eyes staring and glassy. She waved a hand in front of them and he did not flinch. With a pang of anguish, she realized he was blind.

At that moment, I again became his mother.

With his right hand, he cradled his left: in the first joint of the index finger was a tiny black mark, unswollen, which he had already cut with his knife. No blood: the snake bite.

I looked at the fingers with the very short nails and the brass bracelet around his wrist, the gift of a girl he would kiss no more. I took his hand gently in mine and I sucked the small wound from which the life I had given him was seeping away. I sucked and I spat and nothing came out.

Where was the adrenalin? Where did he say he kept it? Was there time to look for it? The serum. In the fridge. Now. In the urgency, I tore the fridge door from the hinges: the uncanny strength of despair and impotence.

'Emanuele. Emanuele *ascoltami. Ti taglio la mano?* Do I cut your hand? Do I cut your arm?' Useless questions dictated by hopelessness and desperation. Emanuele was dying and I knew there was nothing I could do. Bitten in the snake pit with a lethal dose, he had climbed out, walked all the way to the kitchen and collapsed there. Through the exertion, the poison had reached his heart. His blood was coagulating.

'Emanuele.' My desperation to make contact a last time, to hear again his voice, to bring him back to consciousness. Was he deaf too? This could not really be happening to me.

The eyes flickered weakly, focused on mine for an instant with immense fatigue, and there was a faint glimmer of recognition. The strangled voice was no longer his voice. There was no fear and no expression in it.

The pain in my chest matched his. For a moment my vision blackened, and I forgot to breathe.

'*Mamma*,' he whispered hoarsely, slowly, in Italian. '*Muoio, mamma*.' I am dying, mamma.

With irreversible agony I realized he had called me 'mother' for the first time in his life.

These were his last words.

I tried to remember afterwards if there had been any note of fear, of regret, of pain and horror in his voice. But there was only an expressionless certitude of the inevitability of his death. He knew well and accepted what was happening: as he knew — and I did not — that he had already been bitten too many times by vipers, and that another bite would be fatal.

His eyes clouded again and the body became rigid. Still holding his hand I lifted my eyes to Simon's. I read in them what I could not yet accept. Like all the rest he was waiting for a signal, an order about what to do next. My voice sounded unnaturally calm and far away. The other Kuki. 'Simon, Mapengo. *Weka yeye kwa gari maramoja. Beba yeye pole pole. Sisi nakwenda saa hi.*' ('Carry him gently to the car immediately. Do not let him move. We go now').

Of all the things I have ever done and will ever do in my life, the worst by far was having to drive my dying son to bring him to useless help. We carried him like a rigid log of wood and laid him on the back seat. Simon sat with Ema's head on his lap and Mapengo jumped in the boot. The noise of the engine drowned Sveva's screams. I would have to take care of her later. The gardeners and house-servants stood watching, mute, in a line, without waving.

I put my foot down on the accelerator and my hand on the horn. We took off, skidding in a cloud of dust and blaring noise I did not hear, wheels biting the road without mercy, careless of pot-holes and rocks . . . I kept switching my eyes from the road to the rear mirror which reflected Emanuele's grey face and staring eyes. There was nothing I wanted to do more than to hold him and kiss him and touch him, but I had to drive, I had to concentrate on the road.

Two giraffes crossed the track at the Kati Kati *boma* just in front of us, and the outraged trumpeting of a small herd of elephant I disturbed faded in the speed. Just before reaching the Centre I almost hit a donkey cart, and at that moment I felt a surge of pain in my limbs which came in waves, and my womb contracted as if giving birth. A voice, unrecognizable, was wailing loudly: who was it? I moved my head to look at Emanuele in the mirror and I stared at my face with an open mouth: I was screaming. Simon's hand had come forward and turned the mirror towards me so that I could not look.

I stopped on Colin's back lawn. The smell of burnt tyres hung in the air with the noise of the brakes when I erupted from the car. It seemed like a film in slow motion. Colin, Rocky, their children, the dogs . . . coming towards us, a question in their eyes.

I was past minding. I had gone to hell and died with him, and now the world could just crumple and swallow me for all I cared.

It is never so simple.

'He is dead,' I just said. The voice, like my body, no longer belonged to me. There was this disembodied numbness.

Colin was already opening the door, pulling him out, feeling his pulse, listening to his chest. 'No. He is still alive. Just. Come on, Ema! Quick, Kuki. Mouth-to-mouth resuscitation. You. Now. I will do heart massage.'

That other Kuki, with a face of stone, knelt on the grass over the young man's face. Numberless times she blew into his mouth while Simon held his head. It felt heavy on her bare legs. The lips were cold, like some resilient rubber. Air frothed back with saliva. Colin worked rhythmically on his chest. How long it went on I will never know, as time had ceased to matter. Nothing else existed but my boy's face and his mouth and my mouth and my wild hope, and my despair. I prayed to the unknown God who grants us life. I promised Him all I had, all I was, in exchange for that one life.

God did not hear me.

I concentrated on breathing my life back into Emanuele, pouring it out of me with all my love. I went on and on and on until I realized that a hand was heavy on my shoulder and a voice — Colin's voice — was saying: 'Stop. He is gone, Kuki. Oh shit. Oh shit, Ema. He is gone, there is nothing you can do.'

Slowly I lifted my head and looked up at the sky of Africa. The first to break the silence — it seemed to me — were the cicadas. Then the thousand hidden birds. Through the canopy of leaves above, I could see white clouds moving soundlessly. I waited quietly for the earth to crack open and swallow us all. The world went on as ever. The hills were as blue, the breeze as gentle.

From a great distance my voice said, 'He was my son.'

Colin's fingers dug deeper in my shoulder.

I looked up for my boy's smiling face soaring like a freed bird above the treetops.

'Where has he gone?'

Colin's voice had a broken edge when he answered quietly, 'He is watching you, Kuki. He is right up there with Paolo. They are having a good laugh together.'

Good, sane, dependable Colin. He knew these were only words, which could give me no comfort. I looked into Simon's antique eyes and in their mute depths I recognized my grief. I looked at Mapengo. He was crying without noise. '*Wapi yeye?*' ('Where has he gone?') I repeated, and did not need an answer. Time stood still.

A silent group of Africans had gathered around us in a circle. I had not seen them coming. Now I noticed their bare legs like a *boma* of wooden sticks, their patched trousers, old *shukas*, bare feet, rubber sandals, worn safari boots. I looked at their expressionless faces, one by one.

Emanuele's head was heavier on my lap.

I sat there, watching his young dead face, cradling it gently, not to hurt him more. A shadow of moustache on his upper lip. A tiny mole I had never noticed before on the cheekbone. A leather string around his strong neck with a Turkana charm which had not helped. The brown eyes were glazed and open, staring up and reflecting a sky he could no longer see. If I had to go on living, this was the turning-point, the pivot around which whatever happened to me after would revolve forever.

With Simon's apron I wiped his mouth, his nose. A caress on his forehead, to tidy his hair. A kiss, two kisses, to close his eyes forever.

The eyelids felt fragile, like petals of gardenia.

It had happened again. I, too had died. Another stage of my life had again ended. I, too, was now born new.

The other Kuki stood up and I heard her saying: 'Let's bring him home, to bury him.'

A ray of sun touched my cheeks, and it was a cool, lifeless sun, which bore no arrows.

32

The Longest Day – the Longest Night

Meglio morire colla testa bionda
che poi che fredda giacque sul guanciale
ti pettinó, coi bei capelli a onda
*tua madre, adagio, per non farti male.**

Giovanni Pascoli, *L'Aquilone*

Silently, as if in a dream, we put the shell which had been Emanuele back into the car. I slid into the back seat, nestling his head on my lap, kissing his hair, his face, gently, as I had not done since he was still a little boy. Lightly, so as not to disturb my sleeping child. Colin drove. The car moved slowly. The news had spread and everyone was out, men, women, children, expressionless, lining the road, as still as people in a painting. The car drove slowly through the silent crowd.

As in a haze, I saw again the donkey cart, the feeding elephant. The giraffe had gone. The world seemed unconcerned. Warthogs ran away, tails straight, from the menanda at Kuti. Before the gate we stopped, and sent Mapengo ahead to alert people, and make

* 'Better to die while your head is still fair,
and when you were cold, they laid it on the pillow,
your mother combed the curly locks in waves
gently, oh so gently, not to hurt you more.'

201

sure Wanjiru would take Sveva away: she was too young yet for that side of death.

The garden was the same, a green oasis of flowers, bushes, trees, and a thousand singing birds I did not hear. Close to the garage, where he had just left it, lonely and now useless, was parked his beloved yellow-and-blue Yamaha, some empty snake bags hanging from the saddle.

We drove across the lawn with our sad cargo, up to the range of bedrooms.

'Where?' asked Colin.

No hesitation, as if I had always known. 'On my bed, Paolo's side.' Where else?

I waited in the car, under the same tree where Paolo's coffin had been put three years before, while the bed was made ready: a board, a clean green sheet. And there we laid him gently. I remembered the first time I had ever held him in my arms: another world, another life, in Venice. Another me. Snow had fallen in the night, and a grey silence, broken by muffled disembodied seagulls, hung on the canal outside. His crib was white, with lace. Carefully, awkwardly, so as not to hurt my baby, I had slipped on a white dress, trimmed with ribbons. Now, I removed the crumpled and stained khakis, and dressed him ritually in clean ones. Short trousers, a camouflage shirt which had been Paolo's and which I knew he had coveted, as if I had only kept it for this moment. Button by button, with my clumsy fingers, I fastened it in place. Carefully, awkwardly, so as not to hurt my baby.

I was vaguely conscious of Colin's supportive presence in the room. We did not speak. He simply held a basin and handed me in turn a sponge, a towel, a comb. Carefully, with a hollow feeling of 'never more', I did what I had to. When Colin pulled the curtains, I turned my head, and our eyes fell simultaneously on the suspended ostrich egg. It hung still where Paolo had put it, from the central beam of the four-poster bed. It hung white, eerie with its secret message ... of love ... of death ... of hope ... perhaps of wisdom.

'Kuki,' said Colin, 'you must break it now. Now, or never.'

He was right. What more could happen?

Darkness enveloped me in a swirling vortex, and for a while, blissfully, I knew nothing. A few minutes, perhaps, and Colin's face again came into focus, emerging from the shadows, anxiously watching over me. His strained and concerned eyes were saying wordlessly that I had not been dreaming. I was awakening to the true nightmare.

Wearily, I brushed Emanuele's hair. Black unnatural shadows were spreading through his face. The ugly tide of death and poison was claiming him.

Respecting my need to be on my own, to weep, to crumble without any witness, Colin went, not before saying, 'We'll radio-call your friends. Someone must keep you company.' I just wanted to be left alone. To think. To face, alone, what I must face. Yet I knew people would arrive for the burial. Emanuele's burial . . . how absurd. Just a few moments ago — a few hours, lives, millennia — there was a future. Now, nothing. I explained to Colin what Emanuele had told me . . . a few days ago? Was it only a few days? The place, the music, and as many of his friends as could be found: after all, this was going to be his last party. I asked him also to arrange the legal side: to make sure nobody came to take him away and cut him up. No need to torture him. We knew how he had died. Colin nodded. As ever, I could rely on him.

The friends I asked for were especially close and they both had suffered major losses. Carol had lost her man in an aeroplane crash; Aino, her infant son, to leukaemia. I knew they would be gentle on my wound. Colin took my hands in his large ones, and looked into my eyes. I looked back, mute and dry-eyed. He just smiled. For as long as we live neither of us will forget what we had shared. The door closed behind him, shutting away the sun.

*

I sat with Ema for the remainder of that day.

Only once I left the room, went to the kitchen. It seemed they had not moved. They just stood there, grief like a *shuka* covering their faces, waiting for me to give them tasks.

I spoke quietly, thanking them for caring. I told them God had taken what He had given, and we could only bow to what we could not change. I asked them to go about their duties, and to prepare for many people. Food, drink, the silver shining, flowers in every room, in every vase. *'Endelea na kazi. Funga chungu kwa roho, na angalia mbele. Kaza roho, na apana sahau yeye. Akuna inja ingine kusaidia mimi sasa* ('Go on working. Shut away the pain in your heart and look ahead. Strengthen your heart, and do not forget him. There is no other way to help me now').

I looked at Mapengo. Never had I seen a more dejected face. I asked him if he knew which snake it had been. He did. A young female, caught in the game ditch a few months before. Yes, he could recognize her. I asked him then to go and fetch her. She appeared, to me, like any other puff-adder: fat, sluggish, hideous, deceptively lethargic. If she had taken my son's life, she did not know it. Mapengo held her, begged me to let him kill her. I shook my head. It was not the snake's fault. Still, she was not like any other snake. A wild primeval idea was forming in my mind. I told him to put her in a snake bag, and this in a small basket. Tomorrow – tomorrow I would tell him what to do.

I went to look for Sveva. She was playing quietly, while Wanjiru cried. I took her in my lap and told her gently what she should know, in a way I hoped she could understand. If I post-poned explanations for too long, I might not be able to go through this again. I said that tomorrow, and perhaps tonight, she was going to see many people in the house. She asked me why. I said there would be a party. She asked for whom: it was not yet her birthday. 'For Emanuele,' I answered, 'because he has gone away.'

'Where has he gone?'

'He is gone to Papa Paolo.'

'Why?' Her blue eyes darkened with surprise.

'Because he loved him. He loved him and he called him.'

'I love him too. Why did he have to go?' Her small voice trembled. 'If he is with Papa Paolo, I will never see him again.' She knew she had never seen her father.

'No. Not now.' I realized with agony that I was also talking to myself. 'But one day, when they call you, you will see them again. We are all going where they are. He is gone ahead. You know he always walked faster than us.' I kissed her warm hair which smelt of soap, and went back to the room which smelt of decay. The world of living things was shut outside.

I lit a candle and some incense sticks. I sat with him, looking at him forever, at all the details of his young dead body. I spoke to him, and his entire life flashed back, digging deep furrows in my soul. Images of his childhood, fun we had shared, something he had told me, how he walked, how he moved. The time he had proudly given me a snakeskin.

On the bedside table was a photograph I had taken long ago. He looked straight at me with sad, knowing eyes, a small python coiled around his neck: Kaa, his first snake, a gift from his mother. When I had printed that photograph, I remembered, I had had one of my uncanny premonitions: I had seen he was carrying his destiny around his neck, and he well knew it.

The droning noise of an aeroplane: my friends were coming. Hushed voices, steps approaching: they were there. Someone came in gently, and embraced me. In Carol's eyes there was that timeless wisdom. I knew they cared, not many words were needed.

It was now afternoon. A new, strange noise I could not place was filtering through the birds' voices from the closed door. A thumping noise. A rhythmic sound of digging.

The dimming light outside brightened the candles: the longest day was failing fast, like yesterday. Another aeroplane was approaching in almost total darkness. A fleeting thought came and went: Aidan? Would he have heard already? He and Emanuele had liked each other. He would be shattered. He would fly up to his young friend's burial. He would comfort me. The humming noise was now closer, lower, much lower, almost flaying the roof; the windows rattled. Only Iain flew like this. The Douglas-Hamiltons had managed to come back.

The news had spread through Kenya as a bush fire. By nightfall, the house was full of friends, mine, his. Fly-tents mushroomed on the lawn below the pepper trees. More cars. More steps. Whispers outside the doors. And they were there, coming in one by one, like shadows in a play. Young people, some unknown. They had come by car, by air, in the back of pick-up *matatus*. Saba and Dudu holding hands, looking down at their friend. My face was wet with other people's tears.

Night fell, and in the silence the rhythmic sound seemed to grow louder. Closing the door behind me, I went to look. Across the doorstep, ears flattened in distress, tail limp, face resting dejectedly on forepaws, Emanuele's dog Angus kept guard. As if respecting his son's priority to grief, Gordon, my dog, was waiting on the lawn. A fire burned at Paolo's grave, and we followed its light. Subdued voices fell silent at my approach. The thudding noise stopped for a moment. Faces lifted up to look at me from an enlarging rectangular hole deep in the hard soil, which smelt of mushrooms. Someone murmured, '*Pole.*' Black faces, white faces, young and old ones: they were taking turns to dig my son's grave.

I touched the yellow soft bark of the young but strong tree which had been Paolo. I thanked them all, stood for a time in silence, and walked slowly back with Gordon to the closed room which had become a shrine. The wiry grass of April stung my bare feet.

At some point in the night Colin came in, and handed me some papers. I could see from his tired face that he had not stopped since he had left me. It was the death certificate for me to sign. I did not ask him how, but he had managed. Trying to steady my hand, I carefully marked a large cross under 'Killed by animal or snake'. Is a snake not an animal? And signed my name. I had signed his birth certificate − I recalled − sometime in Venice, a thousand years before.

I took a blanket, a pen, a wad of paper. The longest night had just begun, and I would keep vigil at Emanuele's side, writing to him, talking to him a last time. I wrote all night. Time and again, I walked out to the fire and stood there looking at the growing hole, my caftan flapping at my ankles in the chill eastern breeze.

Colin had warned me there would be much bleeding. I had arranged a stack of Sveva's old terry nappies on my side of the bed in preparation. When the first trickle of blood started oozing out of Ema's nostrils, I wiped it away delicately, and went to burn the nappy in the hot-water fire. Angus his dog, I noticed, was no longer outside.

Once or twice, I thought I saw him breathing, the chest just heaving, and I jumped from the bed, put my ear to his heart, incoherently, but it had been a candlelight illusion: his poor young heart was still and cold as stone.

Alone with him for the very last time, I watched, I talked, I begged, I remembered, I tried, groping through the mysteries of destiny, to find the reason why. It was too early.

The egg hung lonely, translucent in the candlelight. It looked the same as any live egg does. Yet its life had been blown away long ago, like Ema's life. The egg was, like the corpse, an empty shell. Was this the message? With leaden fingers I wrote my last words, trying to be brave and not to let him down.

Towards morning the bleeding stopped. All the nappies had been used. Again I washed his face. It had not changed much, but it was now as black as an African's.

I searched my cupboard to find something to keep away the ever-present flies. There was a new bottle of an insect repellent which some friend from overseas must have left. I broke the seal and shook it. I sprayed a bit on a cotton wad to dab it on his body, and once again the unmistakable smell which had pervaded the mortuary the day of Paolo's funeral hit my nostrils, sweetish and vaguely medicinal; exactly the same as that which had saturated the air while I had been tending Paolo's grave. Another uncanny link. A sign. Amedeo, later, would confirm, bewildered at my sudden question, that he had used the same brand for Paolo.

Anything was possible, anything at all, if my own son could die of a snake bite in Africa. Feeling light-headed, I covered his face with a clean handkerchief. The red hibiscus on his chest was fading.

When the stars paled in the pearly sky of dawn the grave was ready, and so were my last words of requiem. The longest night had ended. I walked out and met Iain in the passage. Behind the glasses his bright brown eyes looked strained, and I could see that he had not slept either. I put my head wearily on his shoulder. He took my hand and we walked to the grave a last time. The stones and earth which had been dug stood in a dry mound. The fire was still burning. Crouched on one side, eyes bloodshot, was Mapengo. At his feet, his noble face a mask of canine grief, was the dog Angus. He would for months become Mapengo's shadow.

I told Iain about my words of service, and asked him to say again, for Ema, the poem of Dylan Thomas he had once recited to me.

'I might not be able to,' he told me honestly. He had been so fond of Ema.

'If I find my voice, darling, I know you will find yours.'

A silent pact was sealed. New hibiscus bloomed in the morning dew. I picked some to bring back to Emanuele.

The verandah, the sitting-room, were full of sleepy faces with puffy sad young eyes. My people, faithful to my request to carry on with their normal duties, were setting the table for breakfast, as on every other day. Ema's place at the head of the table had been prepared as usual: only yesterday he had sat there eating eggs and bacon. I could not bear the thought of anybody occupying that place which first had been Paolo's. On the spur of the moment, I chose a flower from the bunch, and put it on the table, where his place had been. With her impenetrable dark Nandi face, Rachel was folding napkins one by one.

'No one is going to sit here, Rachel, in the chair of our *kijana*.' She looked up. 'Not today, not any more. You will pick one of these red flowers he loved at every meal, and you will place it on the table, here. From now on this will be our new *desturi* (custom).'

She nodded gravely. Young and pretty, she could neither read nor write, but this she understood instantly: in Africa, *desturi* was sacred, and always accepted without question. She goes on with this duty still today.

People kept coming. Cars arriving. Aeroplanes. The house, like a beehive, resounded with muffled sounds, whispers, voices. One time, broken desolate sobs and stifled murmurs approached and stopped outside the door, drowning the other noises. They were filled with such heartrendering despair that I caught my breath, opened the door and looked out. Surrounded by a group of miserable young people, crowding around her as if for a mutual comfort, there stood a girl. The boys were all wearing jackets and ties, the girls smart evening clothes, as if they had come to a party. She wore a dress of blue silk, which set off her reddish-blonde hair, rumpled as if this morning she had forgotten to brush it. Her skin was honey-coloured, her mouth full, and she was beautiful. The hazel eyes speckled with gold were red with tears streaming down her cheeks. She hugged a bundle of flowers to her young breast, as if to draw from them strength and comfort. A younger version of herself – her sister? – stood close and mute as if supporting her. I had never met her, but even before she spoke, I knew she was Ferina. She had loved him too. She was perhaps fifteen. I just opened my arms, gently saying her name, and I received her as I would a daughter.

In the night I had decided what to do with the ostrich egg. There was no sense in leaving it there any more. Its message had to be read now, or never.

When the coffin was brought, and the body composed inside it, I asked for scissors. Carefully I climbed up to the beam, as Paolo must have done when he hung it there. I cut the nylon thread close to the knot which his slim fingers had once tied. I would never know what thoughts were in his mind, or what he had written. He had left it to me to choose what to do with it. His turquoise eyes had been inscrutable. Now I carried the egg in my cupped hands, like a ritual offering, and laid it down carefully in the coffin. I would not need to open it. The mystery in the egg would be buried with the mystery of death. Both shells were empty.

Emanuele's soul had hatched.

Again the friends carried the coffin out to where Paolo's coffin had been. Again I sat, my hand on Ema's hand. He held his snake-tongs, our photographs, our letters. Someone had sent gardenias. I looked at him.

Last time   last time   last time.

I nodded. The lid descended. His young friends carried the coffin, and I followed alone.

Across the lawn, to the graves, we walked in silence.

The Second Funeral

'. . . Where has all this love gone?'

In the stillness of the afternoon no breeze moved my long white skirt, a gift from Paolo, the same that I had worn for his last goodbye. Oria stood at my side with a bewildered Livia. Poor, desperate Livia. She had grown up with him and loved him as a brother. Loved and worshipped him. She had been here on a holiday from Italy for a few months. She had come up to Nairobi from the coast, and phoned home, to find that Ema had died. Her adored Ema, after her mother and her father. She would never recover from this blow. Iain asked the crowd to come close. The coffin, shiny and new as only coffins are, rested on the trellis of banana leaves, suspended on ropes of sisal. Garlands of flowers were piled all round. On it, like a large inverted tear, was laid a heart of red carnations, and on the black ribbon rimmed with silver one could read: 'Ferina'.

Paolo's three-year-old acacia spread a thin shade, and in his shade I stood. Mapengo, dressed in his best long trousers, his head bent, Angus behind him, was ready, a small round basket at his feet.

All the ranch people were there. Women in colourful *shukas* and rows of brass and bead necklaces, men in their festive clothes, all wearing masks of sadness and distress. The crowd stood in a half-circle. They all looked at me. I looked at them, and felt as if I, too, was a spectator. There is, I think, a threshold to pain, a limit beyond which a blissful numbness intervenes. Dazed, but aware of the smallest detail, I lived these moments, keeping my composure. Ema would have wished that. I could not yield. Not yet.

A go-away bird croaked from the treetops. The heat sent trembling waves vanishing like water into the sky. I looked around at all those young shocked faces. They had discovered that death could reach into their midst, youth did not shelter them, and they were confused. They had loved him, shared in fun, mischief, adventures. Now they shared the same anguish, and they stood together, like a flock of frightened birds, contemplating their memories and their loss. This experience would forever live with them, and make them grow, and make them better, wiser. Emanuele's last gift had been his death.

I had thought about this moment. I had to keep my voice steady, and conduct the service without stopping to think. One word, another word, like steps in sequence. I could, I must, deal with a word at a time. I remembered my father and what he had taught me. Long gone Italian evenings, dogs running, a little curious girl dreaming of Africa. No one had known what she was meant to face.

Oria's hand touched my elbow with hot fingers. I looked into her eyes, which swam with tears: there was such warmth, compassion in her eyes, such earthy wisdom, and the bonds of understanding which only grow out of maternal solidarity. Her white lace skirt matched mine. Many wore white: it looked as if a procession of mourners in a Greek bas-relief had come alive. The place, the occasion, the same expressions, the stifled sobs, the birds, the breeze, the sun: there was about this scene a dreamlike quality. Perhaps it was a dream, it had not happened . . . Ema would come running to me, now, any moment, he will embrace me, the dogs will bark their happiness, all will laugh, the macabre joke will be over, forgotten . . .

The coffin lay in front of me, suspended over the grave, with Ema inside. They waited for my words. I could not escape. Again, I split in two.

That other me spoke slowly, a tired voice. If the voice trembled, no one would notice, and nobody would care. I cleared my throat, swallowed my sorrow and spoke to Emanuele my last words of love.

> *'Only yesterday morning*
> *we were laughing together;*
> *today I am here with your friends*
> *to bury you, Emanuele.*
>
> *To bury a husband was hard,*
> *to bury my only son is against nature*
> *and a pain which words cannot tell.*
>
> *You were but seventeen,*
> *yet you were a man already*
> *and you could play with life*
> *with a grown man's confidence.*
>
> *You died knowing you were dying*
> *but you were not afraid.*
>
> *You were brave, and you were handsome,*
> *you were intelligent, and you were generous,*
> *you gave love, and you gave friendship,*
> *and you had love, and friends.*
>
> *You shared with all your smile,*
>
> *your charm, your help, your enthusiasm.*
>
> *Your future was a promise*
> *of challenge and adventure.*
>
> *You were but seventeen*
> *but wise beyond your age,*
> *and now you know already*
> *the answer to all questions.*
>
> *I am asking: where are you really*

as this is but your body?
are you now the hot sun of Africa?
are you the clouds and the rain?
are you this wind, Emanuele,
or are you the sky overhead?

I will look for you always
and I will see you in every flower,
in every bird, in every red sunset,
in every crawling snake:
as everything of beauty
will forever be you.

Anything young and proud,
anything good and strong.

You were an extraordinary person,
your short life was extraordinary
and extraordinary was
your cruel, sudden death.

For us — who are left — remains
just to wonder
the reason for such a waste:

Where has all this love gone?

I hope your journey has been good
as you have already arrived.

Just one more thing Paolo wrote to you
one long-gone day:

"Fly for me, bird of the sun.
Fly high":

I love you.'

A gentle breeze was lifting. Sounds of weeping. A few times my voice had almost failed, but now I had finished. I closed my eyes, trying to be elsewhere. Livia's face, wet with hot tears, rested on my shoulder. A hand squeezed mine. Iain kept his word, approached and spoke, keeping his strong voice steady. Just. The verses of the poet from Wales joined the sobs of the people and the singing African birds.

> 'And Death shall have no Dominion.
>
> Dead men naked they shall be one
> With the Man in the Wind and the West Moon;
> When their bones are picked clean and the clean bones gone,
> They shall have stars at elbow and foot;
>
> Though they go mad they shall be sane
> Though they sink through the sea, they shall rise again;
> Though lovers be lost Love shall not;
> And Death shall have no Dominion.'

Then, starting in a hoarse whisper which gained strength word by word, her deep beautiful voice veiled with sadness, Oria came forward, took my hand, and said:

> 'Kuki, you asked me what you and I were doing here:
> we come from the seed of wild men
> we married wild men
> wild children we bore
>
> "Wild men who caught and sang the sun in flight
> And learn, too late, they grieved it on its way,
> Do not go gentle into that good night."
>
> And the mother stands so still
> her clothing seems to have settled into stone.
> In the boy's memory she stands.
> Nothing to animate her face now:
> only the sculpting of the clouds drifting over the brown
> red bush.
>
> She stands that way for a long long time

215

and the sky ponders her with his great African eye.

Two pools of blue in a child's face
will look at you, Kuki.
In the boy's memory she will live and grow.
The snake glides down from its slab
the eagles soar
the sun will rise forever.'

From the corner of the grave where she was crouching on her knees, face buried in her hands, came the broken, desperate sobs of Ferina. Ricky tried to steady her, and her cries slowly subsided into a low moan.

Now it was Colin's turn. I had asked him to make his speech in Swahili, so that everyone could understand and share in this last ceremony. His words were simple, and they touched my heart.

'We have come here today, in the place we well know, — Paolo's grave, which is close to us — to bury Emanuele, our *kijana.'*

His voice failed a moment, and he continued:

'. . . our *kijana*. This young man has left the world.

From the hill of Enghelesha, to the springs of Ol Ari Nyiro, to the mountain of Ol Donyo Orio, it all belonged to him: it was he who led us in our *shamba* even if he was still a youth, and no one could resent him as he was a man of good heart.

We all knew him, and I say there was not a man in this *shamba* who did not like him, as his heart was clean, and he followed the customs of his heart.

A youth is a youth and luck is luck: today is a day of bad luck: our *kijana* has fallen.

All youths have their ways. There is the one who passes and goes and becomes wise. There is the one who falls and we mourn for him. But, people of this place, Ema lived with us.

216

Since he was a little boy this tall he lived with us and we all knew him, and we all loved him because he was, as I say, a man of good heart and we all agree on this.

We must then praise our God, because He let him fall here with us, not far away, not across the sea. He fell here with us and we will keep him here, close to us in the land he loved, as this was his wish, and it is our wish, and we shall not forget him.'

Ravel's *Bolero* started haltingly, progressing gradually to its glorious crescendo. The friends took the ropes, and slowly, inch by inch, lowered the coffin with my baby inside into the deep brown earth, where it landed with a soft and final thud. A murmur ran through the crowd, a baby cried. The music now grew splendid and exalting, absorbing sounds of weeping, sounds of birds, leaving only the mute rising tide of anguish.

Mapengo looked at me, and I briefly nodded. The basket was lowered into the grave to rest close to the coffin. His last snake.

Colin passed me the spade. It was a new one. The shining blade had not yet cut the soil. In the same place I had stood for Paolo. Exactly the same gesture. I dug it in the red earth at my feet. The soil fell on the wood at the bottom. I passed the spade to Livia. The spade went round until the hole was filled.

Mapengo brought me a yellow fever tree, a young one Rocky had dug up from the river. As I had for Paolo, I planted it for Ema. One day, its roots too would reach the body, which would nourish the tree and become part of the landscape.

They now stood in line, Mirimuk, Luka, a chosen group of seven. They pointed the rifles to the sky, and fired their salute to Emanuele. It echoed on the hills. A flight of starlings took off from the thorn trees, circling high. Faces turned up as if all expected to see him there, looking down at us. I had buried only the shell. His soul was soaring. I put my flower gently on the grave. I would go now. I could come back later, today, tomorrow, for the rest of my life.

Some people lingered, some followed me. The music had died down.

The second day went on and on and on. I must confess that I do not remember. I had concentrated my efforts in going through the ceremony with dignity, without collapsing, keeping all my wits. Now I crouched in a corner of the sitting-room, my friends all round, and talked, and talked, and talked. Carol said later she wished she had recorded my words. I do not know. I just sat there with all my love, feeling useless, lost, empty. I spoke of days now past, of never more. A fire burned orange at the graves. At some point I stood up and walked out of the room, towards its light.

I fell without a sound into oblivion, and never knew who carried me to bed.

34

The Last Snake

. . . y hablaran otras cosas con tu voz:
*los caballos perdidos del Otono.**

Pablo Neruda, *Cien Sonetos de Amor*, XCIX, 'Noche'

Smouldering embers of last night's fire sent up a fine gossamer smoke in the cold early-morning air.

On Emanuele's fresh grave the flowers were beginning to fade. The feathery leaves of his frail young acacia were opening tentatively to the light and sun, like live things stirring. Wrapped in sleeping-bags and blankets, some huddled together for warmth and comfort, his friends still lay asleep on the damp earth and grass around the grave. I approached on soft feet, not to disturb them.

I had woken up in my bed still dressed, no recollection of how I had been put there. In the previous two days I had not eaten, or slept. Now I woke up fresh, and for a moment my mind was numb. Then I saw that the egg was no longer hanging light before my eyes. The thin nylon thread had been cut short. It had really happened. I stayed in bed, wondering why I should ever get up and what should I dress for. I contemplated days and days stretching ahead and I felt no desire to see what

* '. . . and other things will speak with your voice:
the lost horses of Autumn.'

the future had again in store for me. No curiosity. A sort of apathy.

On the carpet at the side of the bed, something moved. I looked for Gordon. But it was Livia. Her long brown hair half-covered her face, which rested on a pillow on the floor. She had thrown on a fur blanket and she had slept with me, to keep me company and not to be alone with all her misery. Poor Livia. The pale pink light filtering through the curtains announced another sunny day, but it was still very early, just past sunrise. The birds were waking up with busy morning chatter. I folded my clothes neatly and washed my face. I put on a pair of khaki shorts which had been Emanuele's and one of Paolo's khaki shirts and slipped out of the room. Gordon greeted me, and Nditu, their cold noses sniffed my bare legs, tails wagged uncertainly.

Emanuele's room was as he had left it. His green wind-jacket was slung on the back of his chair. His diary was on his desk, the bookmark at the last day of his life, 11 April. I sat on his chair and looked around. His room was always tidy. Books lined the bookshelves, snake instruments hung shining in a row, the snakeskins stretched on the walls – that enormous seven-foot puff-adder. The sweetish smell of snakes lingered. The page of 12 April was blank. He always wrote in the evening. I took his pen and I wrote in it carefully: 'Today, bitten by one of his puff-adders, Emanuele has died. He was seventeen.' On 13 April I added: 'Emanuele's burial.' I put the pen down, and looked at the bookmark. I was mildly surprised to see it was a letter I had written to him for his birthday, last January. I read it again for the first time since I had written it. It was in Italian:

'. . . I wish you happy days and full of adventure . . . mostly I wish you to learn the lesson of Acceptance . . . as only through Acceptance you will find the secret of existence . . . and you will be happy in a crowd or sitting alone . . . and you will use all that happens in your life, your joys and your sorrows, to become a better person, so that even death at the end will be good, because it is part of the game.'

I stared at my words for a long time. I had forgotten them. But I had been right. The game of life and death. I flipped through the unwritten pages. A note fell out, addressed to Michael Werikhe, the man who loved snakes, and walked for rhinos he had never seen. It was an invitation to come to Laikipia to stay. I registered it in my mind. It was possibly the last thing Emanuele had written.

Blank page after blank page stretched ahead, like the days of my life. Blank pages to fill with what? With whom? All my men gone . . . and Aidan? What had happened to Aidan? Yesterday, he had not come to the funeral of his young friend. Certainly there was a reason. Perhaps he was now walking somewhere up north where news could not reach him. I longed for his presence, for his shoulder on which to rest my head.

Alone . . . with Paolo's baby.

Emanuele was no longer there, but I still was. If the pages were blank, they could not remain empty and wasted. I knew it was up to me to fill them, and the quality and value of what I filled them with was again, as ever, up to me. Another chapter of my life was closed, but as I was still alive, I had to go ahead and make the most of the time I had left. Because of Sveva. Because of Paolo. Because of Ema, and because of me. I had to begin with something new and positive.

I took up the pen again, and under today's date, 14 April, I neatly wrote: 'Today, we set free all Emanuele's snakes.' I closed the book. Breathing deep, I walked out in the daylight once again.

What else could I do with all those snakes? What would Emanuele like me to do with them? We will let them all go. Today. With whoever of Emanuele's friends had stayed behind.

I walked to the grave, and found them there. Someone started to stir. Swollen eyes. Pale, drawn faces, lined by grief. I looked at them with pity and with affection. I had told them yesterday that they were all my children. Their suits and white shirts, their smart dresses, were crumpled. They had come dressed for a party, and I learnt later that Emanuele, a few weeks before, had asked Ferina to come to the ranch during the holidays. She said her parents probably would not let her. 'You will come up anyway,' he had told her. 'You'll come up in April.' 'How do you know?' she had asked, surprised. 'You will come to my funeral.' She had not believed him. Why should she? Young, fresh, death was a far-away, nebulous world belonging to the old and sick. She laughed teasingly. 'What do you want me to wear for your funeral?' His eyes were serious and unreadable, and for a moment she was afraid. 'A party dress. This one you are wearing now. Blue suits you. You must all come dressed for a party.' And so they all did. Ferina could not forgive herself for not having believed him then. That knowledge broke her. She would tell me this, weeks after.

Rubbing their eyes, one by one, the children stood, stretched, and came to hug me. 'Have breakfast. Eat something. Then we'll let all the snakes go.' I went, through the morning garden. On the breakfast table, at Ema's place, was a fresh red hibiscus. Rachel had remembered.

Ricky Mathews and Mapengo emptied the cages and the snake pit, and filled all the snake bags. Hundreds of harmless or deadly snakes were put in bags and pillowcases. The children jumped in the back of my pick-up ... Before leaving, on the spur of the moment, I had picked a bunch of red hibiscus. With Iain, Oria, Carol, Aino, Sveva in Livia's arms, and all the children, I drove down to Ol Ari Nyiro Springs.

We parked the cars at Marati Ine. Two female waterbuck watched with liquid eyes, soft muzzles sniffing, unafraid. It was a strange procession. I led the way with Iain towards the springs. The children followed, in rumpled silks, open white shirts, carrying bags full of snakes. Sveva hung from Livia's back, giggling at the adventure.

In the mud and dust along the shores, tracks of last night's buffalo. Dragonflies darted from pond to puddle, pursuing their mates, disturbing clouds of midges. White butterflies concentrated on fresh elephant dung, trembling wings like fallen petals.

The first to go had to be Bahati, the female cobra Emanuele had revived a few days earlier. She had lived and he had not. Ricky opened the bag, and out she slid, her yellow stomach matching the rocks coated in dry mud. Slowly she moved at first, but soon she darted wriggling out of her apathy, faster, and faster, and I watched her until she disappeared through the low scrub back into life and freedom. Thoughts came and went of Ema, who had found his freedom too, disappearing in the timelessness of death. One by one all the snakes crawled away, some slowly, some jerkily, some sliding into the river. Perched on a rock, I helped to release them, and offered their life silently to Emanuele. Sleek, fast, the green grass snakes, the hissing sand snakes, the white-lips, the pythons, the egg-eaters, the house snakes, swished diving into the restless flow of the Mukutan. Last, were the vipers. Carefully, expertly, one by one, Ricky lowered them into the water.

When the last snake swam away in the current of the Mukutan that hot day of April, on an impulse I threw into the water the red hibiscus I had been holding. Light as a feather it swirled in the ripples and touched the glistening patterned skin of the triangular head fast disappearing into freedom. The head was suddenly heart-shaped, the petals looked like blood. The sun shone on them and caught a drop of water into a rainbow.

From the depth of time a young boy's voice, still unbroken, said to me again: 'Pep, one day you too will understand the hidden beauty of snakes.'

'You are right. You are right. I can see the beauty now,' I told him silently.

The last puff-adder went.

In the hot silence of noon a noise was approaching. A small white aeroplane suspended in the sky appeared through the shade of the fever trees. It could have been anybody. It could have been Aidan. But I knew instantly that it was Mario, and my father, and my mother. The flight they had already boarded to come to the funeral had been cancelled an hour after they were airborne because of engine problems. I knew they would arrive today. I ran to my car, carrying Sveva.

When I reached Kuti, they were already there. None of them had met for years. I could only imagine what their journey to Africa for that tragic reason had been like. My mother had loved Emanuele more than anybody in her life. She looked lost, but as ever in control of her emotions. She embraced Sveva, gently talking to her. I knew what an effort this cost her. My father looked deep into my eyes with his green ones that age had not tarnished. In the strength of our mute embrace we put all that words could never say.

I ran towards the grave, and stopped, a few steps off. Prostrate on it was Mario. Arms and legs spread wide, hands dug into the soil and faded flowers, body shaken by heartrending sobs. I retreated in silence. He was his father.

Soon after, a mad gallop shook the earth, frantic hooves bit the dust, and off went Mario on Emanuele's horse, riding like the Apocalypse. He came back at night. Next day he left, and I have never seen him since.

PART IV

After

35

Walking Alone

... the silence sank
Like music on my heart.

Samuel Taylor Coleridge, *The Ancient Mariner*

The worst thing was the silence where there had been sound, the memory of a fading young voice, of balanced young steps along the passage. The worst thing was his useless motorbike, daily washed, the empty place at the table where a red hibiscus was placed at every meal, the empty chair in the sitting-room where he used to sit to write his diary, the shaded windows of his closed room where all was as he had left it. The worst thing was the letters addressed to him which kept arriving from the university in the States where he would no longer go; the mute grief in Mapengo's face. The worst thing was the newly-printed photographs from Easter which Oria brought up one day for me to see. Serious eyes watched me over flickering candles, unreachable eyes which I had closed forever observed me over a tangle of green grass snakes and a chocolate egg on a festive table. Long legs I had composed in the coffin danced again to a silent music up on the cedar beams of the verandah with Saba and Dudu.

The worst thing was to see him going away, in a shot just slightly out of focus, taken from the back of my pick-up after the last picnic at the Springs. He overtook me a last time with his motorbike in a cloud of dust, leaning forward, half-standing, short trousers and naked young torso, riding towards a dark string of hills without turning to look back.

The worst thing of all was the knowledge that he was dead forever.

What remained was the unchanging magic of the landscape of Africa. The mornings began with the birds, a pale pink-purple grey sky, as in the womb of an oyster. As silver melted into gold and dew evaporated in the warmth of a new day, the clear blue light of another dawn found me awake, and ready to go. In the depth of my grief, I had the sense to recognize the healing power of the undisturbed space which surrounded me. I chose to walk. If before the snake I had loved walking tall in the bush, feeling part of it, discovering gradually its secret language as old as Earth itself, after the snake I chose to walk Laikipia day after day, treading every path I could find, as a form of therapy, as if by tiring my body I could heal my soul. My father stayed on for a few days, during which we walked together, as we had lifetimes before on other hills in Veneto. We renewed silently, through the rhythm and beat of our steps, the ancient link of my childhood, but I knew that the loss of my own son was an experience which I could truly share with nobody.

When my father left, I walked alone.

In the beginning, my senses numbed by grief, I walked as if in a vacuum. I never spoke, my mind was full of thoughts and memories, voices and screams, and it groped through the tortuous labyrinth of my unresolved questions. Then, gradually, a silence descended, and my mind became quiet and relaxed: the outer sounds and the essence of nature reached it once again, and I became more alert and perceptive than I had ever been.

I drove out before sunrise in the freshness of the promise of another new morning, and left the car in any odd place. I asked Karanja, the driver, to fetch me at a given time at a specific spot, and I walked dozens of miles – with Luka or Mirimuk – to reach it. Often we came across sleeping rhino or buffalo, feeding elephant, timid bushbuck. We stalked eland until they smelt our scent and fled, leaping high through the dry shrubs. The odours of the bush started cool and fresh, but soon the warmth of the sun dried the dew and ripened them into heady aromas of sage and exotic fruit. The scent of dust and dung and lost feathers became, with the heat, a smell of fire.

From sunrise to sunset, I trekked up the majestic hills and down the steep valleys. Untouched landscapes are undemanding and in them all pretensions and all acting cease. Nothing was expected of me by the ancient silence of the mountains and of the mysterious gorges. In their unjudging, harmonious existence I found again my own identity, and my place.

I understood that in Emanuele's death I could find the key to the essence of life. A thousand thousand times I went back to those moments, re-living them and suffering them again, in the instinctive life-saving knowledge that the only way out of my sufferings was through them. I could have settled for the constant unease and malaise of the unresolved problems within myself, but they would have crippled me. I chose instead to face directly the pain of my irreplaceable loss. I thought about it, spoke about it, mainly wrote about it. I lived again those hours of agony as if they were happening anew. I called Emanuele's name in the long lonely nights when only he could hear. I contemplated the years to come in the silence and stillness of his eternal absence, which annihilated my hopes and dreams for a future that would never materialize.

There is a bonus in tragedies of such magnitude. You realize that there is no further to go down, and that you have two choices. You can stay at the bottom and get used to the agonizing paralysis of those depths, and use any means — drugs, alcohol — to dull the lucid pain for which you are unable to find any relief within yourself. Or you can decide to rise to the surface again, and begin living once more. This last decision requires a conscious effort, for it is the active choice, and it can only succeed if you truly face your problems directly. It needs perseverance and action to follow it up, and it means change. Once you return to the surface you are as new, you have grown and have left down there your old self like a discarded and useless cocoon; and you have discovered that you can fly. In Ema's death I had found the key to solve the riddle. Only in changing my attitude to it, and in giving my life a new purpose, could I balance the waste and make sense.

About a week after Emanuele's death I heard from Tubby about the memorial service for Jack Block, to be held at his farm on Lake Naivasha. The message also said that everyone in the family would understand if, in the circumstances, I decided not to go.

My friendship with the Blocks went so far back into the past, and Tubby and Aino had been so special to me during both my bereavements, that I did not think twice. I had also learnt how much it matters to see the people one least expects at the time of deepest sorrow, and how touched I had been by those who had taken the trouble to come all the way to Laikipia to be with me when I needed to feel I was not totally alone. And, since I had suffered my losses, I began to discover that in a strange way the pain of others touched me more than ever before, and that there is a soothing bond of human solidarity in standing in silence with our friends in the presence of death.

I took Saba Douglas-Hamilton, who was staying with me, and left Sveva in the care of Wanjiru and my mother. As a precaution I also brought Karanja, my driver, with me as it was the first time I had driven out of the ranch since I had gone to Nairobi a couple of weeks earlier to give Tubby my condolences.

For years the road round Lake Naivasha had been in a very bad state of neglect, and it was getting worse. Deep ruts of soft white dust seemed to swallow the car like water, and, like water, it penetrated everywhere. The thin strip of tarmac in the middle of the track was eroded at the edges and dotted with hundreds of pot-holes, as frayed lace resting on face powder. The grass and whistling thorns at the roadside were white with it.

The green lawn of the Blocks' house, sparkling with enamel-bright flowers and refreshed by sprinklers, was always an un-expected oasis after all the greyness. I parked my car in the shade of the acacia as I had done many times before. A normal and familiar act. But nothing was normal any more. The Blocks, subdued and united in their grief, were gathered on the verandah which looks over the lake. Fish-eagles and pelicans perched on tree-stumps along the shore, as ever, and the lake shimmered blue. Among the thorn trees, below Jack's charming wooden cottage, rows of chairs had been arranged for a very large gathering. The glass door rattled when I opened it and all heads turned towards me. Dressed in black, covered in dust and with my recent grief written all over me, I must have looked like an eerie scarecrow.

I was the first friend to arrive, and my unexpected appearance created a reaction of surprise and concern. I had gone without a second's thought, taking for granted that I could cope. Now I felt uncertain, dizzy and confused. Was it too early to face the world? Perhaps it had been a mistake. Jack's personality, warmth and compassion were known far and wide and he had been loved by a great host of people. Many of them had also been to Emanuele's funeral. But some had not, and when they discovered I was there they came over to the tree under which Saba and I had retreated, and gave me their condolences. The past ten days had been for me a millennium. For the rest of the crowd, they were merely ten days. I had forgotten that the perception of time varies for people. The ordeal was proving harder than I had imagined. It was like living through the agony of Emanuele's funeral a second time.

Somehow the speeches and the ceremony ended, and in a haze, having said a hurried goodbye to Tubby, I slid away unseen. I felt drained of energy, tired beyond words, and let Karanja drive me back to Laikipia.

A few days after Jack's memorial service, looking through the mail which had come from Nairobi, I found two letters.

The first was in a handwriting I recognized instantly. It was Aidan's. I had not heard from him since before Ema's funeral. Day after day the sky had remained empty of his aeroplane. His silence was inexplicable to me.

I took the small white envelope to Ema's grave, and held it a long time in my hands before opening it. I fingered it with closed eyes for some moments as if to divine its contents, as one can know the nature of a tree by the texture and veins of its leaves.

Carefully I opened it. The handwriting was tormented and altered, his sorrow deep. He had felt close to Emanuele. His silence had been enforced by a serious personal crisis which I understood and respected. Although it was not a letter of goodbye, I could feel that Emanuele's death had created a conflict of loyalties, and that our relationship could never be the same again. I had always seen it and accepted it, however, as not belonging to the practical world. There had been an airy and magical quality about our encounters, an unpredictability which made them out of the ordinary, and I could only accept an out-of-the-ordinary reaction as part of the odds.

The other letter planted the seed of a relationship which would prove an exceptionally positive and healing influence on my life. It was from a woman I did not really know, but to whom Tubby had introduced me at Jack's memorial ceremony. It was a letter of sympathy and condolence: '. . . Since the death of your son you have constantly been in my thoughts . . . and my son Robin was distressed to hear the sad news, as I know he is very fond of you.' It was signed Berit Hollister. On an impulse I answered immediately, adding to the letter, as I had for all, a copy of my last words to Emanuele, asking her to forward them to Robin, who had written but whose address in Malindi I did not have. I knew Robin well. I had first met him at a wedding over ten years before, just after we had arrived in Kenya.

In December 1978 he had flown up to Laikipia just to greet us on his way to Nanyuki from Baringo, where he was then working. On taking off, the engine had failed, and the plane had come down like a ripe mango. Paolo and Emanuele had been watching, horrified, but when they reached the spot they found Robin intact, close to the wreck, with his perennial smile, a briefcase in his hand, quietly searching the bush for his sunglasses. The wreck is still there today, or what remained after elephant and hyena had had a go at it, and the rains and winds of many seasons have rusted and scattered its pieces like broken eggshells. Inevitably the accident singled out Robin from other people we knew but did not see often.

For many weeks the mail kept bringing letters of condolence from every corner of the world, some of them unexpectedly beautiful, from people I hardly knew. All expressed the feeling that there was something unusual and unforgettable about Emanuele, and all touched my heart. I kept them in a large box which grew fuller every day.

One day I asked Colin to come up to Kuti, and we drove out together, looking for a suitable stone to put on Emanuele's grave. It had to be large and of a certain shape, but also, like Paolo's, it needed to have some connection with a place he had been especially fond of. It was a weird, unreal feeling, this search for a tombstone for my son, like an ancient ritual. Now and again Colin and I looked at each other, and shook our heads. However, I could not help thinking how different it is to die in Africa and have the privilege of being buried on your own land, where your friends can dig your grave and hold your service, where no paid uncaring hand is hired to perform any part of the ceremony and of the necessary preparations, and where it is your mother, your wife, who sits with you on your last night on earth, guarding your body for the last time.

It was like this in the ancient days, and it is still so among the primitive people who are close to the land and have not forgotten how to live their lives and die their deaths with dignity.

I chose the stone finally from near Ngobithu's Dam, where Emanuele used to practise 'wheelies' with his motorbike. It was a yellow-orange stone, massive, in the shape of a large pillow. It seemed appropriate for his last bed. A tractor was sent in the afternoon, with about twenty people to lift it and bring it to the garden. Sitting on Paolo's stone, I watched the operation with a feeling of unreality. A few days after, Colin came up with his chisel and engraved simply, as he had for Paolo, just EMANUELE and the date underneath: 12.4.83. The day was very hot. Half-way through the engraving, I brought him a beer, and he drank it there, resting a while.

Next morning I took Sveva's hand, and for the first time I brought her to visit her brother's tomb. I had told her he was now with Paolo, and it seemed natural to her that their graves should be together, and that a small version of Paolo's tree had been planted on Emanuele's. She brought a handful of red hibiscus, and her favourite soft toy, a pink mouse called Morby. During the entire time I kept talking to her and answering her questions. Hand-in-hand we offered the red flowers to both our men, and I managed to keep my misery to myself.

36

The Gift of Friendship

Though nothing can bring back the hour
Of splendour in the grass, of glory in the flower . . .

William Wordsworth, *Ode. Intimations of Immortality*

Although only within the silence and solitude of oneself can one find the way out of suffering, my friends made sure I always felt the warmth and comfort of their support and love. They shared my gradual re-birth as they had my sorrow. Strong links deepened. Here, where one could still attune life to the ancient rhythms of nature, friendship and solidarity were nourished by the vinculum of our common choice of Africa.

One was, of course, Carletto. He had been in Europe when Emanuele died, but one afternoon his dusty Land-Rover emerged from the bush, and he was there. He came towards me, a scowl of concern altering the joviality of his rotund walrus face. Below his bushy moustache his mouth was not smiling, and his kind eyes glinted with an unusual shine behind the thick glasses. He opened his vast arms silently and I found refuge in them.

There was no need to recall all the memories and the shared sorrows which had made of our friendship such a strong and unusual bond. Gone were Mariangela, Paolo, Chiara and now Emanuele. We had been together when the first drama had struck, a summer night in Italy, years ago. We were here in Africa for the latest one, and the fact that we had survived and we were neighbours here as we had been in another continent, without any other connection, was so odd that we could only accept it as we did the sun and the rain.

He visited often, as he had in the past — perhaps more, now that there were so few people left around us. He always brought some edible gift of ham or rare wine, asparagus from his garden or a bottle of my favourite Greek ouzo, and always his fishing-rod. He went for black bass in the dams and filled my fridge with fish. As I had in Italy, I allocated to him a special sturdier chair on my verandah, since with his weight he flattened the delicate wicker chairs as an elephant would a basket. Despite his size, Carletto had the inner grace and measure of the great gentleman. I was fond of him, and in his warm bear hugs, which occasionally cracked the sunglasses hanging around my neck, and in his solid, loyal presence, I found comfort and peace. In some sense my company cured his loneliness.

The Douglas-Hamiltons, Carol Byrne and Sam unexpectedly came up for my birthday on 1 June. I had forgotten all about it — I had never made a fuss about my anniversary anyway. Usually it was Emanuele who went out with his horse or bike in the morning and brought back to my room an armful of flaming red wild lilies. Colin and Rocky drove up from the Centre with a few friends they had staying. At coffee time, while I sat at the fireplace sipping my citronelle, the generator beat slowed down and the room sank gradually into total darkness except for the candles and the fire. Looking up from its flame in which I had been lost in thought for a while, I realized that everyone else had left the room and I was alone. At that moment the door opened, and a procession filed in: they were each holding one or two candles, to total forty, and they were all singing 'Happy Birthday'.

Was I forty?

Forty is meant to be a key anniversary in a woman's life. I felt far from being old. On the contrary, an energy and drive practically unknown to me in younger days seemed to have taken over. My long walks had made me more fit than I had ever been. I felt supple in body and mind and, having come to terms with my destiny, I accepted the new challenges of my life. Together with the others, singing in the fluttering candlelight, were Simon the cook and Wanjiru, Kipiego and Rachel, the gardeners. Simon was carrying a cake in the shape of a heart, covered in red hibiscus. Emanuele's favourite pop music flew up to the roof, and I could still see him dancing on the cedar beams where Saba now stood alone, smiling down at me a small sad smile. Long blonde hair, oblique vivacious black eyes of unusual depth and beauty, I noticed she now looked much older than twelve. Her childhood had ended, I knew, when she had looked at the lifeless body of the young man she had worshipped. I remembered my first encounter with death as a teenager in Italy, and how deeply it had affected me and made me grow.

After breakfast next day I drove them to the old airstrip, and took photographs of them and Saba — Dudu was in England — loading their luggage, a sheep I had given them, and a box of avocados. Iain's little plane took off, buzzed over me as usual, its wings undulating in farewell. I stood with Sveva watching the plane fly away like a vulnerable bird carrying my friends over the dark gorges, and growing smaller and smaller as it disappeared over the escarpment and was lost in the clouds.

The time had come for me to go down to Nairobi, to face my house again. I had not yet been back since Ema's death.

The drive of my house in Gigiri looked empty, and the dogs Dada and Duncan, overwhelmed with joy, escorted the car, howling their happiness to see me after such a long absence. My old Kikuyu house servant, Bitu, whom I had not yet seen, came to shake my hand gravely, murmuring 'Pole,' and looking at me with wise impenetrable eyes. Many of his children had died, but many were left. I had had only one son. That was, for Africa, the greatest tragedy.

The house greeted me silently, waiting, like a church. Flowers fresh in the vases, a smell of turpentine and wax. A stack of obsolete daily newspapers. Many hand-delivered letters I did not stop to open. I went straight up to Emanuele's room and closed the door behind me.

237

I stood, back to the door, and looked around. A young man's room. Nothing had changed. Bookshelves filled with rows of neatly arranged books, the desk with papers and pens, a small photograph of a laughing girl − Ferina? − the typewriter, the stereo, the collection of minerals, his shell cabinets. The snake-skins.

I opened the cupboard: all those new suits we had had fun buying when we were together in Italy on our last holiday hung there useless. I caressed a blazer, trying to remember the last time he had worn it. One by one I opened all the drawers. His socks, his shirts, his shoes. On the bedside table were displayed the photographs he had loved and chosen: Paolo and a great black marlin; Paolo and the bull shark whose attack he had survived at Vuma; Sveva and a teddy-bear twice her size; a group of friends at school; a yacht in the Caribbean, and a good shot of Mario; a younger me in a white caftan, hugging the boy he had been; he in khaki shorts, surrounded by all the Security people down at the waterfalls of Maji ya Nyoka. A huge python striking, its stomach swollen by an undigested porcupine . . .

I sat on the bed. The linen had not been changed. I thought I could still distinguish the imprint of his head, smell the scent of his aftershave. I buried my face in the pillow.

Faintly, through the closed doors, I heard the noise of a car stopping in my drive. Hushed voices downstairs. Footsteps coming up the stairs two steps at a time, like Ema's had used to. Someone pausing just outside the door. A knock. My heart stopped. The handle turned and the door opened. I closed my eyes. A very tall figure filled the door.

It was Aidan. I looked at him through the distance of my grief. He wore long trousers, a tweed jacket. A pallor altered his sunburnt face. Tormented eyes bore straight into mine.

'Kuki,' he said in a husky whisper.

I stood up, uncertainly, still hugging the pillow as a shield. He took both my hands in his large rough ones, and kissed them. He pulled me slightly towards him and the wool of his lapel was rough against my tear-stained cheek.

238

I said nothing. There was nothing to say.

A turmoil of emotions, of contradictory feelings. The pain of being again back in the house. Emanuele's presence, gentle, intense and fading. Then, unexpected, Aidan. I felt confused and dizzy. The joy of his presence, of realizing he cared, took me by surprise. I had not had the time and courage to face how lonely I had truly been. An overwhelming temptation. To have a man again. To feel again loved, supported, protected, looked after. To share the cares and problems . . . but not at the expense of someone else's suffering, or of his peace of mind . . . too much, too difficult, and no longer for me. Emanuele's disappearance had been the moment of facing all truths. One could no longer play games. I was free and I was alone, and he was neither. If there was any decision to take, it could not be mine. I had never ceased to care for Aidan. Our relationship had been more than anything a meeting of souls without any ulterior motive. This purity had been its strength. There had never been the need or the intention to change its equilibrium, and this was not the moment for action. Only time could tell.

Aidan went, and from Emanuele's windows I watched his car going down my drive, out of the gate and down the road, for the first time in daylight since the beginning of our relationship.

I did not move from Emanuele's room all night, and I slept in his bed, surrounded by the memories of his childhood and interrupted youth, and by the essence of his loving spirit. I slept on his pillow wetted by my tears which refreshed the smell of his aftershave. And again I dreamt that same dream which had been haunting me for months now.

The boat floated on crystal-clear water so transparent I could distinguish every pebble, every shell on the bottom of pale turquoise, standing out in every detail as in a child's naive drawing. Only Emanuele and I were on board the small wooden craft, grown old and polished by many seasons of sun and seawater. Emanuele had been bitten by the same old viper and he was dying. Dressed in his khaki shorts as on that last morning, snake-tongs dangling from his waist, he was sprawled face up on the planks, eyes half closed, half staring. A disembodied voice – Colin's voice? – echoed and magnified vocally the reverberations of the sun on the ripples, saying unemotionally: 'The only remedy for snakebites is water. You must put him in the water.' His body was as heavy as dead stone, yet with the strength of despair I managed to lift it painfully and to push it out, inch by inch and pausing to rest, until I balanced it for a few seconds on the edge of the small boat. Then it rolled overboard as if in slow motion, touched the water and sank out of my reach. I watched him sink and I could not drag him back, his arms outstretched, legs out-stretched, and the ripples on the surface playing golden reflections on his sleeping face. He sank deeper and deeper, smaller and smaller, until he became one with the bottom of pebbles and the clear clean shells, and as green. My voice would not come out. Impotent, frustrated, and with all the weight of my renewed inadequacy, I watched him sink away into the unreachable.

'He will drown. I can't pull him out. He is too heavy. He is too far.' I ended the sentence in broken sobs.

'He is dead,' the voice out of the picture said. 'He is dead; there is nothing you can do.' At this moment, as always, I woke up. The telephone was ringing.

It was Iain. There was a strange hesitant note in his voice.

'Are you all right?' I asked him, suddenly awake.

'I am. So are Oria and Saba. It's the aeroplane. I am afraid I crashed it.'

On the top of the Kutua hills the engine had failed. There began what Oria described later as a 'silent fall'. Only Iain's excep-tionally cool head and his skill as a pilot saved their lives. He managed to spot an abandoned cattle *boma* in the thick bush, overgrown with shrubs and trees, and he crash-landed in the small clearing. The plane lost both wings. Saba was drenched in aviation fuel. He managed to call a 'M'aidez' which was received by a station standing by on the Laikipia Security network. Then the battery failed. They could see Jonathan Leakey's aeroplane –

alerted by radio, he had taken off immediately — circling, searching for them, but the wreck had been swallowed up by the luxuriant vegetation. They were invisible. It was only in the evening that a *moran* of the Gemps tribe found them, and ran to alert the village and the police. In typical Rocco–Douglas-Hamilton style they celebrated that night with the young warriors, feasting on the roasted lamb and avocado I had luckily given them. A police Land-Rover rescued them the next day, and drove them to Nairobi.

I immediately radio-called Colin to send our lorry down to fetch what was left of their plane, and they carried it off to their farm in Naivasha. That courageous little plane has lain there ever since, under a canvas on the lawn, like a crippled dragonfly, memento of past dreams and lost adventures.

37

Out of the Skies

On Man, on Nature, and on Human Life,
Musing in solitude.

William Wordsworth, Preface to *The Excursion*

Before Emanuele's death I had commuted between Nairobi and Laikipia because of his school. Sveva was not old enough to attend nursery school, so I could now stay on the ranch.

One day I received another letter from Aidan. It was the letter of a man torn apart by his obligations and it was of goodbye. In a postscript he noted: 'For as long as I live you will sit on my shoulder.'

I felt a desperate sense of loss, and, although I managed to write back saying that he could forever count on my friendship and on my understanding, I felt forlorn, and memories of our flying carpet and of the joy and depth of our encounters haunted me for a long time.

Emanuele's death had ended even this dream abruptly, but perhaps this was always meant to be.

The sun kept rising every day. Sveva grew beautiful. And my life went on. If fortune had for a time deserted me, my spirit, however, never failed me. It is really our last resort, our spirit. When everything seemed to be lost, when I was standing alone in the wind over my graves, I felt this was a unique time to raise my head and with my eyes look out again at Africa.

When I was a little girl of nine or ten, one evening while we were walking with the dogs my father told me, almost abruptly, 'The most important thing you can ever learn in life, Kuki, is to be able to be alone. Sooner or later the time will come when you will be alone with yourself. You must be able to cope and face your own company.' I have never known what had prompted my father to tell me this, but I have never forgotten it. Now was the time to prove it if I could, as I was now truly on my own. So I learnt to live and to think alone, in the weather of my own mind, and I discovered that I was not afraid, that I could accept whatever happened to me, and that in this I was lucky.

My friends visited often, and they mostly came out of the sky. There is a feeling of unbounded freedom and space in flying over Africa. In Kenya, flying in small aircraft is the natural way of getting around, and a popular one since the early days when roads were often non-existent and distances to be covered enormous. Private airstrips are common on farms and ranches, easy to build and to maintain with adequate farm machinery, and there are no complicated procedures to follow. Flying is not regarded as a luxury, but is accepted as an invaluable way of speeding communications, doing business and maintaining friendships. One can literally land in friends' paddocks and walk to their houses for a drink. One can have breakfast on the coast in Lamu, lunch in the Highlands of Laikipia, and dinner by Lake Turkana, a journey which could take weeks by car. It also guarantees speedy rescue in an emergency. From the flying doctors to most of the zoologists and ranchers in the Highlands, many people in Kenya fly their own aircraft: Wilson airport in Nairobi is the largest airfield for private aircraft in Africa. But our airstrip in Ol Ari Nyiro was twenty minutes' drive from Kuti. Emanuele had been hoping to get his pilot's licence, and we had planned another airstrip close to the house. I decided to carry out this plan and to build the new one almost at my doorstep, so that whoever landed could just walk home. There were other reasons for this. I never wanted to find myself again in the position of having to drive for help all those miles, as I had for Emanuele.

I went walking with Iain and Colin one day and chose the site, just outside the garden at Kuti. The old D6 Caterpillar came up in a clangour of chains and cut a scar through the bush from the hill below Kuti to the thatched huts of the labour lines. People came up to remove the largest rocks and roots by hand. The land was graded and flattened. Sveva and I planted grass seed, throwing it out of the back of a pick-up with much giggling. It would germinate with the rains. Now I had an airstrip at Kuti.

One day before the summer Richard Leakey flew me to Koobi-Fora, 'the Cradle of Mankind', where he regularly went to supervise the excavations and research on our early ancestors, carried out by the National Museums. 'You need to get away,' he said perceptively. 'Koobi-Fora will be good for you.' He was right. He picked me up at my new airstrip and we flew to Turkana.

I had always loved Lake Turkana. Its ancient emptiness fascinated me. A ceaseless hot dry wind blew from the endless silence of millennia. On the calm surface of the lake the sun set purple and indigo. We walked on the black volcanic sand which smelt of soda, where strange gigantic fishbones had been washed ashore from its mysterious depths. When we swam the water was warm, as if a continuous slow fire, burning underneath, made it simmer.

A splash, very close, rippled the surface. 'Just a crocodile,' grinned Richard, undisturbed. 'Don't worry. They are well fed.' Eyes protruding above the water level, these huge scaly reptiles spend their torpid uneventful lives as part of a larger scheme, fitting into the wise equilibrium of Nature.

Sitting on the open verandah of Richard's windswept cottage that night, sipping some excellent chilled wine, I felt cleansed and renewed by the majesty of the lake. The stark, undecorated simplicity of those rocks and bare shores was a contrast to the lush vegetation of Laikipia. It seemed as if we were at one with our ancestors, and I felt the wind of time blowing away my unresolved pains, blending them with the pains and sorrows of all the people who had trod the Earth, from their very beginning up here to this moment in my own history. The healing effect was what Richard felt it would be and I was grateful for his intuition.

On my return Laikipia looked greener, richer and fuller than I had ever experienced it. Up there I had faced my deepest nature: alone but not lonely, without excuses behind which to hide, I had again felt that I could well and fearlessly be in my own company. Slowly my open wound was forming a scar.

I started flying more often with Iain Douglas-Hamilton. Iain flew with total ease, very low, a glorious way of exploring the African bush. He may have taken risks, as some said, but I knew he could cope with competence and courage in any emergency. For me, flying with Iain was not just exciting, it was pure pleasure. Although his nonchalance about details was found alarming by some, I was totally confident in his ability to deal with any drama with nerves of steel and a cool head. He flew very low, scanning the contours of the terrain as if searching it with his eyes, so we could catch every detail of the animals we were trying to spot. You saw more from Iain's plane than from any other.

One weekend Iain was staying in Laikipia with a couple of friends and their children when on a cool morning, just after breakfast, our attention was attracted by some cries coming from the direction of the swimming-pool. There, behind the 'baby enclosure' I had built to prevent Sveva, who could not swim yet, from falling in, her small figure stood alone, calling 'Mamma'. Even from the distance I could see there was something strange about her looks, and her voice was weird. She was drenched in water. Overturning the chair where I had been sitting, and without stopping to apologize, I reached her in a few fast, desperate strides, Iain following. She was dressed in heavy overalls, socks and Wellington boots, and a sweater. She was soaked to the bone, her boots full of water, her clothes and hair dripping. I took her in my arms, and she was so heavy that I staggered under her weight.

Only then did she begin to cry. The story came through broken sobs while I undressed and dried her, and it left us all bewildered.

She had been playing with the other little girl, who had accidentally pushed her into the water; terrified by what she had done, instead of calling us she had run away to hide. Sveva had sunk straight to the bottom, her tiny body weighed down by all her heavy clothes, incapable of floating and unable yet to swim. And then?

'And then, Mamma, I opened my eyes under water and it was all blue and cold and I could see the white ladder, a bit far . . . I could not reach it . . . so I kicked my feet on the bottom and just managed to grasp it, and I climbed out . . . as Ema had taught me I should do if I ever fell in . . . like a frog. I am cold now, I am afraid . . . but there, I wasn't . . .'

We stayed speechless, looking down at her, a wet toddler of not yet three. I knew she could not swim at all . . . there was no explanation. I felt faint at the image of what would normally have happened . . . and had not. I started trembling with delayed shock. Iain seized my shoulders in his hands to steady me, shook me a little, looked deep into my eyes. 'Kuki,' he said slowly, trying to sound calm, 'Kuki, your daughter is going to live for ever, can't you see? She managed to swim out on her own – by God! – fully dressed from a deep pool at the age of two, before she has learnt even to float. I'll be damned . . . there are truly things science cannot explain.'

Sveva was unusually quiet all day long and so was I, unable to take in the implications of what could have happened. To distract us from this pensive mood, Iain flew us to Carletto's for the morning, Sveva wrapped in a blanket in my arms. Absentmindedly, I watched the shadow of the plane moving fast through the dry shrubs, scaring away warthogs down their holes, pink-necked ostriches trotting off, and zebra running in the dust a few feet below us.

In the early afternoon, the sun shining, I put Sveva into her swimming costume and went into our pool with her.

'Show me how you did it. Let's see if you can manage to do it again.' But she could not. Although practically naked and light, in the warm midday water, with my reassuring presence, she sank down and I had to grab her by her hair, spluttering wildly . . . in the morning, she had not even swallowed any water, she had not coughed . . . Iain and I looked at each other unbelieving, and to this day neither of us can explain what really had happened, what force benign, unknown, had saved her life.

Often, in the months and years to come, when at night she sometimes woke up because of a cough or a nightmare, by the time I reached her bedside I found her already quiet, soothed, and she told me that Emanuele had been there sitting with her, just as he used to do, and she was now consoled. When something uncanny happens, something beyond the parameters of what we call 'normal', when fantasy, memories and magic meet and disconcert us, we label it 'unbelievable' and dismiss it, since contemplating the unprovable makes us uneasy as if treading uncertain and insecure terrain. But such things do happen, and not to be able to explain how or why is only our limitation; our inability to understand is our problem, and does not affect their authenticity. The day Jack Block died and disappeared under water in a river in Chile, his boat, moored at the jetty of his farm in Naivasha, sank for no apparent reason. There is no question that Paolo knew he was going to die soon, and that when he died, before anyone told me, I instantly knew, and I grew pale, laid my cheeks upon my hands and cried in anguish.

There is a tune Sveva later took to whistling — I *cannot* whistle for the life of me, and she can, like a nightingale — the very tune Paolo whistled all the time. And when I ask her who taught it to her she naturally answers, 'Nobody. I just know it.' There is her left index finger: perfectly normal, lovely and flexible. But when she is concentrating, she curls it up and it becomes like Paolo's broken finger, the one he could not move after the first accident. We do not know how or why, but it remains a fact that she does.

A few days after the swimming-pool episode I heard one morning on our internal radio network that a dead leopard had been reported by a herdsman on the Sambara hill, close to Enghelesha. I drove there, and, with the young assistant manager and a couple of trackers, we went to look for the carcass. It was a rule in Laikipia never to leave a dead animal without trying to find the reason for its death. We left the car and proceeded on foot. It was further than we had thought. In the June sky, slate-grey clouds had started to gather and it looked heavy with imminent rain. Finally we found the bloated, stinking leopard below a combretum tree on the side of a hill. It was a young male, badly mauled, scratched and with signs of bites: possibly a fight with a stronger competitor for the favours of the same female. The skin was already damaged and the fur peeling off in tufts of matted hair: no chance of skinning it, and we decided to leave it there.

Just then, the first large warm drop of rain fell from the skies on my head, and thunder shook the earth. A cold wind began to blow in scattered gusts. Soon rain mixed with hail started falling, biting like icy needles into my bare arms and legs. There was no escape. The car was about five miles away. It was the first heavy shower of the long rains of 1983. It ran through the dry steep paths like a river, carrying twigs, leaves and branches, small dead birds, a grass snake, lost dung beetles, and in places reached up in muddy swirls from our ankles to our knees and hips. We could not seek refuge below the sparse trees for fear of lightning. The sky seemed to have descended on the Highlands like a grey lid of water, squashing us, drenching us to the bone. I think I have never been colder in my life. Often, white lightning zigzagged across the sky, closer than I dared to think, and thunder exploded in magnified rumbles. Wading through churning torrents in the billowing wind, we walked back to the car, and it took hours.

In those hours, through the blinding rain, deafened by thunder, scratched by thorns and branches, in the howling gale, a sort of catharsis took place in me, as if the storm had symbolically washed away the old clinging skin and the debris of the old searing pain.

When, with chattering teeth and wet hair, we finally reached the car and the assistant manager's house he lent me a pullover and one of his *kikois*. Towelling my hair and body dry in the bathroom with a rough towel, I looked at myself in the small rusty mirror, as I had not in weeks. Wet locks hung around my thin face. New grey showed through the blonde of my hair, and new deep lines marked the sides of my mouth. Yet my dark tanned skin was fresh and dewy. My grey-green eyes looked washed also, and bigger and clearer in my haggard face. My shoulderblades were showing, my hands with the short nails were slimmer, my arms thinner: I looked in an odd way much older and much younger.

Wrapped in clothes too big for me, barefoot, I crouched in front of the fireplace where a roaring fire of mutamayo had been built by the house servant, who now brought me a tray of strong sweet tea and slices of thick brown bread, just baked, with home-made farm butter. I ate as if for the first time in my life, ravenously, savouring every mouthful, as I had not in weeks, while slowly the warmth of the fire penetrated my bones and a sense of physical wellbeing pervaded me; I felt pleasantly drowsy, and fit. I think that was the best meal I have ever had in my life.

Outside, the storm had subsided, and night was falling fast. Someone came in with an unusual report: seventeen steers had been sheltering from the storm under a tree in the grass ley, lightning had struck the tree, and they had all been electrocuted. The young man went out to check, and I slowly drove the thirty kilometres to my house at Kuti, on the other side of the ranch. From the open car window came the song of life of a million frogs. The car kept sliding in the dark red mud, leaving new tracks, like a decoration on creamy chocolate fudge. Just before Kuti, green eyes shone in the car beams – a spotted body – and the live leopard, a dik-dik hanging from his mouth, was gone, swallowed by the night.

The beauty and privilege of being here, now, made me euphoric. On bare feet I walked to Emanuele's grave, and to his orange fire. My head on Paolo's tree, as on his shoulder, I sighed deeply, and the night air smelt new and good.

An idea was beginning to take shape in my mind, a positive,

triumphant idea to turn their irreversible end into a new beginning. It matured slowly, and it became my purpose. If Emanuele and Paolo were no longer here, the place, the animals and I still were, and so were the reasons for my choice.

Looking through Emanuele's things one day, I had come across a book Paolo had given him on his last birthday: that tragic, gruesome and yet prophetic book of Peter Beard, *The End of the Game*. Paraphrasing the famous piece 'Desiderata', Paolo had written:

> Emanuele, you are a Son of the Universe. No more, no less than a tree or a star or a stone. You have the right to be here. With all its Ends and putting out of the Fires, it is still a beautiful world for the one who can see a new beginning every time the sun sets on our Mukutan. Be careful. Be happy. I love you. Paolo.

There was a finality in these words, as in an epitaph, but I could now see in them a new meaning: like stones, like hills, like anything with shape in nature, we had the right to be here. Yet we did not have the right to pollute or to destroy the environment which surrounded us and which had an equal right to existence. In Emanuele's open, dead eyes I had seen reflected the sky and the trees he could see no longer. He had passed and gone ahead, but Nature survived as before, and in it we had to live and go on and be gentle.

This was the lesson in Emanuele's death. The love of his life had been his death: but it should not be also his end. If he had physically gone, his spirit lingered, and the place and I were still there. Like Paolo, Emanuele had been an idealist. He would have gone to university in the following September to read Zoology and Range Management, and would have come back one day with all the new ideas. He would have implemented his acquired skills on the ranch, combining innovative techniques with traditional knowledge and the principles in which he believed: keeping the balance between the wild and the tame, learning the secrets of Nature and applying them to its protection and balanced development.

I considered the future of Africa with its growing population of people, children of today in whose hands the destiny of Kenya will soon lie. Children brought up on the outskirts of the towns, where nothing wild had been left, their minds confused and polluted by alien religions, by poverty and lack of worthy goals. These children had never seen and been taught to appreciate the beauty of their country. The average urban African has never seen an elephant; how could these people make a policy which would enable them to protect the environment and at the same time ensure their survival? Was all the wilderness destined to disappear through lack of knowledge and planning? I certainly could not change everything, but I could not tolerate the thought of this happening to Ol Ari Nyiro.

The only solution was education, offering the chance of ex-periencing at first hand the land and traditions of their forebears and proving that one can and should coexist with the wild, in harmony . . . that one can, and should, learn how to utilize Nature without spoiling it, in fact protecting it at the same time. In Ol Ari Nyiro, we already had it all. The wildlife, the indigenous flora and the people and the domestic animals and the crops. We not only had the springs and the Mukutan stream, but also the man-made reservoirs; the well-graded roads, and the narrow paths made by generations of buffalo and antelope going to the water. The place was an oasis where animals were welcome, and where they found refuge, food, their ideal habitat. But the place was an operating ranch, with domestic stock, plantations and people on it. We had already proved that it could happen. We should try harder, do it better, become a model of how to achieve this goal.

The elephants walked here from the north along their ancient routes, which they had known and used since the beginning of elephants on Earth, but which were now increasingly interrupted by cultivated fields, mushrooming along their safari paths faster than they could possibly adapt to the change. Inevitably, they would not resist the temptation of ripe fields of maize, and they would forage on it as they would on the grasses and bushes which the maize had replaced. Although innocent, they would then be seen as destructive, branded as crop-raiders, shot on control: the rights of man would always win over the rights of the wild animals, unjust as this might be, unless a way could be found to combine the wild with the tame, and to plan a safe route for them to tread. Something needed to be done urgently to avoid the injustice of their gradual elimination.

The descendants of those first rhinos Delamere had met at the beginning of the century were still here, in Ol Ari Nyiro. But how many did we have? What was known of them? Why had they chosen this area as a refuge? What were they eating?

The people of the ranch still used the indigenous plants they gathered locally to cure a myriad of diseases: which plants? Which diseases? Why could we not find out more about them, learn these secrets from the old people who still remembered, and record them before it was too late? There was no end to what one could do to utilize the land as well as respect it. It was a matter of taking a step, several steps further, to get adequate help, and there was no reason why I should not succeed. I became determined to do all I could to make of Ol Ari Nyiro a unique example of how this ideal could be achieved. The ranch and its animals, wild and domestic, and its plants, cultivated and indigenous, and its people, living in a changing Africa but still remembering – just – their traditional skills, would be established as a living monument to the memory of the men I had loved. If the country and its nature and people could benefit from their deaths, they would have served a purpose.

There was the time when an aeroplane flew low over the house, and a friend emerged who had come especially from Italy to bring me a message. 'Enough is enough. You do not belong to this place. What more do you want to lose? Your friends are worried. Come back to Italy.'

I walked with him to the graves at the bottom of the garden: birds chirped on Paolo's tree; in its shade Emanuele's was already growing sturdily, as a young boy in the shelter and protection of

16. Alone with Gordon (far right)

17. Iain, Kuki and Sveva at the graves

18. Pokot dancers at Emanuele's rodeo

19. Kuki and Cheptosai Selale, the medicine woman

20. Kuki and her dogs

21. Breakfast, and Simon at Kuti

22

23

22. Sveva and rhino skulls

23. Rhino in thick bush at Ol Ari Nyiro

24. Kuki with Michael Werikhe, who raised funds for black rhino by walking through Europe and donated some money for their protection at Ol Ari Nyiro

25. Elephant rescue: Colin reviving a wounded elephant

26

27

26. Kuki: the ivory fire

27. Sveva: the ivory fire

28. Richard Leakey at Kuti

29. Kuki with a baby rhino

30. Kuki, Sveva and Rastus in the garden at Kuti

his father's love. Two red hibiscus had been laid on the graves by Sveva and by me, as happened every day. I stood there in the peaceful shade and looked at my friend. The life of town and business had not been kind to him. Deep wrinkles lined his face and he had the hurried look of people who have no time to stop and listen to their inner voice, and care for things wild and free.

'I have buried them here because here is home,' I said gently. 'I have planted two African trees because one day their bodies will be transformed into them. I have decided to stay on and to make a success of it; otherwise all these lessons would be wasted on me. I am here to stay. You are kind, and I appreciate your concern, and I thank you. But I will not come back to live in Italy, I will not escape and give up. I am in Kenya to stay, but I must earn this privilege.'

Making up my mind about this had given me a new feeling of clarity and serenity. A peace descended which I had never experienced before, and with it a determination to succeed in my new life and a strength I did not know I possessed.

38

A New Foundation

The real voyage of discovery does not consist in seeking new landscapes, but in having new eyes.

Marcel Proust, *À la Recherche du temps perdu*

The first people with whom I shared my idea were Oria and Iain. They had flown up from Naivasha and spent the night.

In the morning we went for an early walk to Paolo's Dam. The first rain had washed the air of the memory of old dusts. Slipping in the mud which bore the tracks of last night's animals, we circled the twin dams below Kuti hill and looked down at the peaceful, majestic expanse of the ranch.

A wilderness to protect. Overcome by a special mood, we came back in silence, reached the garden through the back road where it appears unexpectedly through the bush in a surprise of flowers and green lawns, and walked straight to the graves. Paolo's tree was strong and healthy. Emanuele's was producing new buds, and everything smelt fresh and new. There, with Sveva in my arms and my dogs around me, I told my friends that I had decided to dedicate my life to the ideal of the coexistence in harmony of mankind and the environment and that I wanted to create in Ol Ari Nyiro, in memory of Paolo and Ema, an example of how this goal could be achieved. I asked for their help. We embraced.

The Gallmann Memorial Foundation was born that morning.

*

I left for Europe in the summer. Emanuele had died only a few months before. It felt as if he had been gone forever.

His room in Laikipia was now closed. I had moved, changed nothing. His books, his clothes, the snakeskins stretched on the walls, the snake instruments in a neat row, the jacket as he had left it, slung on the back of his chair. Everything in his room seemed waiting for his return at any moment, and I had been unable to touch anything. It felt as if he had never left at all.

Every day, three times a day, a red hibiscus was put at the head of the table where his place had been.

Every night a fire was lit at the graves, and its light could be seen from far away on the ranch. It kept away the animals — mainly elephant, who are so fond of yellow fever trees — and I felt there was a symbolic meaning in the flame which burned night after night. Looking after a fire is in a way like looking after a plant; it needs care, constancy and dedication, a sort of love. There is something ancient and unchangeable in a fire, as in the waves of the sea, or the current flowing in a river, or the restlessness in the wind. Their mutable shape and constant movement forever changes, and therefore is forever the same. Every fire is the same fire. Every wave is the same. Today's wind is millions of years old.

Before leaving Kenya, I spoke of my plans with a number of close friends who, I hoped, could help.

The first was Richard Leakey. He drove up to my house from the Museum, and we sat in my study with the Venetian wallpaper I had bought at an auction years before. There, surrounded by Venice as if for comfort, I told him about my vision. He listened quietly.

'I have the idea. I have the place. I need the people. I need your help.'

'You have it,' said Richard. He never wasted words. 'What you want to achieve is valuable. Just take your time. Do not rush into things. Be sure of what you want. I will support you'. He meant it. Richard suggested I should get in touch with Maurice Strong, a friend of his. This, he said, was exactly the sort of thing he would be interested in helping with. I had never met Maurice Strong, although I knew of his extraordinary achievements in the United Nations and in the environmental world. I spoke next to Tubby Block, the friend from the early days. He was also very supportive. At the end of our conversation he said, 'You ought to meet Maurice Strong. I will write to him.' I was struck that both Tubby and Richard, so different in interests, character and background, should suggest the same person. My curiosity to meet this man was stimulated instantly.

I said goodbye to my dogs as if I were leaving for a crusade. Last time, Emanuele and I had been together in Europe. We had met in Rome. He was coming from a sailing holiday in Greece with Mario, and I from Venice with Wanjiru and Sveva. We were all to fly to Sardinia, where we would stay with friends. He had come through the crowd of passengers from the Athens plane, and I saw him first. He carried a blue bag on his shoulder and wore a new sailor cap on his head, and he walked easily, long legs in jeans, handsome and distant behind the thick glass of the Arrivals area. He could not see me and he could not hear. For long moments he had seemed unreachable, I had feared the crowd would swallow him, and I unreasonably panicked, barely over-coming the urge to bang on the glass to attract his attention. Then he had turned his head and discovered us, a smile had transformed his face, Sveva had waved delightedly, and the fear had dissolved.

Europe was grey, hot, crowded with the aimless, weary tourists of August.

I wanted to visit people in various countries, to feel how my idea would be received by those who did not know me and would therefore not be emotionally biased in their judgement. In London, I stayed with Aino and Tubby Block, while Sveva and Wanjiru remained with my mother in Italy.

There were days when I felt I could not cope with the world. I remember one morning when I was not capable of leaving my room, and cherries and champagne were brought and left outside my door by Anthony, Aino's son, who had been a friend of Ema. He was young and he was kind. I had known him since he was a child, and in him – as in any young man – I had started to see the reflection of Emanuele. The cherries remained uneaten and the champagne lost its sparkle, and I stayed quiet in bed until night came, listening with closed eyes to the echo of my memories, knowing that my friends would forgive me.

There were nights when I was haunted by nightmares and woke up bewildered in the tousled darkness of my bed of pains, clinging miserably to the wild illusion that the impossible miracle had happened, and Emanuele was alive, and well, and still with me. Then in the shaded light of the bedside table I met his eyes, enigmatic and unblinking from the photograph in the silver frame. The alien humming noise of London filtered in through the curtained windows, and the reality of his eternal silence crushed me yet again.

I longed to be in Laikipia, listen to the birds, walk with the dogs, get lost in the valleys, sit at the graves, let the wind of the Highlands dry my tears with its wise, gentle hands. But there were things to be done, and this was the time to do them.

I left for Zürich, to meet a lawyer who had been recommended to me as the ideal person to help in setting up my memorial. The plane was crowded with unknown people. Head against the window, I looked down at the snowy peaks of the Alps. I felt suddenly drained and lonely, going to meet a stranger to tell him about a dream, a story of people he had not met, of a place he had not seen, and of my desperate desire to make out of my personal anguish, of which he knew nothing, something positive, lasting, worthwhile.

Meeting the lawyer, Hans Hüssy, was a pleasant surprise. His office was in an old house set in a garden of trees by the lake. The large rooms, with ancient stucco and carved stone fireplaces, were in attractive contrast with the modern and ethnic sculptures and paintings. He quoted for me the words of Chief Seattle to the

Americans who wanted to buy the land from the Indians. They were words which I believed and experienced as true: 'How can you buy or sell the sky and the warmth of the land? . . . if we do not own the freshness of the breeze and the reflections of the water, how can you buy them?'

We discussed my plans, and he undertook to take the necessary steps to formalize them legally. It was a major practical step forward.

I was encouraged by the response of everyone, especially my friends. Iain agreed to serve as Chairman of the Scientific Advisory Committee whose task it was to establish the research priorities, and to advise and help to implement them. Richard and Tubby had each contacted Maurice Strong separately, and to my amazement a letter came back to Tubby which said, *'. . . tell Mrs Gallmann I will be delighted to help her in her courageous and unusual tribute and I look forward to meeting her.'*

I met Maurice first in Nairobi, some time after my return. Richard had given me a copy of an international magazine with an article about him. It described a sort of wizard, an inspired and farsighted environmentalist with a knack for business, an uncanny perceptivity, and the idealistic drive and persistence of all true leaders and innovators. On the cover of the magazine, an ordinary-looking man with a small moustache, in a grey suit, emerged from a taxi, carrying a briefcase.

Tubby had asked me to lunch at the Norfolk, to introduce me to him. I arrived early and waited in the lounge, looking at the continuous string of cars stopping at the entrance to deliver businessmen and tourists. From a taxi like any other emerged an ordinary-looking man dressed in grey, with a small moustache, carrying a briefcase; so identical to the photograph that I almost burst out laughing. He looked around, and his eyes focused on me, instantly singling me out of the crowd. They were eyes which missed nothing: vividly intelligent, acute and mischievous, yet with an unusual depth of concentration.

'Mr Strong, I presume?' I could not resist it.

'Mrs Gallmann.' The eyes twinkled. 'I am glad Tubby is late, so we can get to know each other.'

Maurice had a way of putting people immediately at ease, and his questions were never futile. I was amused to hear him say that, like me, he had been extremely intrigued by the fact that friends as different as Tubby and Richard could recommend me for the same reason at the same time. Maurice had a wealth of interests, an unexpected spirituality and a knowledge of Eastern thought; we ended up talking about everything from nature conservation to life and death. It felt as if I had known him for ever. Like Richard, Maurice in time agreed to join the Foundation as a trustee.

It was Richard who one day flew an important visitor up to Laikipia. The aeroplane stopped on my strip and I went to meet the guests with Sveva and the dogs. Like a magician with his bag of tricks, this time Richard had flown up Prince Bernhard of The Netherlands. He wore green khakis, a beret studded with pins portraying all sorts of animals, a glint in his eyes and a smile on his mouth. Few people, I think, have more stamina than this gallant gentleman who has dedicated his life and most of his time to the wildlife cause. Tirelessly he travels the world, to bring to heads of state and conservationists worldwide his message for the protection and survival of the wildlife on this planet.

He jumped out of the aeroplane like a young man. There was a great kindness about him, and he was touched by the story of the loss of my son so soon after my husband. He was fascinated by the beauty and freedom of Laikipia, and the possibilities that the place offered for the protection of the animals and flora. We discussed much of what I hoped to achieve in Ol Ari Nyiro, and he took an immediate interest in my cause.

Prince Bernhard loved walking in the bush and stalking rhino and elephant. He had a passion for cigars, pink champagne and Mexican music, and once he told me with a grin that he had chosen for his funeral the tunes 'Paloma' and 'Boca de oro', which the Royal Band in Holland had to practise regularly in preparation for this – hopefully distant – occasion. He spent much of his spare time doing the most complicated crosswords in Dutch as a form of 'mental gymnastics', which obviously worked, as he carried his years with grace and his mind was sharp and lively.

After this first visit several more followed, and in the course of the years Prince Bernhard supported and helped the Foundation generously in many ways. Finally, to my eternal gratitude, he agreed to become its first Patron.

When the Foundation was finally registered in Zürich and I received all the official documents, I felt a great sense of achievement. It was time to start on our first project. It had to be significant, and it had to succeed.

Ol Ari Nyiro was already well known for its abundance of wildlife and for our concentration of black rhino. We also had a unique record of zero poaching, thanks to our Security. I discovered to my surprise that there had been very few studies of these endangered and shy pachyderms. Iain suggested that the first project for the Foundation ought to be the monitoring, conservation and ecology of our elusive black rhino, which still survived undisturbed in the gorges as they had since their beginnings on Earth.

With the help of Jim Else, an American scientist working with the Museum, and Colin's contribution, Iain wrote up the project proposal. We had to discover how many rhinos there were in Ol Ari Nyiro and how they interrelated; what their chosen browses were in their natural habitat, and what we had to learn about their ecology and habits in order to be able to protect them. This knowledge would help the various rhino sanctuaries that the government was planning to set up around the country. Once the proposal was ready, we decided to contact the Zoological Society of London to see if there was a young scientist who could take over the project and be responsible for training Kenyans in the same skills, since education was an integral part of the Foundation's programme.

From the suggested names, we chose Rob Brett, an Oxford graduate in Zoology who had Kenyan experience as well as an impressive CV. He had spent two years in Tsavo studying the elusive naked mole rats for his Ph.D. An intelligent and competent young man, with a ready wit and pleasant manners, Rob Brett fitted immediately into Ol Ari Nyiro's community and life. I established a simple camp for him, the core of which became, over the years, the GMF Research Camp, and to which we gradually added facilities and extensions. It was planned that Rob would spend four years in Ol Ari Nyiro. Helped by our Security people, and with Iain's and Colin's advice, Rob set out to count our mysterious rhinos. The bush is extremely thick in Ol Ari Nyiro, and rhino are generally solitary, with the exception of mothers and calves, or females and courting males. Iain theorized that rhino footprints, like our fingerprints, differ for individual animals: Rob perfected and refined the technique, and identified forty-seven black rhino in Ol Ari Nyiro. This made our population of natural rhino the largest known in East Africa outside National Parks. But they needed our protection.

After the sale of Ol Morani and Colobus for settlement, and the increased price of and demand for ivory, what had been a rare occurrence now became more and more frequent: animals wounded or with snares made of wire embedded in their flesh started finding refuge in Ol Ari Nyiro.

Our askaris and cattlemen kept reporting buffalo, eland, in one case a giraffe, and mostly elephant, limping and aggressive, with suppurating wounds, spears hanging from their sides, or snares in their legs.

One day one of our Turkana herders was gored to death by an infuriated elephant which, the day before, had killed two heifers and next day killed Kijana, a fierce bay stallion Emanuele had loved to ride. The herder's name was Loyamuk, the same half-blind old man after whom Emanuele had named his one-eyed favourite sand snake. The idea of a mad elephant crashing through the bush with enough speed and fury to catch up with a galloping horse was horrendous. Colin went out to find him, was charged by the screaming bull and had to run for his life. The elephant left a trail of rotten pus behind him: reluctantly, Colin shot him. The tusks were still covered in dry blood. His upper trunk was hideously swollen, broken and gangrenous. Embedded in it was a bullet.

A young elephant crippled by a snare was sighted soon after. Snares, like traps, are the most vile and cowardly way of catching game. Made of heavy wire, twisted often three, four times or more, they are set along the beaten paths animals use to go to water or salt licks. The smaller ones, like dik-dik or impala, or even bushbuck, remain imprisoned, unable to disentangle themselves, defenceless and trembling in terror until their captors come to kill them. Leopard have been known to bite off a leg or foot to get away. Larger and stronger animals, like buffalo and elephant, usually manage to rip off the metal wire, but the noose, tightened in the desperate struggle, remains deep in the flesh and cripples them, cutting off the blood supply. The limping animal becomes weaker and weaker as the wound becomes infected and the leg swells. Soon the herd will abandon him to his fate. Unable to run, debilitated by lack of food, he will then become an easy victim for any predator, from man to lion. The vultures will discover him and will patiently gather on nearby trees, waiting their turn. This unnecessary suffering is intolerably tragic and gruesome.

For this young elephant we managed to get hold of Dieter Rottcher, a veterinary surgeon with a passion for the wilderness and tremendous experience in immobilizing wildlife in the bush. The elephant was darted, injected with antibiotic, and the snare was removed. Colin assisted him, and after a series of similar successful operations he learned and mastered this complicated technique, which requires the accurate aim, courage and bushcraft of the hunter and the medical training of a competent vet. We finally managed to acquire our own darting equipment, and I gave Colin *carte blanche* to take time out from his ranch duties, whenever necessary, to pursue the task of rescuing wounded and maimed elephants which were reported more and more frequently, even in our neighbourhood. It seemed a different era from that time up in the north frontier when he and Paolo, like most men in Africa, were hunting the same animals we were all now trying to save.

At about that time the Head of our Security, Luka Kiriongi, had been honoured with the David Sheldrick Award which went each year to a Kenyan who had performed extraordinary services for the conservation of wildlife. We went to State House, where President Moi presented Luka with the Award and a substantial cheque. Straight and proud, dressed in his best uniform, saluting smartly while cameras clicked, Luka looked even taller. Thanks to our Security efforts, no elephant or rhino had been poached in Ol Ari Nyiro for years.

In Ol Ari Nyiro, thanks to the careful protection of the environment, the indigenous plants were still there, and the climate and terrain difference between the top of the hills and the bottom of the Mukutan Gorge allowed for an amazing variety of flora.

The rains have come to Laikipia, and it is an awakening. No seed is ever lost, no root sterile, in Africa. Dormant life sprouts again. Grass seems to grow greener overnight. New buds and fresh shoots appear on apparently dead old wood and dry grey branches. Between rocks, on barren tracks, extraordinary lilies bloom, pink and fleshy, and the light balls of fire of the aemantus, like bright red pompons, beckon in the breeze. Gigantic mushrooms break the hard crust of the termite hills. Termites swarm in their nuptial flight, quivering in millions, like golden snow. With this bounty, animals seem to go wild with the pleasure of partaking in this gigantic banquet. Well fed, with lustrous coats, the antelope and buffalo contentedly chew their cud. Fat elephant and healthy giraffe reach up to feed on the tender new leaves of the upper branches of the acacia, white or yellow with powdery round flowers. The weaverbirds are busy building their nests with the new blades of grass. The air is balmy with the heady perfume of jasmine and mimosa, and the carissa bushes are frothy with clusters of white flowers. The surprise and wonder of the abundance of luxuriant vegetation is renewed every rainy season.

For years I had noticed that our people in Ol Ari Nyiro went out to gather a variety of plants, berries and fruit, wild spinach and twisted roots, which they brought home to cook. Most were delicious, with a tangy unpolluted flavour. People used strange seeds and pods, and the bark of trees, for medicine. In most of their homeland and in native villages these plants are now disappearing, owing to ploughing and the planting of foreign crops, weedkillers, and over-grazing.

I became very interested in the traditional use of herbal remedies, and felt that to record this precious and vanishing knowledge, to discover and use these plants, would be a useful study for the Foundation. I found out that the recognized expert in herbal medicine in our area was a very old Pokot woman, the mother of Langeta, a man we employed to check on the Pokot boundary. I decided to go and find her, to see if she was prepared to share her knowledge and co-operate in a project on ethnobotany, the traditional tribal use of indigenous plants.

I found her sitting outside her hut, children and goats playing around, and in her old eyes an unreachable wisdom. When she saw me she stood up, surrounded by small children, covered with flies, in the red dust and litter and dung of the little yard. Many brass rings, discoloured by age, dangled from the elongated lobes and sides of her ears. Rows of brown bead necklaces encircled her neck. Her skull was shaven along the sides in the traditional way, leaving a crown of long curly hair in tight ringlets like a mane on the top of her head.

I had met her before. She had come with the group of young Nditus and warriors clad in black, walking miles in the hot sun of noon. The dust which their marching feet sent up could be seen in the distance, and their safari song heard high above the treetops. The strong smell of wood-ash, curdled milk, smoke and sweat had been as dense in the still air as the odour of the herds of buffalo, and as recognizable. Like all the rest of them she had danced in the sun of noon, and in the windy night by the light of the fires. She had danced as if time did not matter.

Her name, I now discovered, was Cheptosai Selale.

A small, wizened old woman of the tribe of Pokot, she is the only remaining recognized shaman left in our area. When she dies — and many seasons have added wrinkles to her skin and sapience to her old greenish eyes — all her knowledge will die with her. I went determined, with patience and gentleness, to enlist her help in finding and recording the precious plants whose secrets she had mastered.

I brought her a gift of sugar and tea, soap and salt. I could not find tobacco, but on meeting her I guessed she would seek in her herbs and roots any such remedy for herself.

I remembered Paolo and the special relationship he had had with the *wazee* of Pokot, and the powerful medicine they had shared with him. I told her I respected and recognized her knowledge, and that I felt it was too valuable to lose. For all the time of our meeting she stood there, small and proud, listening to her son interpreting. She could speak little Swahili and mostly answered in Pokot, and her eyes never left mine; I read in them something powerful and unique. I understood that, before it is too late, we must have the humbleness and the wisdom to ask such people to teach us. We must shed this self-imposed blindness, which veils our perceptions — our peripheral life at the surface — and go down to our core, the source of all things, which we all share.

It was the strangest thing to feel this communication with her, a fund of buried common knowledge, a deep recognition, as of two beings who had shared the same vision and perhaps the same wisdom, almost as if I too had been a medicine woman in another life, and as if she knew this well.

Not once did she blink, yet she was not staring. Without her eyes ever leaving mine, at the end she just nodded. I offered my hand and she took it in hers without shaking it. Her hand was dry and hot, like a stone in the sun.

For the first time betraying any emotion, her face broke into a toothless grin, and I just smiled back: nothing more was needed, and I knew she would help.

I drove back in an elated mood. Suddenly the sky of Africa was more than ever my sky, more than ever I felt rooted in the old dust of the red murram tracks ... in the smell of sage from the tall leleshwa mixed with jasmine and elephant dung and hot dust and fire, which is Laikipia's smell.

A few months after this meeting, our project on ethnobotany began and progressed with great success, in partnership with the Herbarium, and with the invaluable help of Cheptosai Selale.

If in the beginning I had dealt more with men, I now gradually discovered the women of Ol Ari Nyiro. In Africa rural women seldom get a chance to come out of their shells. In their native villages they till the fields and tend the small herds of domestic animals. On a ranch where the men are employed and there is no land for them to plant, they are confined with the children, dependent on their husbands, and with nothing more than the mere chores of survival to stimulate their lives. They rise with the sun and sleep with the moon. They gather wood which they carry in enormous tidy bundles on their bent, supple backs, to build a fire inside their dark huts which become saturated with dense eye-stinging smoke. The huts are safe and hot like dens, but the temperature drops outside, giving children dangerous chills: chest congestion and pneumonia are among the most common diseases. In the old days in the villages the women would still make utensils and ornaments out of the natural materials gathered in the forests, skins of animals, wood and roots and wild coloured seeds, oddly shaped gourds, and with the trade-beads peddlers used to barter for game trophies and goatskins.

Now the traders do not come any more, and at the weekly market in the village they sell no beads, but garish nylon garments, plastic basins and tin mugs for tea. The skill of making cleverly decorated utensils out of any material available is disappearing fast.

I noticed the amount of empty time the women spent looking into the distance, sitting with children around their huts, waiting for the time to cook their maize meal and vegetables. I discovered that they were keen to do something to occupy their days, and I provided them with beads and cottons, wool and skins, leaving them free to show me what they could produce. I was surprised by the quality and skill, the ingenuity, the meticulous care and the imagination they brought to this task. Blankets and lace, wall-hangings and belts, necklaces and earrings, delicate and exotic, appeared as by magic from their worn, clever hands. With care and patience, a small thriving Art and Craft Centre gradually began in Ol Ari Nyiro, and it was a true satisfaction for me to see the pride and enthusiasm the women put into their work; the proceeds gave them money of their own, and helped them to make their lives better and more fulfilled. There seemed to be no end to what one could find in the cornucopia of Africa.

The Gallmann Memorial Foundation was now firmly established and we needed a logo. It had to be the emblem of the memorial and it had to be evocative of Africa. I felt the two acacias, one small and one bigger, growing on Emanuele's and Paolo's graves were ideal. Our friends and I knew their meaning, and to strangers they symbolized the quintessential African tree. I asked Davina Dobie, the artist and friend who had painted the flight of seagulls in Sveva's nursery, to portray the trees for the logo. She spent a week in Laikipia, and did a sensitive job of love and artistry.

A larger and a smaller tree growing close together, their branches touching.

39

Robin

Biondo era, e bello, e di gentile aspetto . . .[*]

Dante Alighieri, *La Divina Commedia*

One evening soon after my return from Europe a car stopped in my Nairobi drive. From the door I watched a pair of legs in jeans run down the steps. Slim young legs, safari boots, a spring to the walk, and for an instant, crazily, I thought of Ema. A blue shirt, dark skin, straight fair hair almost bleached to silver, merry blue eyes under bushy blond eyebrows, an elfish smile of full sensuous lips turned up at the corners, brightening a good-looking boyish face: and there was Robin, whom I had not seen in years.

Now he came in from the dark of a night which looked so much like any other, to my lit lounge with the candles and the fire, and sat smiling on my white sofa, legs stretched out on the carpet, as if he had always belonged. He listened intently to my story, and time passed as I told once again of my pain and my sorrow and of the new-found sense of purpose and re-birth. He then spoke easily about his own life, and it was a pleasure for me just to sit there listening, letting my cares slide off like running water.

Robin had been born in Kenya of an English father and a

---

*'He was fair and handsome, with a gentle countenance . . .'

Norwegian mother. His father had been a Wing Commander. His mother came from colourful ancestors who had left the luminescent north of Europe to live in Cuba, Mozambique and finally Kenya, where they became prominent coffee-planters. She herself was born on a ship in Madeira Harbour. She had met the dashing Wing Commander during the war, and he had once smuggled her – and a grand piano – to Cyprus from Nairobi for a party. They were married soon after, and have been devoted to each other ever since.

From his mother Robin inherited an uncommon love and understanding of animals. She – like Robin – was always surrounded by a bizarre assortment of pets; turtles and dogs, cockerels and cats, bushbabies and ducks, and talking parrots.

There was a lightness about Robin. As a new-born baby he had been very sick with blood poisoning, and the doctors at Gertrude's Garden Pediatric Clinic advised the parents just to go home and let him die. He unexpectedly survived, and for years he remained thin and pale and faintly ghost-like, to bloom, in his later teens, into an unusually attractive young man. An engineer by training, versatile with anything to do with water, machinery and engines, when I met him Robin was working on films, mainly in the art, construction, or special effects departments.

There are people who walk in gloom, and others who walk in sunshine. Robin was one of the these. There was a positive aura about him, a cheerful, pleasant disposition, as if he could cope with whatever happened and could tackle any problem with a light heart.

After that first evening, he came back the next day, and the day after. To my surprise, he admitted that for years he had regarded me as his ideal woman; but I was married to a man he liked and respected. He himself was going through a short and unlucky marriage, and he was nine years younger. He told me that my eulogy to Emanuele had affected him deeply and had made him feel he wanted to meet me again.

Since Emanuele's death I had nursed the desire to go away one day to a beautiful unknown place with a beautiful person, gentle of soul and understanding — man or woman, it did not matter — and in the new and pure landscape relax and let all memories come and go as they would. I felt Robin would be the ideal person for this, and I confided in him, getting an immediate, positive response. He brought me to a place where I had never been, close to Lake Magadi, and it was a times of perfect magic and mutual discovery. The weather changed many times in only a few hours, from rain to sun to wind to clouds. We watched sacred ibis fish with fluid movements, their reflection in the water of the salt lake as vivid as their real image. We drove back bewitched, holding hands like teenagers. Our relationship was no longer platonic and soon after, as he had moved from Malindi to his parents' house in Muthaiga because of his work, I invited Robin to come and live with me.

Apart from my husbands, I had never lived with a man. We shared days and nights. We laughed. Again the house echoed with a man's voice. Men's clothes hung in the wardrobe and his car was parked in our drive. Robin helped me to exorcize some of the shadows which had been haunting me, and which I had not dared to face. Since Paolo's death I had wanted to visit the place of the accident, where he had died. Yet up to now I had been incapable of driving again on that road, heavy with traffic and, for me, pregnant with memories of my own. I asked Robin to go with me.

I gathered some gardenias, and one morning he drove me down the Mombasa road. The place was called Hunter's Lodge, after a famous professional hunter, and was now a hotel. We often used to stop for refreshment at the Lodge on our way from the coast, and I knew it well.

He parked the car at the side of the road, and I got out. I looked up and around, trying to guess what Paolo had seen last: a row of gum trees, the sign of the petrol station, the mutating clouds of Africa. I searched the tarmac for marks of brakes on the smooth grey surface, but the weather had obliterated them long ago. Where was the exact spot? Would the people working there remember? No point. The attendants at the petrol station would certainly be new ones. It did not matter.

I found a place where the grass seemed to grow greener, and some wildflowers bloomed naturally on their own. I closed my ears to the noise of the passing traffic, and my eyes to the curious glances of passers-by. From the speakers in Robin's car the music of Boccherini floated out, loud and evocative. I arranged my gardenias on the grass. Silence descended on my soul in peaceful layers, while Robin stood by me, quietly supportive, respecting my healing tears of remembrance.

Sveva was three at the time. She missed Emanuele and the crowd of his young friends of whom she had been the mascot, and Robin's presence and attention filled her unexpressed yearning. At the ranch, he rode out carrying her in front of him on his motorbike, with me on the back. The air smelt of resin, buffalo and things growing, and elephants often crossed the road a few metres ahead, shaking their heads at us and getting on tranquilly with their elephantine life. Laikipia stretched around us in its intact beauty and I felt young and carefree. Sveva laughed, shaking her blonde hair in the wind. Robin was what we both needed at that time in our lives. The dogs ran after us, fighting playfully, barking at every dik-dik, chasing hares in clouds of red dust.

One night Gordon followed my car, and we did not notice he was missing until next day. When we found him he was stuck in the mud in Ngobithu's Dam, unable to move. He had been there all night. His warm, loving eyes looked at me in acceptance of his fate, with an expression of desperate devotion which haunted me for weeks. Robin drove him straight to the vet in Nairobi, but his kidneys and his battered brave heart could not stand the strain. As soon as the car disappeared along my drive through the avenue of candelabra and I turned to go back inside, with a lump in my throat I noticed that Emanuele's dog, Angus, who since his death had gone to live with Mapengo and followed him everywhere, had materialized again on my verandah. He sat across the passage in Gordon's place; he had taken over the leadership of our pack of Alsatians. I knew from this that Gordon would not survive.

When Robin passed me the news on the Laikipia Security network that night, I cried for my old friend and for another severed link with the past. Robin brought him back to Laikipia, taking a day off filming, and we buried him close to the graves in the shade of the bush where he used to watch over me when I sat in remembrance. On his grave I planted little yellow flowers.

There was a serenity, a positive attitude about Robin, and it became my cure. To the delight of my friends, who adopted him immediately, in his love I bloomed. In his company I felt freer and happier than I had been in months. In the chaos of my psychological life, he was a steadying and positive factor, and he helped me to come to terms with my solitude. I slipped into a period of sunlit happiness, and of intense physical well-being which lasted for a long time. Our relationship was to continue for years, and eventually, when our paths gently moved apart, it evolved into a deep friendship made of love, memories and total mutual trust, which is precious to me and which I shall for ever treasure.

Through Robin I had my first inside contact with the strange world of make-believe of cinema. Seeing people playing the game of films and reproducing reality helped me to come to terms with the real part I had been given to play in life. It was a weird world, where nothing was what it appeared to be. In its novelty, fantasy and absurdity I found distraction and solace for my true pains. I often visited Robin on location with Sveva.

During the filming of *Out of Africa* I joined him on the coast. A yellow Gypsy Moth biplane had been especially flown from England for the film, a shiny jewel of a flying-machine, unexpectedly sturdy, which could land and take off practically anywhere. In this case it had to land on the beach, and once they let me fly in it. It was like flying in a romantic time-machine. As light as the moth whose name it bore, the yellow biplane took off from the thin strip of deserted beach left clear by the receding tide, guarded by scraggy dunes and fringed with palm trees, which had been fenced off so that seaweeds could still draw their characteristic natural patterns on the shore and the mob of tourist feet would not interrupt the smoothness of the sand.

Robin, carrying Sveva on his shoulders, a blonde four years old in a white caftan, waved up to me, smiling. We circled high over a choppy sea rippled by the monsoon, the plane surged agile in the stormy sky into the wind which blew in my hair through the open cockpit; I wanted to scream with pleasure. In a moment one overtook the boundaries of time and space, and I passed from the silence and natural rhythms of the sea as it used to be, to the upturned faces of strangers, buoys and outboard engines, and from the past to the present, in a few seconds. When we landed again to the sudden quiet and stillness of the beach left only to the mercy of nature, the impact was almost physical. I emerged from the plane with the dizziness of one who has travelled seventy years in a few minutes. The inadequacy of our conception of time hit me once again, positively, ripping through the limiting certainty that we know everything and that time and space must conform to our rules. I clearly saw that time, as we perceive it, is man-made, tied precariously to this dimension, and so is the boundary of death. 'As sure as the sand, it is written, we shall be together again,' Emanuele had written in his diary one 19 March, Paolo's death anniversary. It was true, and it was a wonderful feeling.

With Robin's help, my wound was healing.

40

Sveva: A Child of Africa

'Paulo' — said Mirimuk — 'Paulo ni mama mzee.'

At the end of the passage past my bedroom at Kuti, Emanuele's room was still locked. Strange rustles were heard at night, and I suspected that bats and mice had started to nest in it undisturbed. Emanuele had been tidy and I knew he would not have liked to see his things messed up and ruined, but I had felt any intrusion as a profanation of a precious relic. It was Robin's healthy influence which helped me to dispel many ghosts, and one day I decided the time had come to open that room again.

What triggered this action was the fact that I had undertaken to complete what Emanuele had begun. Discussing rhino with Iain had made me remember the letter to Michael Werikhe I had found in Emanuele's diary the day after the funeral, when we had let all the snakes go. The diary was still on his desk. The lock was slightly rusty, but the door opened easily enough. An almost solid, sweetish smell of snakeskins and rat droppings hit me even before I entered. I opened the windows wide and the sun once more lit up the rows of books, now covered in dust, the cherished objects. The floor was littered with fragments of snakeskins and dirt. A beehive hung in a corner: for some unknown reason, bees had always liked that room.

While the light of day shone on the mildew, and insects buzzed, I sat at Emanuele's desk and opened his diary; it was musty, but intact. I found the letter to Michael where I had left it. I read it again. Emanuele had asked him to come and stay and I decided to honour his wish. That evening I wrote to Michael in Mombasa, where he worked as a dog-trainer in the security section of a factory. I explained what had happened to Ema, and invited him to come up to Laikipia anyway and see his first rhino, as this had been Ema's desire. A few days after, I received his answer:

> . . . I greatly respected and admired him . . . I am shattered that fate never allowed us to meet . . . the sense of loss will forever be a part of my being. I will always think of him and strive to keep his memory by loving nature. I would like to pay my respect to him by visiting his grave whenever I get a chance to take a few days off work . . . Please keep in touch. Yours Michael.

This was the beginning of a correspondence which lasted for months, and the beginning of a friendship which will last for ever. When finally he got his leave, I met Michael in Richard Leakey's office at the Museum and we drove up to the ranch. It was for him the discovery of a new world: a private place of beauty, where people cared for the wild, and animals thrived. Michael was a serious, bespectacled young man, with an inspired way of talking, a purity, an ideal, and the energy and drive to work hard at making his dream a reality. I liked him instantly, and saw his potential: not only was he dedicated to the survival of the wildlife and specifically rhino, but he was an African, and he did not belong to any organization. In a conservation world mostly dominated by European Ph.D.s. paid to do their jobs, Michael's idealism and commitment were precious and rare. He could appeal to people of his own race, to whom finally the destiny of African wildlife was entrusted; he could be their hero, inspire them, speak a language they could understand. At a time when Kenya was being constantly reported by the international media as killing its wildlife, here was a Kenyan who could be quoted positively in the news as doing something extraordinary to save it.

A few years later, in fact, Michael would walk through East Africa, and finally Europe. He would raise an immense amount of money for rhino conservation, and would become an internationally known figure, sought by the high and mighty, loved by the media and respected by all. The recipient of prizes and awards, he would travel the world far and wide, but he would never lose his simplicity, he would remain loyal to his old friends and to the cause. When his daughter was born he called her Acacia, after the tree on Emanuele's grave. It all began with that first visit.

As I expected, he fell under the spell of Laikipia. When he left three weeks later, having seen his first rhino which was nicknamed Michael after him, and having caught and released a gigantic python as Emanuele would have done, we were friends. He wrote me a few days later:

> Laikipia ranch will forever be in my mind. I'll see it in my eyes, and hear its songs in my ears, wherever I go. The serenity of the environment there made me so ecstatic . . . to me it is a heaven, an oasis of love and hope . . . With lots of love from Michael.

There was a postscript:

> P. S. He was not there in person to take me around. He did in spirit. Everyone must have a hero. Well, he is mine.
>
> P. P. S. I left my belt and water container behind purposely, so that whenever I think of them, memories of Laikipia will flush back into my mind and rekindle my interest before it gets dark.

Days rolled away like clouds, and they were suddenly years.

From his grave, and fed by what had been his body, Emanuele's tree grew sturdy in Paolo's shade, and up above, their branches touched again, intertwined as if they were holding hands. Weaverbirds built their nests in Paolo's tree, and bees came to the pale creamy flowers, bringing the pollen back to their hives behind our house. We ate that honey at breakfast, and when the first pods and seeds appeared on our trees Sveva and I spread them around the ranch, brought some down to Nairobi to plant, and gave many to Michael Werikhe, who was starting a scheme of indigenous trees in some wasteland down at Mombasa. It gave us immense pleasure to feel that their bodies were truly now returning to Africa, and to us, in other shapes.

Sveva grew tall and long-limbed in harmonious grace, radiant and gentle, sunny and compassionate, adored by all for her charming ways, and fully deserving her nickname of Makena, the Happy One. There was a quiet maturity about Sveva as there had been in Emanuele, although they were different in many ways; she was more physical and more extrovert than he had been. Her hair had grown long and a darker gold, streaked with silver; her eyes remained that astonishing deep blue. Apart from her small nose, which had nothing of her father's Roman profile, she was Paolo's identical image: her way of walking, the bronze colour of her skin, the long runner's stride, her smile, her mannerisms, and her gift for music.

She used to ride out on her horse Boy, or on the tall camel Kelele, in the sunny mornings at the ranch, and after that first inexplicable incident when she had fallen into the pool and had swum out on her own before she knew how, she became an extremely good swimmer, as natural in the water as Paolo had been.

Sveva was fascinated by the wildlife. From the beginning, with Mirimuk as her mentor, she had learnt about the ways of the bush like an African child. The moment he had seen Sveva, a baby of a few days, she became 'Paulo' to him, and his devotion to her was touching and unstinting. She returned his affection with her natural grace and her shared love of the country and its creatures.

When we were alone we often spent a night out, Mirimuk and Sveva and I, as in days past we had done with Paolo. We would find some spot overlooking a dam or a valley, and build a fire of dry leleshwa roots. Mirimuk sat with Sveva, telling her stories of the Turkana, of Paolo, of hunting adventures in days past; the old man in green with the worn jacket and the much-used .303, and the blonde, long-haired little girl with eyes like blue pools. I looked at them in the great darkness of the African night. The fire played orange shadows on the ebony and on the golden skin, they held hands, they laughed, they whispered. The old and the young, two worlds coming together in total sympathy in this corner of ancient Africa where all is as it used to be. I felt yet again the rarity of the privilege of being here as I am, of giving Paolo's daughter these unique experiences and the extraordinary memories which will always live with her and make her special.

One night, in the wake of the years, I holding Sveva's hand, we watched with Mirimuk, crouched in the hide he had built with Garisha during the day, a huge leopard leaping up the acacia a few yards from us at the bait of a sheep, the branch creaking under the weight, cackling guinea-fowls, and the black shape silhouetted in the full moon. Only six, Sveva was as quiet and fearless, composed and calm, as a much older person. She held her breath, squeezed my hand, and absorbed this experience for ever. Next morning, Mirimuk commented: 'Paulo' – he touched her head affectionately – 'Paulo ni mama mzee.' The greatest compliment: 'Paulo is a wise old woman.'

Memories of the past kept coming back in unexpected ways and places, again and again, taking me by surprise.

I went back to Pembroke House one afternoon to fetch Colin's son Andrew, a great little chap and a close companion of Sveva, to bring him to Laikipia for half-term, and, for the first time in years, I went in to show Sveva the school where her brother had been. There was the same smell of carbolic soap and everything looked smaller.

With a pain in my throat, and looking for Andrew, I automatically searched hopefully through this new generation of children for the slim little boy with the blond straight fringe and serious eyes who had been mine, and whose shadow will always mingle with those of the children grown and gone. The grey uniforms made the boys look identical, like a swarm of ants, and in the small chapel the stained-glass windows cast an aquarium light.

A shining brass plaque just inside the chapel door froze my blood and choked me in renewed pain and remembrance: in a short row of names, under the heading 'In loving memory', I read with surprise and shock:

EMANUELE PIRRI-GALLMANN 1975–1978

Three precious years of his life engraved there for ever for all to see.

Emanuele's friends from Pembroke and Hillcrest had mostly gone abroad to study, as he would have done, but they returned, and some remembered us; sooner or later they appeared again on our doorstep.

A new Mercedes stopped one afternoon in my drive in Nairobi, and a sophisticated young man in smart clothes, with a moustache and glasses, tall and well-built, came towards me smiling. He was Indian, and I had a vague recollection of having met him before. 'I am Mukesh,' he said warmly, 'don't you remember me?' Of course I did. He had changed a lot from the thin teenager in the same class as Ema, one of the gang of his best friends. He had finished his studies in England, and was joining the family business in Kenya. I was impressed by his courtesy and maturity, and by the genuine concern which had brought him back to my door years after to 'pay his respects'. Mukesh became a regular visitor. At least twice a week he came to see us on his way home after work, and, over a cup of spiced tea, we spoke about Emanuele, about his future, his interest in flying, of life and death, and of the Indian philosophy of his ancestors, which had always interested me. He often brought Sveva small presents, the oriental sweets she loved, he worried if she was unwell, he advised me on business matters. We came to look forward to his visits, I counted on his friendship, and I adopted him in a way as a new-found son. He always came to Laikipia for Emanuele's anniversary, joining the group of our friends.

Since their trees had touched, Paolo's and Emanuele's anniversaries were now celebrated together on whichever weekend was closest to the dates. As ever, friends drove or flew up. We sat around the graves which were covered in flowers, and it was Sveva's task, now she was no longer a baby, to stand with two glasses of champagne in her hands and throw them against the gravestones in a toast. She took her responsibility with serious grace, as with everything she did. Once, straight and lovely with her long hair and in her long dress, she stood in the light of the bonfires which burnt into the night. With a small voice which only I and Wanjiru and the few who sat close enough managed to hear, she whispered, 'Papa Paolo, Emanuele: I miss you and I love you, I love you, I love you for ever.' Overwhelmed by her daring, she sat back, hiding in the shadows, next to me.

That night, after Emanuele's anniversary, on my way to Sveva's bedroom to wish her goodnight, I was overcome by a sense of solitude and melancholy. I put my head on Wanjiru's ample shoulder as I did occasionally, and kissed her fresh cheek. Made bold and emotional by the same mood and perhaps by the glass of champagne to which she was not accustomed, Wanjiru looked at me with her kind, motherly eyes and said, almost shyly, '*Gina yangu . . . Gina yangu si Wanjiru . . . gina yangu ni Gallmann*' ('My name is not Wanjiru. My name is Gallmann'). I was touched and honoured beyond words. She could not have said anything more valuable to me at that time.

'Kuki darling', wrote Oria,

a little girl in white sat on a stone shaded by a tree, lit by a moon, looked at her mother with a deep blue look, separated by a piece of earth, her brother. Around her, five red flames kept guard. The wind played a tune. No other little girl has a father and a brother made of stone, made of trees. Can we ever be the same, can we ever forget? Something happened to all of us: in your pain, in their loss, we all became better people.

41

Shadows

---

*Sed fugit interea, fugit inreparabile tempus.**

Virgil, *Georgics*, II

Life followed ancient patterns, as life does; new friends joined us and old friends went. Like shadows in the memory, they drifted in and out of our story. We watched them go. One should not cling to shadows.

One day, Mapengo decided to move on, as the Turkana often do. After Emanuele's death and with all the snakes gone, life had lost its shine for him; like all young men, he needed other fields and new challenges. I gave him Emanuele's favourite knife, as I had given Luka Paolo's favourite binoculars. We embraced, and I watched him go his way with his lanky gait in the worn boots which had belonged to his 'brother'.

'*Mama*,' he told me, showing his naked gums in one of his now rare smiles, '*Mama, kama wewe taitua mimi, mimi tarudi tu*' ('When you call me, I shall return'). I learnt in time that he had found a good fat wife, and a job to do with horses; he had a few children, and was happy enough.

Luka began to develop a fatal passion for an unforgiving drink: the intoxicating and addictive brew of *changaa*. Within a few years

---

* 'But time flies meanwhile, flies never to return.'

he became a shaky shadow of the brave, agile and fearless tracker he had been in the early days. After a particularly unhappy episode, and after many occasions when I had tried to talk to him and restore his pride in the memory of his glorious record, Colin was left with no alternative but to dismiss him. I shall never forget the day he said goodbye.

A car drove him to Kuti, and a small stranger got out, dressed in ill-fitting clothes. Without his gun, his green khaki uniform, the black beret askew, the belt studded with ammunition, stripped of his pride, he looked like any anonymous little man with nowhere to go. I met and held his weary, bloodshot eyes, the same sharp eyes which had spotted wild game first, invisible signs of buffalo on grass blades, a bent twig, the freshly cracked branch, prints of running hooves on dusty paths. Between us stood the memories of days gone, of people gone we had both loved in our ways. I kept his hand for a long time in mine, a trembling hand, and I could only say: 'Pole,' the all-encompassing word for 'Sorry'.

'Pole,' he answered, and added with a touch of the old cockiness: 'Mimi tarudi' ('I shall come back'). We both knew he would not. Changaa does not forgive, and brings an early old age and an early grave.

I nodded. 'Ndiyo.'

'Salamia Kainda' (his name for Sveva).

'Kuenda na Mungu' ('Go with God').

He turned and went, but before getting into the car he stopped a moment, and looked back at me. A shadow of a smile. A faded brilliance caught again his eyes. He shook his head to chase away his pain: 'Awesi kusahau' ('I shall not be able to forget'). The car door slammed, and he was gone for ever.

I entered in my diary that night:

> ... the story of Luka climaxed again today as he left the ranch most certainly for ever ... and yet it appears to me that the 'rise and fall of Luka Kiriongi' is symbolic of what the white man has done and does to black Africa ... as the

rise and fall of Luka would not have happened had he not met the white man. He had been the best, and he took it for granted, until he was made to feel special and different. He had only done what he well knew instinctively. A new foreign perspective of his worth upset the balance and became his ruin. Stripped of his pride, sacked in shame, no longer respected by his men, there goes the man who cried on my two graves. The gallant hunter, the superb tracker, the fearless bushman, the companion of uncountable days and nights of unforgettable adventures . . . how long has he been drinking? Why did he start slipping towards *changaa*, losing his dignity . . .? Slight of body, minute, a splitting grin below the fine moustache, brave in the face of danger, genuine in your loyalties, I am sad for you tonight, Luka Kiriongi . . .

It was a sad day indeed for us all in Ol Ari Nyiro, and mostly for Colin, who had known Luka for twenty-three years. Hussein Omar, with Mirimuk as deputy, took over the difficult task and responsibility of leading our anti-poaching Security.

Then Mirimuk became sick, and after three months in hospital they sent him home to die. The diagnosis was advanced cancer of the oesophagus, and the American doctors of the mission at Kijabe, where we had sent him, gave him two months to live. I went to visit him at his little house on the ranch, at the Centre. They had laid him out on a blanket in the shade, his head on a log of wood, the traditional Turkana pillow. No flesh was left on his dry limbs, and the hand he gave me had no strength, but he tried to sit up, and to drink a spoonful of the liquid food I had brought him. His face was more haggard, the skin tighter on the protruding cheekbones, a greenish film on the eyes. Holding my hand and looking at me with an affection which brought a knot to my throat, he whispered hoarsely: '*Kama Mungu nafungua melango, sisi napita tu*' ('When God opens the door, we must pass'). He looked behind me hopefully. Sveva had not come. '*Salamia Paulo*,' he said raspingly, before falling asleep.

A month later, back from Europe, I went to see him. I brought him a warm new blanket, a radio, a torch: miserable tokens to try and make his last few days more comfortable. He was just a living skeleton now. The body had shrunk, all strength had left him, the pale eyes shone unnaturally like those of a haunted animal trapped in the night. He could swallow no food. He was starving to death. In the next room a few Turkana girls, the wives of his sons, chatted gutturally, unconcerned. I wrapped the blanket around him, and for a long time I held his hand in silence. I thought about the risks he had taken in the bush, the fights with poachers when he had been wounded, the narrow escapes from dangerous in-furiated animals, the time when he could still run and fight back, and the many deaths he had eluded. The cancer was devouring him too slowly; any lion would have had more mercy. Before I left, he murmured, slowly, *'Paulo . . .'*

Sveva knew Mirimuk was dying and was more upset than I had seen her in a long time. Even if death is for us now a familiar name which evokes no fear, she had lost so much that any new loss was painful. But she owed it to Mirimuk and to herself to find the cour-age.

'He will be gone for ever in a few days. He has asked for you. You would feel very bad if you did not go and see him. We'll go to-morrow.'

'I'll come.'

'I brought you Paulo.' The shape on the blanket moved slightly, and with an immense effort what was left of Mirimuk sat up awkwardly. Simon, my cook, had come with us. Hugging her gift of a pot of honey and holding Simon's hand, biting her lips and staring hard at him, she came forward. When she was close she walked alone, and bent towards him. His hand, like a claw, grabbed her arm, and from his leathery lips an invisible spray of spit landed on her long blonde hair.

'Kwaheri, Paulo,' we think we heard, and he fell back on his blanket. Sveva stood, eyes swimming with tears. Her pink lips quivered. *'Ejok,'* we think we heard: 'Thank you' in Turkana. She

284

walked straight to the car, quiet tears streaming down her cheeks, wrapped in her dying friend's blessing as in a rainbow.

Mirimuk died in the night.

When the news came on the ranch radio network, Sveva and I looked at each other for a long, long time. They buried him next day in his *shamba* just outside the Nguare gate, in Ol Morani, still called Nyasore, in Colvile's honour, by the old people.

His last night, feeling his end was close, Mirimuk had asked to be brought home, and there he had died. Until recently, the Turkana custom had been to put the dead out for the hyenas. Now the law demanded a proper burial. A deep hole had been dug in a dusty field by the people I had sent to help. There would be no priest, as Mirimuk, like most of his contemporaries, had not belonged to any church. Many mud huts in a circle, each surrounded by its own fence of sticks for privacy, formed Mirimuk's *manyatta*. Women and children sang mournfully, stamping their feet in the rhythm of a slow dance. His son Ekiru, a tracker in our anti-poaching squad, and Simon my cook, whose younger wife is Mirimuk's daughter, brought me in to see him.

If anything had been in the hut before, it had been taken away. He lay on his side, on the bare beaten-earth floor, wrapped in an old sack from neck to foot. The head was small and shrunk, as in an ancient mummy, and white with ashes and salt to keep away insects and decay. I reached to touch his shoulder in goodbye. His ear looked like a fallen dry leaf. From the little window, a ray of sun emphasized the darkness.

They had all come, his companions and friends of a lifetime. There was Ngobitu, the Meru headman, and Tunkuri; Ndegwa, the sheep headman, and Silas, the small Tharaka, with most of the Security squad, dressed in their green khaki uniforms, a stillness on their faces. There was Arap Chuma the mechanic, with all the workshop people; Karanja the driver, Garisha the cattleman, Ali, Nyaga the horses headman, and John Mangicho, the assistant manager, dressed in a blue suit. They took turns to speak, his old wife, his friends. Then John turned to me and asked me to say something. I had not prepared a speech, so I let my heart talk. I spoke of early days when Mirimuk had taught me the ways of the bush. I spoke of other graves, and of the salute he had shot in the air to the souls of my men. Of his courage and endurance. Of the gap he had left. With my hand on the coffin, I thanked him in Turkana: 'Ejoknui, Mirimuk.'

Then there was a small commotion, the crowd parted and a woman came forward. She was young, with a baby in her arms. Bead necklaces were round her throat and brass earrings hung from the elongated lobes of her ears. She came with her hand stretched out, found the coffin and touched it. She had a proud face, with white, blind eyes. Someone murmured to me that she was the daughter of a dead brother. She spoke in Turkana with a shrill strong voice. A man translated aloud. There was such presence about her no one stirred, and we listened.

'I have come to Nyasore to say this man was a man. I used to have a father, and when he died he became my father. I had a home, but I have forgotten where. I used to have a name, but I have forgotten it. I have forgotten because he became my father and my mother and my home. My name is his name, and I am grateful. He looked after me and after my children, and he did me no wrong. He has died and he is in this box. The people of the church say it matters to follow the Book. We Turkana have no book. The people in the church tell us that if we follow their book we do not die. I tell you that the sun dies, and it comes back. I tell you that rains die, and they come back. But when a man dies, he does not come back. He is dead. Whatever the people of the church say, a dead man remains dead, and their book does not help. We are the Turkana and God knows our ways. I remember this man, and the window he has left will be filled by no other. And so be it. Ejoknui.'

In the heat of the afternoon a dog barked. Uncaring of the crowd, she turned her back and went.

The free soul of Mirimuk would have loved that.

*

Despite the loss of Luka and Mirimuk, Hussein Omar and our rangers managed to carry on the anti-poaching operations successfully and with selfless dedication. But this was still Africa, where wild is the bush and its unpredictable animals, and where accidents are always bound to happen.

Oria's voice sounded dull and distant on the Laikipia Security network, and the message was chilling. Saba, who was taking a year off before university, had joined a walking safari around Lake Turkana with Rob Brett and Bongo Woodley — son of Bill, the famous game warden of Tsavo. During the night she had been bitten on the ankle by an unknown poisonous snake — either a cobra or a carpet viper.

Snakes are not rare in Kenya, but like all animals they are shy, and seldom attack unless they feel cornered. It is most unusual for Europeans, who do not normally handle reptiles or walk barefoot among tall grass or cracked desert rocks, to be bitten accidentally by a snake. But the Douglas-Hamilton girls seldom wore shoes.

The news, passed by radio-call from Koobi-Fora, had been luckily intercepted by Robin, who was working on the film *Mountains of the Moon* at Loyengelani, and whose radio was linked to the Laikipia Security network frequency. Iain, distressed beyond his usual self-control, was going to fly her back.

I drove with Sveva immediately to Nairobi and straight to Wilson airport, where they were due to land. Oria was already there, a mask of petrified anxiety, which I understood only too well, painted on her face. We embraced wordlessly and we waited there, looking up at the enigmatic sky and willing the elusive aeroplane to materialize and bring a certainty to the agony of waiting without knowing. In those moments Oria and I silently shared again the unique feelings which cemented even more strongly our extraordinary bond.

The plane landed and a pale Iain jumped out. Saba was alive and grey-faced, dark circles around her stunning black eyes, an evil shade spreading through her body and enhancing every single blemish of her skin in ugly purplish marks. A hideous blue-red blister, the size of a large light bulb, swelled the side of her foot, like a repulsive sea creature. Amazingly, Emanuele had had no visible reaction at all. She tried to smile when she saw us, and broke down into sobs in my arms. There was no need to underline all the associations and memories that this incident had brought back for us all. She survived, brave and strong as one could ever wish to be, and after weeks in hospital she limped home and gradually recovered. Bongo Woodley had been prompt in applying a new method, discovered in Australia, of curing snake bites: by repeated electric shocks from the car battery, to break down and neutralize the venom. Although this was her first snake bite, most probably he had saved her life. I have ceased long ago to believe in coincidence. This uncanny episode was another uncommon link which tied me for ever to the Douglas-Hamiltons.

I worked, my life went on; sounds and images came like drifting mists, dimming sometimes the mirror of remembrance. One evening in Laikipia, I switched on the radio, and a voice I had not heard in years came through the Security network. So vivid was it, and so unexpected, that I was violently thrown back to other days, and in a wave of memories the old pain and longing swept over me again. It sounded so close, it was so out of reach.

It was Aidan's.

I often thought about him. I could imagine him walking alone in the early mornings, when the dew is still trapped in the dry grasses, easy strides of the long slim legs, and the shadows of his camels. In the hot noons, when we shared the same sun and the birds' concert at Kuti took over all other sounds, I could see him rest under the rare acacia. I knew he would walk again in the late afternoons, when the shadows are long on the silent dust and sand of the short red sunsets, and, for a brief time, everything glows with fire. In the starry, windy nights in Laikipia I imagined him facing the same wind and looking up at the same stars. At this hour, I felt, he would sometimes evoke my presence as a smiling unjudging companion, to soothe his brow, and to guide him through the night.

As long ago, before I had met him, people often talked about him, but he was seldom seen.

He still, I knew, lived the privileged life of the first explorers, often following the call of his adventures to the remote wilderness of deserts yet undiscovered – or already forgotten. A mutual friend had telephoned me a few years earlier, on my return from Europe, to tell me that Aidan had been captured, with no documents, far inside Ethiopia where he had been wandering alone, and had been put in jail. He had been there a month. Only Richard Leakey, who had contacts in that area because of his archaeological excavations, could help. I called him. He knew about it, and he said he would try. A while after, I heard Aidan was free, and I was relieved. I could not bear the thought of him confined, his long legs restless, trapped in a narrow room, looking out of a window at the tempting, inaccessible mountains he had hoped to climb.

Soon I was told of another incident. He had been delayed and had had to land at night. He was one of the most experienced pilots, and night-flying was not new to him. But private up-country airstrips have no lights. A boy was instructed to stand at the end of the airfield, holding a hurricane lamp, to mark its limit, so that Aidan could calculate its landing length. Alone in the dark with his lantern, the little boy waited for the noisy bird – *ndege* in Swahili means both bird and aeroplane – to fall from the sky. But when the invisible vibration roared too close, he panicked and ran with his lamp into the night. Aidan followed the light, and landed deep in the bush among the treetops, damaging his aeroplane. Sitting on my carpet, head on my knees, I listened to his disembodied voice, which soon was gone.

A few days later, the mail brought me an unexpected parcel, the paper worn and brittle as if posted from a far-away place and carried by many hands. It did not contain sand or dried leaves or butterfly wings, but a new book. On the first page, I read with a pang of surprise, in a once-familiar handwriting:

If you like this little book, think of me.

If you find wisdom in these pages, think of me.
I thank you for your friendship,
and many lessons of how to care.
Your old friend Aidan.

I opened the book, and these were the first words which caught my eyes:

> . . . every bit of unspoilt nature which is left, every bit of park, every bit of earth still spare, should be declared a wilderness area as a blueprint of what life was originally intended to be, to remind us.*

Rob Brett was learning to fly, and Mukesh was doing the final tests for his licence and had decided to come up to Laikipia for his first solo, during the Easter holidays, just after Emanuele's anniversary.

I saw Rob's green Suzuki approaching down my drive of euphorbia candelabra, and I noticed how much they had grown in a few years – now a tall and majestic colonnade of straight green trunks. I poured two cups of coffee and waited to hear what news there was about the next planned rhino operation.

Rob kissed my cheek, sat down in front of me, and looking me straight in the eye in his frank manner, began with uncharacteristic hesitation: 'Kuki, you have heard there was an aeroplane crash in Nairobi yesterday. My instructor was killed.'

I had heard. 'I am sorry.'

'There was a student pilot with him, and he was killed too.' He paused. I looked at him blankly for a moment. 'The student was Mukesh. I am terribly sorry.'

He handed me the daily paper. From a badly printed grey photograph, Mukesh smiled the white warm smile I had grown to love. The cup of coffee never reached my lips. I paused a moment,

---

*Laurens van der Post, *A Walk with a White Bushman*.

paralysed by shock, then I rose and I walked blindly out to the garden, wanting only to be alone with this new, choking grief, and I found myself at the graves. I had come to regard them as my 'magic circle' and there I went to find comfort, advice and peace in my moments of solitude and confusion.

I had expected Mukesh that very day for his first solo flight. The lunch had been ordered and the table was being laid with an extra place. This blow stung needles of pain in my soul. Mukesh had been so special. Gifted, kind-hearted, promising: is it then really true that the best die young? Never again would his car stop in our drive, and never again would he sit on our white sofa telling us stories of his day at work and tales of India. He would no longer join us for Emanuele's anniversary. Wanjiru cried when she heard, and all the staff were upset beyond words by this tragedy, as they had loved his quiet manners and had valued the genuine affection and care he showed towards us.

Back in Nairobi, I went to offer my sympathy to his parents in the house in Muthaiga where I had not yet been. Dozens of Mercedes were parked in the drive, and the sound of chanting came from the inner rooms. Passing the threshold was like crossing an invisible barrier of time and space, and I was in India.

It was the tenth day after his death, on which, by Hindu tradition, the soul goes to join the gods of its ancestors. In a few days' time his uncle would take his ashes back to the river Ganges. It seemed impossible. In the crowded kitchen, legions of people cooked complicated curries, chapatis and papadams, and ceremonial sweetmeats. Men in traditional white robes and women in white saris filled the richly decorated rooms, which smelt of incense and spices. A thin Hindu priest chanted mournfully with closed eyes, sitting cross-legged on a cushion.

His father, an older version of Mukesh but without moustache and glasses, came to meet me. I knew he was influential in the world of business and banking: in his grief and traditional dress he looked younger than I had imagined, and so did his wife, a tall

291

handsome lady in a sari of white silk, her face wet with tears, who embraced me and said in a lost voice, 'I was so proud of my son. I go to his room, and I don't find him.' She looked around. 'Where has he gone?'

From a life-size photograph set on a sort of altar, garlanded with marigolds, a dot of saffron and rice on his forehead, above the drifting incense smoke I met Mukesh's eyes. In the light of the candles they seemed to twinkle. They reminded me stunningly of Ema's.

I turned to his mother. 'He is with Emanuele. I have no doubt. They were friends. They were brothers. Even I, I have lost another son.'

I went out into a night heavy with the first rain of April, carrying in a yellow handkerchief a handful of almonds and cardamon sweets for Sveva, Mukesh's last gift.

42

Emanuele's Rodeo

Remember me when I am gone away,
Gone far away into the silent land.
Christina Rossetti, *Remember*

The mornings always begin with a wind, a blue and pale golden light, and the cool wet dew on the grass. At the edge of my garden, where the trees of remembrance grow together guarding the horizon and the hills, my graves are covered in purple-pink and red flowers. On the lawn in front of my house, tables and cushions, carpets and tents decorated with palm leaves and bougainvillea, and the long lines of barbecues in preparation for the evening feast.

The red banner flies in the early-morning breeze, and the one word written in black, EMANUELE, appears and disappears again, pulsating in the gusts of wind.

It is the day of his party.

Among the things I did not want to change was the rodeo Emanuele and I had discussed during the last months of his life. It was to have been his eighteenth birthday celebration and would involve all the employees of Ol Ari Nyiro, our friends, people from the neighbouring ranches. I had never given Emanuele a party when he was alive. I now give him one every year, and it is in his memory.

A long line of cars is parked along the road at Kuti and more

293

keep arriving. Aeroplanes circle low to land on my airstrip. A multicoloured crowd of Africans and Europeans of every age move closer to the enclosure of the cattle dip, where preparations are under way. From the four-wheel-drive cars emerge the teams: grinning Africans neatly dressed in T-shirts printed with the name of their ranch, all ready to participate in today's event. On a large signboard the programme of events. This time there will be a relay race with camels, donkeys and horses. A running race for children. A tug-of-war. Several games of skill to do with cattle, crowned by the most popular event, the steer-riding, in pure rodeo style, in which the participants must ride a kicking steer bareback, using only one hand and staying on as long as possible. A champion at this is Simon Evans, Jasper's son. There is an art competition for the children of our school on the theme 'Animals on our Ranch'. The best handicraft will get a prize, and so will the best-kept garden planted with indigenous trees. Later, there will be traditional dances and food for all. A New Year party, a disco.

Friends I have not seen in years come out to greet me; familiar faces, young men and women, Emanuele's friends now grown to a physical maturity he will never reach. What would the Emanuele of twenty, thirty, have been like? From a large framed photograph arranged on a table next to the trophy for the winner, a snake coiled around his neck, he smiles his sad, knowing smile which will never grow old.

There is cheerful, red-headed Toon Hanegraaf, taller than anyone. Michael Werikhe, who has come once more all the way from Mombasa. Carletto and all his daughters and ten guests. Another aeroplane approaches, low, scanning the ground, the engine noise changes, low, lower, buzzing over the *menanda*: it must be Iain . . . it is. Saba and Dudu — beautiful women now — and Oria emerge, bronze Italian skin, earrings and bangles, long skirts and bare feet jingling with anklets. Our Toyota lorry arrives in a cloud of red dust, full of supporters, voices chanting aloud some Meru song of joy and celebration.

In the middle of the cattle dip enclosure, a whistle in his mouth, blue cap shading his eyes, Colin is in charge of the preparations. Cattle are chosen and marked. Camels and donkeys with their keepers wait nearby. New sisal ropes are arranged for the tug-of-war, prizes are lined up. A large target painted with a charging buffalo is set up for the archery competition. The Mugie team is a group of Samburu, handsome in their red and white *shukas* and red bead earrings, spears shining, and each resting on one leg like a proud flamingo. The Ol Ari Nyiro team mixes with the crowd, helping, and performing their duties as hosts; they are all wearing khaki T-shirts printed in bold red: FOR EMANUELE. Among them, a feather stuck in his hair, I see Mapengo. One day each year he returns to Laikipia from the far-away place where he now works, to compete for his *ndugu* (brother). On that day the shadow of the old Mapengo takes over again, his cocky way of moving, and the toothless grin seems unchanged while he rides a steer 'for Emanuele' among the cheering crowd.

To shouts, clapping and applause, the rodeo begins. How many times now? Five, six? It is the last day of the year, the closest festive day to his real birthday. For the newcomers, at the moment of distributing the prizes I remind the guests once again that in this land there was a young man who loved Africa, and loved its animals and its people, and he is dead. But as love is the bridge with the beyond, he is alive in the hearts of those who knew him and loved him; as he also loved parties, like all young men, this party is to celebrate his memory and we will rejoice for him.

In the shade of a tree, ready for the evening dances around the bonfires, the Pokot wait. They have walked for miles to be here again, dressed in their old greased skins, to sing their song of remembrance about the *kijana* who loved the people, and who loved snakes too much. Among them, her skull and her gaunt face ceremonially oiled with red ochre, I recognize the old medicine woman, Cheptosai Selale. They will join the people of Ol Ari Nyiro in the dances which will continue all night by the light of the bonfires, and when the sun of the New Year rises again tomorrow a guttural chorus will salute it, vibrating from a thousand throats as from the very depth of the African heart.

The pop music slows down, fades away, stops. The dances interrupted, the guests walk out on the lawn, looking at their watches: it is almost midnight.

An older, slower tune begins, a haunting Spanish lilt, building up to a crescendo, gaining volume and beat: Ravel's *Bolero* rises up in the cold starry night through the roof of *makuti*, and the crowd listens bewitched, in awed silence, to Emanuele's music. The fire burns at the graves, as on every night.

Through the shadows towards the end of the garden, brilliant with hundreds of twinkling candles like a fairyland, Robin moves on light feet, holding a torch. With a hiss which sends a murmur through the crowd, the first of many fireworks, in a rain of sparkles, shoots up like a comet, exploding in a myriad stars and brightening the sky.

Even the elephants know something great, unusual, is happening tonight.

Wine flows in the proffered cups. 'Happy New Year.' Friends come to embrace me. 'Another great memorial to your son.'

In the dark, no one can see my tears. I look up at the mysterious depth above, searching for him. 'Happy birthday, my love,' I say silently.

He would be twenty-two. Another year has gone. Another has begun.

43

The Ivory Fire

If the great beasts are gone, man will surely die of a great loneliness of spirit.

Chief Seattle of the Nez Percé, 1884

In the late eighties, bands of Somali *shiftah* and deserters from the Somali Army infiltrated Kenya's Northern Provinces and, descending in a wave of terror, killed their way through the parks, leaving behind them mutilated carcasses, helpless orphans and decimated herds of elephants. Dramas unfolded daily in the open savannah and thick bush of Africa. The existing wildlife system, poorly equipped and lacking funds, leadership and proper planning, seemed powerless to stop this organized offensive of poaching. We watched in despair, trying to do all we could to stop the slaughter.

Although in Ol Ari Nyiro the situation was under control, wounded animals were often reported on neighbouring ranches, and limped into Ol Ari Nyiro to die. Elephants crippled by wire snares became a common event, and whenever we came to hear about it, Colin and our team went to help.

Standing in the stubby grass under a small *Acacia gerardiœ*, I look down at Colin working on the sleeping young elephant. Under the shade of a large bush, perfectly camouflaged in their green uniforms, is a group of our Security people who have come to help. Three of them will stay behind to check on him, to make sure no lion, no Pokot, no Samburu hunter will take advantage of his weakness and limping gait. They will watch him for as long as he takes to recover or to be re-adopted by the herd which had to leave him behind when he could no longer walk and keep up with the pace of the group.

In a few weeks the wound gradually healed. He no longer limped. His mother came to check on him every day, and his own herd, called back possibly by the infrasound messages he transmitted, returned to fetch him, and he joined them. Our three askaris, who had looked after him, fed him lucerne and water, guarded him around the clock, talked to him to make him feel secure and not threatened, had come back to Ol Ari Nyiro. Until next time.

Tsavo National Park, once the kingdom where elephant roamed free, now became the theatre of the agonizing solitary death of hundreds of defenceless pachyderms killed by human greed. A count co-ordinated in 1988 by Iain Douglas-Hamilton showed that only a few thousand elephants were left in Tsavo and their number was diminishing daily. Despite the international uproar, and help pouring into Kenya, nothing seemed able to stop this indiscriminate and irreversible destruction. The elephant, like the dinosaur, seemed doomed to extinction.

In April 1989, Oria passed me the news on the Laikipia Security network that Richard Leakey had been unexpectedly nominated by the President of Kenya as the new Director of the Wildlife Department, soon to become a new parastatal organization, the Kenya Wildlife Services. Practically overnight, Richard became responsible for rearranging and reorganizing the desperate situation of the wildlife in the country. The task he had been given was daunting and would have been regarded as impossible by most people. Richard put all his competence, time and courage into it.

'Congratulations or condolences?' I asked him on the phone, as soon as I came down to Nairobi.

He laughed his small meaningful laugh: 'Both.'

I did not doubt for a second that he would rise to the occasion, and he did, with his usual impeccable flair.

The priorities were many and intermingled, but certainly stopping the slaughter of elephants was the highest and most immediate one. How? It was clear that for as long as people bought ivory and ivory products there would be someone there to kill elephants. Richard, like many, felt that the only way to stop the slaughter was to stop the trade. He decided that Kenya should set an unprecedented example of coherence.

The Association of Private Land Rhino Sanctuaries, of which I was Vice-Chairman, met at a different sanctuary each time. Now it was our turn, and the meeting took place in Ol Ari Nyiro, in my house at Kuti. The Director of Wildlife was always invited, and this time it was Richard. Unexpectedly – as there were so many demands on his time – he was able to come, on his way to visit Koobi-Fora, which is in a park. He opened the meeting in the morning, and everyone was impressed by his clear-minded and confident statements.

Back to Ol Ari Nyiro from Turkana that evening, Richard told us that the President had agreed to burn publicly all the ivory accumulated in the Ivory Room in the last two years. The ivory was meant to be sold at auction and the buyers had already arrived. It amounted to twelve tons, and it was worth over three million dollars. Richard had cancelled the sale.

'Twelve tons!' I gasped 'How do you burn twelve tons of ivory? Does ivory burn?'

'I am not sure,' said Richard, unperturbed. 'There must be a way. Why don't we try?'

We keep the broken ivory fragments collected by our people in Laikipia. To encourage them to hand it over, rather then selling it under the counter, we compensate such finds in proportion to their size. We then number the pieces and enter them in a register. When we have enough to fill the back of a car and justify a long journey, Colin – who is also an honorary game warden – brings them up to Nanyuki and hands them in to the Wildlife Department. With Richard's permission, I asked Colin to send up some large pieces, and with a certain feeling of unreality we burned them in my fireplace during dinner.

It took a long time and quite a bit of wood, but the fragments finally did burn to flaky ashes. Lots of heat was needed, and the proportion of wood to ivory was about ten to one. Richard asked Colin to help. The thought of destroying twelve tons of elephant tusks, and the respective hundred and twenty tons of firewood, was staggering. Burning a forest to burn the ivory was perhaps as environmentally unacceptable as killing elephants, and although the wood used would be the domesticated and 'imported' gum tree, very abundant in Kenya, it was still, to me, an uneasy feeling. The decision was obviously not mine, but I kept looking for another solution.

The best ideas of my life have always crept into my mind at the moment of falling asleep. To be sure of remembering them in the morning I keep a notebook and a pen on my bedside table. A couple of nights after that weekend, on the verge of sliding into oblivion, I saw with sudden clarity that the real purpose of burning all the ivory publicly was to show to the entire planet Kenya's commitment to end the ivory trade: when the President lit the pyre in front of the assembled world press, the flames had to catch and flare up instantly and dramatically. Even a short delay would be an anticlimax. More than anything, the fire had to be *photogenic*.

I sat up in my bed, suddenly awake. Robin.

Robin would know how to burn the ivory without using all that wood, *and* he would know how to make the event photogenic. It was his job, and he had achieved just this dozens of times for the special effects in films. He had just come back from Norway, and I knew he would soon be going to the Far East for a film. I called him immediately. It was past midnight. He answered sleepily.

'If you had to burn twelve tons of ivory – for the press – how would you do it?' I asked him.

'Very simple,' he answered, and produced a practical explanation. He would douse the tusks, one by one, in inflammable, invisible glue. He would arrange them on a pile of wood on a system of hidden pipes connected to a generator which would spray up fuel to keep the heat and the fire going for as long as it was necessary. He would be perfectly capable of achieving this, and volunteered, there and then, his help and that of his special effects crew.

Next morning I called Richard. 'I think it would be useful for you to see Robin,' I said. 'He has some ideas about the ivory-burning which make lots of sense.' I explained them to him briefly.

'Tell him to come here at nine,' said he. Robin got the job, while Colin was going to be responsible for organizing the stacking of the gigantic pyre.

One way or another, I was now deeply involved in the last act of the elephant drama.

It was 18 July 1989.

A shiver like a wave ran through the crowd in Nairobi National Park. The African brass band in blue started a tune. People clapped, stretching their necks to see better. Cameras clicked.

Tall, a fresh rosebud in his lapel, out of the shiny car stepped President Moi. The National Anthem rose high above into the almost cloudless sky. In the haze of distance, Nairobi's skyscrapers stood as a reminder of man's pressure on the untouched environment.

Nearer, but still in the background, was a pile of neatly and dramatically arranged elephant tusks, the emblem of a holocaust representing almost 2,000 dead elephants. Only yesterday we had helped to carry those tusks, Sveva and I, Colin and Robin, Oria and her girls, and the people we had sent from Laikipia to help. And, of course, Richard.

Faintly, through the pressing mob, I saw Robin stepping forward on light feet, holding a long stick doused in glue, ready to ignite it.

Among the crowd were many friends, people who over the years have become part of my life and of my work, of what I have become. I scanned the crowd, focusing with a certain wonder on one or the other of those familiar faces. The *Who's Who* of world conservation was here. The National Anthem's last notes drifted in the hot air of the afternoon. President Moi, followed by Richard, stepped on the podium, which was draped in red, in front of the press bench. Behind him stood the mound of ivory which soon would go up in smoke to prove to the world that Kenya practised what it preached. In the high silence the microphone crackled.

In a clear voice the President read his historic speech. A mountain of ivory worth over three million dollars, the symbol of man's thoughtless destruction of the environment, would now be destroyed in this wildlife sanctuary. To me, the burning appeared like a cathartic way of exorcizing the evils and corruptions of the past, and of starting again, clean and new, from the beginning.

Amid cheers, the speech ended. The President stepped from the podium. Robin lit the stick and passed it to Richard, who offered it to Moi. I held my breath and closed my eyes for a moment.

The tusks, doused in the special glue, caught fire instantly. Flames flared up in a scalding blaze. Fine, then thick smoke lifted in the air in a dense cloud which smelt of dead old bones. Through the smoke I could see Sveva's figure, light as a fairy, move in the distance, holding Wanjiru's hand. The ivory blackened and started burning, crackling. Deafening applause burst out from the crowd, while television crews from all over the world showed to every corner of the earth this new sacrifice of Africa. Robin was lost in the crowd, manoeuvring the fuel pump and the generator; I could still vaguely see him through the smoke, and I knew he was smiling.

I watched, mesmerized, while the scorched tusks in the orange fire changed slowly into charcoal, well aware that this was another turning-point and the climax of years of preparation. Gradually, in the following hours, the crowd dispersed. Some lingered. Oria asked me to tea, and I went with Sveva. A new yellow cloud was drifting in the afternoon sky to join the white clouds of summer.

We returned in the evening. The crowd had left hours ago.

Night was falling fast on Nairobi National Park, now left once again to its animals.

The askaris in camouflage gear stood guard with their guns on what remained of thousands of tusks, the emblem of the lost herds which once roamed the plains. The fire still smouldered. In the incandescent embers, charred shapes of long curved teeth disintegrating into ashes could still be recognized. I stood watching in the scalding heat, bewitched and lost in thoughts of other places, other people, other fires in my life, of which this was the last.

A lion, very close, roared his hoarse, throaty salute to the rising moon. Nairobi's lights dotted the night like fallen stars.

A little hand slid into mine — the index finger curled up, as always when Sveva is deep in thought. The sizzling blaze of the last tongues of the ivory fire played coral flickers on her skin; her hair glowed like bright flame. For as long as she lives she will remember this unrepeatable moment. It was another ending, another beginning, and it summarized, purified and made sense of all that had happened so far in all our combined lives.

The future stretched ahead, with all its challenges. A circle had closed; another had opened again.

44

Epilogue

———————

For the word is Resurrection
And even the sea of seas will have to give up its dead.

D. H. Lawrence *Be Still*

Driving up to Laikipia from Nairobi after the ivory fire is like going back in time. The tall buildings are left behind, and after the dark forests over the escarpment planted with cypress and pine trees, one has the first breathtaking view of the Rift Valley and Lake Naivasha with its crescent-shaped island.

Along the newly surfaced road beyond Nyahururu there are small farms, villages of wooden huts, patches of forest, where it is now rare to see any wild animal.

The tarmac ends abruptly. We pass through densely settled areas: ploughed fields dotted with huts, roofs of corrugated iron, small herds of goats and scrawny cattle guarded by vulpine dogs, bare stretches of land with stumps of half-burnt trees, which once was Colobus. From the side of the road Kikuyu children wave to us, and we wave back. Some of them come to the ranch with their teachers once or twice a year, in the lorry I send out for them, to see the wildlife which no longer has a place in the cultivated fields where they now live.

A little man seems to materialize by the side of the dusty track in front of us, and raises his hand in greeting, almost shyly. Intent on the road, eager as ever to arrive, I slow down slightly, but I do

304

not stop. There is something familiar about his figure . . . Wanjiru and Sveva turn their heads towards him, and cry in unison with the same surprise, 'It's Luka!'

I slam on the brakes and the car stops in a cloud of red dust, through which he runs towards us, small lithe body bent forward obliquely to beat the pressure of the air and gain speed: his characteristic way of running effortlessly which I would recognize anywhere. Too many times we had run together after or from another running beast, and I had tried to copy his natural suppleness, the angle of his gait. In pearly dawns in coral fiery sunsets. He stops in front of my open window.

'Luka.'

'*Memsaab. Kainda. Wanjiru. Kumbe, wewe badu najua mimi!*' ('You still recognize me!').

He has aged. Some teeth are missing. He is much thinner, the skin tight on his cheekbones. The red eyes glitter with a hint of the old spirit. He tells us he has a shop, a *shamba* at Lariak, he is fine . . . he misses the bush. '*Habari wa faru?*' ('How are the rhino?'). Nostalgia veins his voice. He will come to the house one day to see us. Soon. Next month, perhaps. We say goodbye. In the mirror, his diminutive figure becomes smaller, the hand raised, unmoving. Sveva waves until the dust settles on the memory of his shadow.

At the end of the murram track we reach the gate. From massive posts hangs a sign carved out of old cedar: OL ARI NYIRO RANCH. LAIKIPIA RANCHING CO. Underneath, newer: 'The Gallmann Memorial Foundation.' The gate opens, the askari smiles his welcome. Like all visitors, I sign the visitors' book. My first question is always, '*Habari wa nvua?*' ('Any news of rain?'). The gate closes behind us, and we have arrived in Africa.

Rolling hills. Pale green leleshwa. Vivid red soil. Guinea-fowl in large flocks. To the south, at the feet of Ol Ari Nyiro's side of the Enghelesha hill, spreads the untouched forest where colobus, leopard and buffalo, rare birds and butterflies, still find refuge. Next to it the grass leys where herds of fat Boran cattle graze, and the fields planted with maize and oats, sorghum and wheat and beans.

The game with Sveva is to be the first to spot a four-legged wild animal. It does not take long. A herd of impala. Running warthogs. A male zebra, massive, twitching tail over the round fat rump, surveys us from the middle of the track, snorts through black lips and trots after his females.

'Elephant!' cries Sveva. Feeding quietly off the thorn trees, a group of females and young ones hardly notice us. Trunks lift up tentatively to catch our scent, ears flap, stomachs rumble. A flock of pelicans fish the Nyukundu Dam. On the east side, a large herd of Dorper sheep, white bodies and black heads, drink, tended by their herders. Next to them, gentle waterbuck look on untroubled, handsome and harmless like hairy cartoon does. Buffalo drink at the Big Dam, deep in water to their knees. Black heads lift, wet muzzles dribble, oblong ears listen.

The road climbs up to Kuti through clearings and *luggas*, and round the corner of the airstrip, my garden appears, ablaze with flowers, the euphorbia grown to a colonnade, resonant with bird voices. The twin thorn trees are now visible from a distance, and I salute them. Simon comes to the car smiling, and we shake hands. 'Ejok.' 'Ejoknui.' The dogs jump around, howling their pleasure.

Every return home to Laikipia seems the same, yet something is always different. Small things. Perhaps there are new puppies to meet, or orchids have bloomed for the first time; elephant have defied the electric fence and uprooted another pepper tree or broken the water pipe; the leopard has come to steal the dogs' meat; a rabid jackal has had to be shot at the gate; a cobra has chosen to nest in the fish-pond. Someone has been taken sick with malaria, and has had to be sent to hospital; wild bees have swarmed again above the ceiling in Emanuele's room.

Unusual and memorable events, like one special evening not long after the ivory-burning.

My dogs were ready for the evening walk, when Simon's silent shape materialized at my door. His impassive face seemed to have lost some of its normal composure.

'*Memsaab*', he whispered gravely, '*Warani wa tayeri ya Pokot alikuja kusalamia wewe. Ni saidi ya mia. Unajaza kiwanja.*' ('The young circumcised Pokot warriors have come to greet you. They are over a hundred. They fill the entire airstrip.') He seemed awestruck. '*Ni kitu kubwa sana.*' ('It is a very big thing.')

I went out on the lawn with the dogs. The golden light of the late afternoon silhouetted the black of the hills; the ridge of Mugongo wa Ngurue looked like the profile of a whale about to plunge down into the mystery of the Mukutan Gorge. Orange tinged the clouds as if an invisible fire burnt below the rim of the horizon.

The dogs tensed, straightening their ears and pointing towards the west. Black noses quivered, sensing a strangeness in the wind. Alarm ruffled the longer hair on their backs, as in a pack of hyenas alert to the hunt.

With a cadence of numberless cattle, of pounding buffalo hooves, an army of marching bare feet stamping in rhythm approached slowly from the plain. From it lifted a weird moaning sound, low and vibrating, powerful and eerie, coming closer: the circumcision song of the young Pokot warriors.

I took Sveva's hand, her blue eyes widened by curiosity. The dogs surrounded us. I turned to Simon. 'Tell them they are welcome. We shall wait for them.'

It was a long way from Italy, from the tame surroundings of my childhood: blackboards inscribed with Greek, classrooms shaded in greys, ancient paintings, bells calling from churches, history hovering in the fogs of autumn.

An unending procession of identical brown shapes moved like wooden spirits between the acacias and the euphorbias of the drive. Their faces were covered by long plaited hair falling forward to the waist. From breast to knee they were wrapped in skins, made soft and clinging by grease and red ochre. Their features hidden and their bodies concealed, they appeared sexless and remote, like ghosts or angels. They shook their hair from side to side, dramatically, like moving masks, revealing nothing.

It was as if the earth had come alive, taking the shape of humans. Each held a new ceremonial bow, and arrows burnt with intricate patterns of rusty brown and ivory white. They sang their haunting song, and they were well over a hundred. They approached spiralling in a single row, endlessly circling round and round, advancing indirectly in sign of friendship. In front walked the old chiefs. I recognized a few of them, ostrich feathers stuck in their skull-caps, black *shukas* fastened to their shrunken hips, sandals of uncured hide tied to their gnarled feet. They carried spears, the blades covered and lowered as in peace.

Before we knew it, the warriors stopped around us in an almost perfect circle. Sveva and I waited in the middle, on the manicured lawn carved out of the wilderness, among the flowers, our large dogs surrounding us. Our fair skin and hair stood out, and I realized that she and I were the only females present at this ceremony. Our European origin, my position as guardian of this land, gave us, I supposed, the status of men.

Yet there had been a time, only few years ago, when these same Pokot had come to kill our rhino.

The chiefs advanced to shake our hands. *'Sopai'* ('I greet you'), the oldest chief said. *'Epah.'* ('And I greet you'), I answered.

Langeta – the son of Cheptosai Selale, the old medicine-woman of the herbs – came close to interpret for me.

'Kuki, we come in peace, to greet you and wish you prosperity. Our war with the Turkana rebels is over and this is a time of rejoicing for the Pokot, because it is the end of our first circumcision ceremony in twenty-three years. Every *manyatta* has sent some of their young warriors to you, and none of them shall forget this day, and what it means.

'We have walked across your boundary to state our friendship and our co-operation. You, Musungu, have been fair to us, and we shall be loyal to you and we come to thank you. We want you to know that we consider you as one of us. You have helped us, and we shall help you. We shall not disturb the animals for which you care. What we are saying now cannot be undone and shall not be forgotten, for this is a sacred ceremony for the Pokot, and God is watching.

'These young men were circumcised and are now healed. Tomorrow, and forever after, they shall dress as men, but today they will sing and dance for you. If you have any wish, speak.'

What more could I wish for? They had come to greet me in my home in the heart of Africa. I had become a figure in their life, as they had in mine. These wild Pokot warriors stood among my flower-beds, under the trees I had planted and seen growing, to honour me, a girl of Veneto, whose name they knew, accepting me as one of them. My childhood visions were realized beyond hope.

At the edge of the garden two yellow fever trees stood, reminders of the price I had paid in loss and sorrow to gain the privilege of protecting this land. They evoked in my mind Paolo's and Emanuele's faces. If the God of Pokot was watching, so were they. Love could not die: my awareness, responsibility and sense of belonging had grown out of my love for them.

As if in a well-rehearsed choreography, eight of the man-shapes advanced and closed around us in a tight circle. They smelt of smoke and sweat and animal fat. They put a gourd on the ground in the middle.

I looked at Simon, who stood watch at the limit of the circle waiting for my signal, and now came forward and gave me my pouch. Instinctively I knew what should be done. I bent and put a symbolic offering in the gourd.

In unison the eight young warriors spat on us in a drizzle a ceremonial blessing, and at that moment from more than a hundred throats the moaning began again. As the hair shook over their covered faces, I could make out the sound of three words I recognized: 'Therra gnow-gnow, Mama Kuki' ('Thank you, Mama Kuki').

'Therra gnow-gnow,' I answered humbly.

As one man, they shook their heads, the hair fell backwards, and for a fleeting moment I could see their exposed features.

I knew instantly that this was the highest honour. I went around the circle with Sveva, thanking each of them. I shook every hand, one by one, in the triple Pokot handshake I had learnt in Paolo's days. Faceless once more, the young men sang 'Therra gnow-gnow' over and over again, hypnotically in refrain, so that it became a natural sound like the voice of an animal of the earth or a bird of the wind, lingering long as an echo well after they had gone.

After the last Pokot had left, Sveva and I walked to our trees at the end of the garden. The fire of wild olive burned below these, as it did every night. Like the ivory fire a few nights before, it was reflected from her golden hair and skin, while her eyes seemed to reflect the experiences of her unusual childhood.

The limpid sky of the equator, fringed by the leaves of our thorn trees, was studded with millions of bright stars unknown. 'Some of those stars,' I remembered Emanuele saying to me one night when we had camped out at the Nagirir Dam, 'died millions of years ago. Yet we now see their light.'

I told Sveva, and we looked up together, feeling fragile yet strong, part of the universe, in the comforting perception of eternity. What she will be one day will come from the experiences of her childhood. There was hope. A time long gone I had been a little girl who dreamed of Africa.

Hand-in-hand we walked back to the house. It had been an extraordinary day and I wanted to think about it, and to record it in my diary.

The box of ebony inlaid with brass where I keep my pens has a false bottom. There I have kept Paolo's letters. I took them out. It was years since I had read them.

On the top of a page of brittle airmail paper, he had written: 'Kuki'. Below, he had traced the contour of his hand. A singularly slim hand.

At the bottom, he had written: 'I love you. P.'

Now I put my hand over the outline of his, wishing I could still feel its warmth.

There were little notes. One, scribbled on the side of a label said: 'I WANT your baby.'

On a folded page torn from a school book, that Paolo never had the time to give me, and strangely I did not remember having seen before, I now read with the choking awareness of after:

> . . . you empty your heart in POETRY. As a last thing I ask you to write poetry, and one day to let us read it. You have the gift of seeing, feeling and communicating. I have wasted the time I was given without pausing long enough to see and to feel, but you have not. Perhaps you have paid much for what you have achieved. Perhaps it is the simplest thing of all, but because it takes a lifetime to learn, it is the only important gift you can give us. Only in this way will the whole belong again to us who loved you; good and bad, joy and ecstacy, melancholy and pain, people and places, *e come era il tempo* . . . the only true quality of real love is immortality . . . I shall always see you, darling shadow, on the lawn in Laikipia, with the dogs, writing your poetry. And in your poems I shall find again, with persistent devotion and unending joy, the dazzling country of your butterfly soul to which I have given my heart. Be happy. Your P.
>
> P.S. If you do not do it for me, do it for Ema.

I stared at that letter for a long time. The silence in my bedroom was broken only by the crackling fire. From a black-and-white photograph on the mantelpiece, Paolo in the rubber dinghy at the Big Dam, Emanuele in front of him riding bareback deep in water, waved to me a last goodbye. Still tied to the central beam of my four-poster bed was the severed nylon thread from which the ostrich egg had once hung, protecting a mystery. From the side of my chair, like another ostrich egg, hung Emanuele's white motorbike helmet, which had protected his head. In the next room Sveva slept with her dreams.

I pondered on the past, on all the omens. I had no choice. 'The only true quality of real love is immortality.'

Surrounded by my memories that night, I took my pen and I began to write.

Laikipia, July 1989

Glossary

Ayah	Nurse, maid, nanny
Boma	Enclosure made of sticks or shrubs
Bunduki	Gun
Bwana	Sir
Chui	Leopard
Duka	Shop
Fundi	Craftsman
Ganduras	Flowing mantle
Gari	Car
Hapana	No
Ilelechwa	Wild sage
Jambo	Hello
Jikoni	Kitchen
Jina	Name
Kanga	Traditional loose garment for women
Kanzu	Long robe
Kati kati	Middle
Kidogo	Small
Kifaru	Rhino
Kifo	Death
Kijani	Young men

Kikoi	Traditional loose garment for men
Kisima	Spring
Kisu	Knife
Kondoo	Sheep
Kubwa	Large
Kufa	Die, dead
Kwaheri	Goodbye
Kwenda	To go
Lugga	Small valley
Maji	Water
Makuti	Thatch made of palm leaves
Manyatta	Traditional dwellings for a clan, built within an enclosure
Maramoja	At once
Matatu	Local taxi
Mbogo	Buffalo
Mbwa	Dog
Memsaab	Madam
Mistuni	Forest
Mlima	Hill
Mnyama	Animal
Moran	Young warrior
Moto	Hot, fire
Mpishi	Cook
Msungu	European
Mti	Tree
Mugongo	Back
Mutamayo	Wild olive
Mutaraguo	Cedar
Ndege	Bird
Ndiyo	Yes
Ndovu	Elephant
Ngoma	Traditional dancing ceremony
Ng'ombe	Cattle

Ngurue	Pig
Nugu	Baboon
Nyama	Meat
Nyasore	The Thin One
Nyoka	Snake
Nyukundu	Red
Nyumba	House
Pole	Sorry
Posho	Maize-meal porridge
Rudi	Return
Sahau	Forget
Shamba	Small farm, field
Shuka	Shawl, scarf
Simba	Lion
Taabu	Problem
Wapi?	Where?
Wazee	Old wise men